BUILDING
TION

REBUILDING CONSTRUCTION

Economic change and the British
construction industry

MICHAEL BALL

Routledge: London

First published in 1988 by
Routledge
11 New Fetter Lane, London EC4P 4EE

Set in 10/12pt Sabon
by Input Typesetting Ltd, London
and printed in Great Britain
by T. J. Press (Padstow) Ltd
Padstow, Cornwall

British Library Cataloguing in Publication Data
Ball, Michael, 1948–
  Rebuilding construction: economic
  change and the British construction
  industry
  1. Construction industry — Great Britain
  I. Title   II. Series
  338.4'7626'0941   HD9715.G72

ISBN 0–415–00208–7

Contents

Figures

Tables

Tables

CHAPTER 1

Construction: the image and the reality

Of all industries in Britain, construction has one of the worst public images. High cost, poor quality and chaotic working practices are believed by many to be synonymous with building work. Folk tales abound about what goes on in the industry. The derogatory word 'cowboy' is often used against get-rich-quick construction firms and workers. It sums up well the general view of construction – not quite proper, full of sharp practices, dangerous, inefficient and definitely not like any other modern industry.

Like all folk-lore generalisations, such views of the construction industry are based primarily on myth, but they do have close links with many people's experiences of the industry, either as consumers or as building workers.

Over the past fifteen years, the industry has contracted heavily in the face of declining orders for new work. Substantial restructuring has taken place, leading to considerable reductions in capacity. In the context of such reduced potential, it is virtually impossible to expect any rapid increase in the output of the construction industry, even if a government decided to pump millions of pounds into building work. It is also unclear what shape the new slimmed-down construction industry is in. Has it improved its hopeless record of high cost and low productivity? Are shoddy work and building failures aberrations from its past or an ever-present threat? In the midst of the rapid changes taking place, it is difficult to piece together adequate answers to such questions without an understanding of how such problems first arose.

This book explains why the building industry is like it is, and why and how it has changed over the recent decades. The popular view of construction is shown to be misplaced, but a dynamic, vibrant industry cannot, unfortunately, be revealed to replace the mythology.

The core chapters look at the organisation of the industry; the relationships between employers and workers; the role of architects and other professionals; the slump in construction workloads over the past decade; the shift away from new building to repair and renovation; how firms have managed to survive the slump and the resultant impact on the industry as a whole; and the consequences of

1

the changes that have taken place in the industry over the past fifteen years.

When looking at the construction industry, some guiding theories are required to interpret, organise and evaluate the mass of available information. So a sub-theme running through the book concerns theories of the construction industry. Competing views are examined, and it is suggested that the industry can only be adequately understood in terms of the complexity of its social relations, its history and the overwhelming dominance of large-scale capitalist enterprises. Such an argument contrasts, in particular, with interpretations of construction which externalise its problems. Governments, economic fluctuations, trade unions, planners, even nature itself have been blamed for construction's ills, while remarkably little analysis exists of the peculiarities of capitalism in construction itself.

Before proceeding further, an introduction to the industry and its contemporary problems is required. The rest of this chapter is devoted to this task.

Construction: an overview

EMPLOYMENT

Around a million and a half people were estimated to work in construction in the mid-1980s.[1] The trades unions reckoned in 1984 that another half million construction workers were unemployed, and the situation did not change much in the following two years. Since 1982 the government has stopped collecting unemployment returns by industry. However, as the official statistics estimated that approximately two million worked in the industry in 1973, the trades unions' guess should be about right, though Conservative ministers throughout the mid-1980s vociferously denied the claim, suggesting instead that many of the unemployed were moonlighting (see also *Building*, 19 December 1986).

Manual workers in construction are employed in three ways. An unknown number are self-employed, others are employed by private contractors, while a large number (17 per cent in 1985) are employed by public authorities, particularly undertaking repair and maintenance tasks in local-authority direct-labour departments. Not all employees are manual workers. Roughly one in three of private contractors' employees are administrative, professional, technical and clerical staff (APTCs), reflecting the sophistication of the modern building enterprise.

Few manual workers now do the traditional labouring jobs associated with construction; over the past thirty years machines have taken over many of the heavy digging and lifting tasks. Roughly 70 per cent of private-sector building workers are classified as having some sort of skill, according to Construction Industry Training Board (CITB) returns. 'Skill' is a social construct denoting status, earning capacity, industrial power and the ability to exclude others, as well as indicating a capacity to undertake certain specified tasks. Construction is riddled with skill and status divisions. They have benefited certain types of workers but have created enormous rifts between trades, as well as between those workers officially designated as having a trade and those classified as unskilled. One group clearly excluded from construction has been women. Only a handful of manual workers are women; a construction site is usually an all-male preserve (Gann, 1984).

The hard, physical nature of much construction work, often under-taken in a poor working environment, is frequently combined with images of masculine stereotypes to create impressions of what construction work is like. At best a half-truth, the idea of 'hard men' dashing around construction sites with devil-may-care attitudes in attempts to make the most out of piece rates and bonuses may be used as part explanation of poor site safety, the young age profile of the workforce, and low-quality work. From this perspective, management may be said to do its best to contain the worst excesses, and is conveniently absolved of responsibility for their causes.

It is wrong, however, to take the converse view of construction workers as being united against a common enemy – the employer – or to see beneath brusque exteriors a workforce bent on mutual support and caring and sharing. Divisions within the workforce, the types of workers entering the industry, and the means by which individual and groups of workers have tried to sustain their positions and living standards have had an enormous influence on the development of the construction industry, as later chapters show.

CONSTRUCTION'S ROLE IN THE ECONOMY
Construction is one of Britain's major industries – it is the creator of the built environment within which most other economic activity takes place. Buildings and other construction products have a pervasive influence on social activity in modern societies. The built environment of a society expresses its cultural values, and is a major influence on the visual beauty or squalor people experience. However they look, houses, roads, factories, offices, schools, hospitals are also part of the complex physical infrastructure of daily life. A well-provided built environment facilitates efficient production and distribution. The costs of building products, on the other hand, affect

firms' profitability, peoples' living standards and, with publicly-financed construction, the level of taxes and public borrowing.

The state is heavily involved in funding construction work – even after years of public expenditure cuts. In 1985, 32 per cent of all new construction work was undertaken directly for the public sector, while much private-sector work receives public subsidies or tax reliefs (such as mortgage-interest tax relief for owner-occupied housing, and investment allowances on new buildings for companies).

Involvement of the state in construction expenditure has qualitatively changed over the past fifty years, reflecting trends in capitalist economies. Certain services and transportation facilities, for instance, have to be provided publicly for economic activity to continue. The state has also intervened to varying degrees in attempts to resolve the inability of unregulated private markets to provide basic consumption goods like housing. Investment by private industry, in addition, is often encouraged by free state infrastructural provision.

Apart from the uses to which construction products are put, the industry is a major source of economic activity in itself. In 1983, 5.8 per cent of total national income was generated in the construction industry. To get an idea of relative size, such a percentage is over three times as great as agriculture, larger than all the transportation industries, and about a quarter of the contribution of the whole of manufacturing industry.

Construction is also a labour-intensive industry. In 1984, manufacturing industry had a fixed capital stock equivalent to 3.13 times its net output for the year, whereas construction had a fixed capital stock equivalent to only 0.81 of its annual net output.[2] Construction is also overwhelmingly a domestic industry. Overseas work, though significant for some individual firms, was only 9 per cent of the value of gross UK construction output in 1984.[3] Imports, on the other hand, constitute a relatively small, though growing, proportion of construction inputs. Many construction materials are too heavy or bulky relative to their value to make extensive international trade viable. Only when there is a lack of indigenous sources (e.g., for Britain, timber) or when domestic prices rise well above foreign prices – perhaps because of monopolistic pricing or the use of outmoded plant – does the importing of materials like bricks, plasterboard and cement occur. Overall, the value of its imports constituted just over 5 per cent of the industry's output in 1974, and the proportion is unlikely to have changed much since then.[4]

ECONOMIC REGULATOR

Construction's position within the British economy has encouraged its use as an economic regulator by successive governments since the Second World War.

In terms of the *usefulness* of the existing built environment, variations in construction output have little short-term effect. Given the durability of most construction products and the sheer size of the existing built environment in relation to either new output or repair and maintenance expenditure, a rundown of construction output takes a long time to have any significant influence on users. Increases in construction output take a similar time to have much noticeable effect. How much is spent on construction can, as a result, vary quite sharply from year to year without significantly affecting the state of the built environment.

Such limited short-term physical consequences, plus the high proportion of public expenditure in total construction output, make the industry prone to the adverse effects of public expenditure cuts. It is virtually impossible for building workers to resist such cuts, making public construction expenditure a soft option for the Treasury knife. The labour-intensive nature of much construction work and its low reliance on imports produces the opposite effect when a government wants to stimulate overall demand. Expenditure on construction, within limits, becomes a good means of reflation, and one frequently endowed with moral superiority over other potential forms of reflation – 'investing in the nation's future'.

Construction's role as an economic regulator should not be exaggerated, however. Building-employers' organisations, in particular, have used fluctuations in construction demand as an excuse for many current practices in the industry, which, as will be seen later, are more adequately explained by factors internal to the industry. It is also not that easy to turn the construction tap on and off in the short run. There is usually a long gestation period between the decision to implement a construction project and the actual commencement of building work, while on major projects the job may take years to complete. Cancellation may be prohibitively expensive once contracts have been let, when extensive pre-planning and design has been done, or when the project is semi-completed. So, overall, the possibility of rapid cuts in construction expenditure may be limited, and sudden increases in construction work are even more difficult; all the planning and pre-construction stages have to be gone through for any new projects proposed. The construction industry may also not have the ability to take on much more work in the short-term. Such structural rigidities in the industry were clearly seen in the years following the two World Wars.

The rundown of the British construction industry since the early 1970s has been of major concern to many. Key features of Britain's built environment are now in bad shape. There is a growing shortage of decent houses; roads are poorly maintained; new public transportation schemes are sorely needed; inner cities, and soon the interwar suburbs, will have to be rebuilt and renovated; while Victorian sewerage and fresh-water systems are on their last legs. For virtually every use to which construction products are put a long list of much needed projects could be drawn up. Mass unemployment in the building industry has also generated considerable concern. Furthermore, consumer groups and outraged 'bona fide' building firms want to do something about the 'cowboy' enterprises that seem to have blossomed as a result of the industry's decline.

Given the importance of construction in the economy and widespread concern over unemployment and the state of the built environment, it might be expected that the health of the industry is high on the political agenda. However it is not. After a flurry of legislation restricting the activities of local-authority direct-labour departments in the early years of the first Thatcher administration, the Thatcher government has subsequently turned a deaf ear to pleas from building employers and unions, the CBI and the TUC, the Labour opposition and others to expand construction output substantially. Yet Thatcherite *laissez-faire* policies alone cannot explain the current political *impasse* over the construction industry. All the politicians and pressure groups pushing for action over construction were and are concerned only with the industry's role as provider of buildings and as an economic regulator. Apart from some complaint from building trade unions, little concern is ever voiced over the nature of the industry itself. Yet the record of the construction industry is little short of appalling in terms of the quality of its products, its waste of resources and lives, and the poor working conditions most of its workers have to face.

It would be tedious to go through all the problems of the construction industry and the debates that surround them. Just a few indicators suggest that serious difficulties exist, and that they cannot simply be put down to a contemporary lack of public-sector demand. Product quality, employment conditions and general productive efficiency are three areas which bring out the extent of the industry's failings.

A dismal catalogue

PRODUCT QUALITY

Consumer power can hardly be said to rule in construction. Virtually no client of the industry seems happy with its products. Construction projects frequently take too long to build, cost too much, do not meet user requirements, and fail to last as long as they should, often quickly requiring extensive remedial work. Agents in the construction process are usually adept at ensuring that blame does not stick to them. Who, for instance, is to blame when it is reported some ten years after a structure is built that it has to be extensively repaired or demolished? The causes of building failure are usually ascribed to the catch-alls of poor design and bad workmanship. Few aggrieved clients can seek redress through the courts, as the offending parties cannot be identified, have gone out of business, or the case cannot be sufficiently proved beyond doubt to be the responsibility of the offending party.

It is impossible to know the proportion of design and building work which is substandard. However, a brief look at the few surveys which exist and the general press suggests that the proportion could be high.

Industrialised housing systems Perhaps the most famous and spectacular building failures over the past forty years are the ones associated with proprietary industrialised housing systems.

Industrialised systems can take many forms. Generally, substantial parts of the load-bearing structure are fabricated out of non-traditional materials, usually in an off-site plant. Early large-scale use of industrialised systems was associated with the application of concrete systems to houses – Wimpey's No Fines (fabricated on site) and Laing's Easiform were used on both council and private housing estates in the inter-war years, and 'prefabs' like the Airey house were common in the early post-war housing drive. Later, in the 1950s and 1960s, large blocks of flats became the principal form of industrialised building, using concrete-based systems like Concrete Limited's Bison Wall-Frame and Taylor-Woodrow Anglian's Larsen-Nielsen system (used in the construction of Ronan Point), and again Wimpey's No Fines (the most commonly used of the systems).

The problems of the industrialised systems and the enormous misery they have brought to thousands of council tenants are so well documented that they need little further elaboration. Bad design and building combined to produce one of the most costly failed experiments in British post-war history. The Association of Metropolitan Authorities, for instance, has calculated that £10,000 million needs to be spent on correcting 'design defects'.[5] Newham Council is likely to have to spend £6 million on demolishing each one of its Ronan Point-style blocks,[6] and 600 such blocks were erected in this country. The failings of the concrete systems have meant that since the mid-1970s virtually no dwellings have in Britain been built using them, though in other European countries, like Denmark, concrete systems are still the norm (except that nowadays only low-rise housing is built) (Ball, 1988). Industrialised building technologies in Britain instead have developed along new lines. Timber has taken over from concrete as the new load-bearing material for industrialised systems, and emphasis is back on houses rather than flats. Timber-framed housing is now used widely in private housebuilding. Until 1983, it looked as though the majority of new owner-occupied houses would in future be built using timber-frame techniques; many of the volume builders had already switched to it. But media publicity brought to light technical uncertainties about its long-term structural viability and the frequently appalling way in which it was erected.[7] The debate over timber frame still rages, and no-one can unequivocally guarantee the long-term structural viability of timber frame nor that it is erected according to specification. Meanwhile, many volume builders still use the system because it saves them millions of pounds in working capital each year. Owner-occupiers faced with the threat of large repair bills and unsaleable houses might not feel so sanguine.

One major question overhangs the whole saga of industrialised systems: Why are they built when the apparent risks of design faults and incorrect building are so high? The explanation can only lie in understanding the way in which the overall building process is organised, and the conflicts and contradictions associated with it.

Calcium chloride rots concrete During the 1950s and 1960s a variety of additives were experimented with to increase the strength or speed up the drying of concrete. In laboratory conditions, calcium chloride seemed to offer much quicker concrete drying times. Its subsequent widespread use as an additive is now creating a substantial programme of remedial work which will continue as long as buildings and other concrete structures exist that were built with calcium chloride added.

One documented case of the mid-1980s is illustrative of a problem whose extent no-one knows. Harlow council spent an estimated £2 million on repairs to its twenty-two-year-old town hall because of calcium chloride attack (plus poor workmanship at the time of building). The Post Office is another agency with enormous repair bills; it has spent millions in attempts to remedy the effects of calcium chloride on its central city sorting offices built in the 1960s.

Perhaps no-one could have foreseen the long-term effects of calcium chloride. Some say it should have been predicted (e.g. Scott, 1976). However the important question raised here is why do some parts of the building process have to be speeded up to such an extent, while, at the same time, the industry overall is so notorious for its slow completions?

Motorway blues   Failures have not only been associated with buildings; other products of the construction industry have faced similar problems. Motorways, as anyone who drives on them knows, are forever being repaired. In general, they have not lasted as well as they were supposed to. The roads were not designed for the loads they have had to carry; not all new technologies tried in their construction have worked; and at times specifications were not adhered to during building.

The Midlands-links motorway system is the most notorious, and in this case failure to build to specification was a significant contributory cause, not only in the initial building but also in the repairs – and in the repairs to the repairs! Frequently, the same contractors were used time and again. Eventually, some of the contractors had to repay money to the Department of Transport, but the full story of incompetence has never been revealed, despite active campaigning and numerous Parliamentary questions.

A general problem   Building failure should not be seen solely as something associated with high technology. It affects all fields of building work. Sometimes the faults can be niggling; at other times they can cost millions.

In a survey of house purchasers, the Consumers Association magazine, *Which* (July 1984), found that only one in eight houses were fault free at the time of moving in (although a quarter were said to be overall in very good condition), and that only a quarter of purchasers would definitely buy from the same builder again. On individual private estates some remarkable failures seem to occur. In February 1983 a Conservative MP lambasted Tarmac, Britain's largest building firm, in the House of Commons for building faulty walls on its private housing estates and failing to repair them. In 1984 Barratt had to put in missing wall-ties on all the houses on a new estate near Lowestoft.[8]

Repairing, maintaining and improving housing seems to raise particular difficulties. It is in this area that most people come into direct contact with the building industry and the experience often does not seem to be a pleasant one. Even the employers' organisation, the Building Employers Confederation, has expressed concern about this sector – blaming the problems on the 'moonlighter or cowboy builder'. The Department of the Environment instigated an investigation into the escalating costs of refurbishment late in 1984 and why, in the words of the then under-secretary, George Younger, 'projects done ten years ago are falling apart already' even though they were supposed to last thirty years.

Housing projects and public-sector work get the most publicity, but the problems extend to the private sector as a whole. One 1984 report by a firm of remedial architects suggests that users of private commercial property would have to spend around £1,000 million on remedial work over the next ten years. Typical faults include curtain walls that leak, external mosaic tiles or stone that come loose, brickwork badly supported, seals that depend on mastic in impractical situations, roofs with saturated insulation, floor screeds that break up and leaky basements.[9]

The government's Building Research Establishment (BRE) in its 1985 Annual Report stated that quality control in general was a big problem in building. 'The greatest problems arise not because people do not know the problems but because they do not apply what we know.' The biggest difficulty identified by the BRE was that of 'motivating people at all levels to do things well' (reported in the *Financial Times* 9 September 1985). A NEDO report on construction research and development (R&D) in 1986 voiced similar criticisms of a lack of use of technical information; of new materials and methods being introduced much faster than experience and feedback were generated about them; and of a general lack of R&D in the industry (NEDO, 1985).

It is difficult to believe that construction firms deliberately build substandardly. Most advanced capitalist industries are obsessed with quality control in order to maintain business in the face of competition. Something in the construction industry seems to override that obsession; later chapters will try to find out what.

PROJECT DELAYS AND COST OVERRUNS

Construction projects have been notorious for not sticking to cost estimates and for overrunning time schedules considerably. In public housing in the 1970s, the situation was so bad it can only be described as incredible (see Direct Labour Collective (1978) for a lengthy, but by no means exhaustive, list of such unfortunate schemes). Every sector has experienced similar difficulties to varying degrees, although in the mid-1980s the situation seems to have improved somewhat, as later chapters will show.

There can be few industries whose cost and time performance has been lambasted as thoroughly as construction's. In the late 1970s, a chairman of Exxon, the US oil company, justified the extensive regional grants given to build process plants on the grounds that they were in effect simply a subsidy to bring construction costs in Britain closer to those elsewhere (*Financial Times*, 7 January 1981). In 1986, at a building conference in Oxford, the secretary of NEDO's Building Economic Development Committee claimed that the situation was so bad it affected the level of construction demand; he said that 'customers were frightened to start building projects, because they feared that costs and time factors might get out of control', adding that construction problems were one reason why British companies had been slow to update their premises (quoted in *National Builder*, September 1986, p. 227).

EMPLOYMENT CONDITIONS

Mass unemployment is not the only problem facing building workers. Construction is not a particularly attractive industry to work in. Much of the work is unhealthy and dangerous. Exposure to the elements, the dirt, damp and dust of a construction site, and the speed at which heavy manual tasks have to be undertaken, all take a long-term toll on building workers' health. And accidents are common; construction has one of the worst safety records of any industry.[10]

Employment in construction is overwhelmingly casual in nature. The epitome of casual work is a worker turning up to a site, getting a job, and then being laid off when it is finished. Traditional dockwork (before the Dock Labour Schemes) was of this casual sort. Self-employed building workers fall clearly within such a definition of casual employment; they are only employed for specific tasks. Directly-employed workers also tend not to be employed for long periods of time; a survey in the late 1970s (Marsh *et al.*, 1981) found that 60 per cent of workers had been in their current jobs for less than five years, and that many had had a number of jobs over the period, some entering and leaving the industry several times. The survey was of all employees, including office workers and technicians, and failed to distinguish adequately between public- and private-sector employment (councils are supposed to be better employers). Its results, therefore, only hint at the extent of how dependent many workers are on the project in hand – the threat of layoff is ever present. Frequently, layoff takes the covert form of a rapid drop-off in bonuses, so that workers leave 'voluntarily' in the face of large cutbacks in take-home pay. The survey did show that relatively few older workers (aged forty years and over) are employed in the industry, and most of them are in the public sector. Such an age profile is a sign of casualised hire-and-fire policies as much as the physical nature of the work. In some sectors casual work is now almost universal; speculative housebuilders, for instance, rely virtually entirely on self-employed labour.

Building workers' pay does not compensate for their poor working conditions and casual employment. Table 1.1 shows male full-time building workers' reported weekly earnings and hours. It can be seen that nationally they corresponded roughly to the norm for all industries and services in the mid-1970s, but there was a slow relative decline in pay over the subsequent decade. The figures are very aggregate, however, and do not indicate the complexity of the wages structure in the industry; a complexity that leads to a wide distribution of earnings. The governments' New Earnings Survey for 1985, for instance, showed that the top 10 per cent of male manual workers earned 44 per cent more than the industry average, while the bottom 10 per cent earned less than two-thirds of it. This skewed distribution meant that most (i.e. 50 per cent) earned at least 10 per cent less than the average earnings for the industry.

Table 1.1 *Construction earnings and hours compared with all industries and services, 1975–85*

	Relative full-time male manual workers (all industries and services = 100)	
	Earnings	*Hours*
1975	100.5	102.6
1976	99.2	102.3
1977	99.5	100.4
1978	98.6	100.4
1979	98.1	100.6
1980	98.2	101.8
1981	99.1	100.4
1982	98.2	100.7
1983	97.4	99.8
1984	97.8	100.0
1985	95.8	99.8

Source: Housing and Construction Statistics

Four interlinked divisions help to create the spread of earnings: skill, differences in wage setting in the public and private sectors, regional factors and self-employment. Table 1.2 shows some of the wage variations caused by craft differentiation. Not surprisingly, foremen earn more than the norm, followed by a hierarchy of wage levels related to particular types of skill, with ordinary labourers trailing way behind. Pay in the public sector also tends to be lower. Local-authority manual-worker wage negotiations have a strong influence on direct labour building workers' annual pay awards. In general, given successive governments' explicit or implicit incomes policies towards the public sector, local-authority building-workers' pay has tended to lag behind the private sector. Another cause of pay differences is regional variations. Generally, areas of high demand for construction work generate the highest earnings. Building workers in the South West, for instance, earn almost a quarter less than those in London, although in some of the more depressed regions it would seem that, relatively, construction wages have remained firmer (see Table 1.3).

Table 1.2 *Construction earnings by craft, 1985 (full-time men over 21)*

	£	Index
Foremen	187.8	120
Carpenters	153.3	98
Bricklayers	145.4	93
Roadmen	139.2	89
Mates and labourers	134.6	86
All workers	156.8	100

Source: *Housing and Construction Statistics*

The final, and most controversial, of the listed causes of earnings differences is self-employment. Earnings from self-employment are generally understated for taxation reasons, and it is often believed that earnings data for the construction industry are grossly understated because of the self-employment effect. At the time of writing, for example, contractors in London were advertising for labour-only bricklayers at £60 or more a day – a considerable sum in comparison to the New Earnings Survey data. Such anecdotal evidence helps to create the impression of carefree, well-paid, self-employed building workers – they are said to be the ones that take the initiative and who work hard and get rewarded for it.

Table 1.3 *Regional variations in construction wages, 1986*

	Male manual workers' average weekly earnings	
	£	Index (GB=100)
Greater London	188.20	120
Scotland	162.50	104
South East (non-London)	158.20	101
North West	155.00	99
North	154.80	99
Yorks and Humberside	152.10	97
East Anglia	151.40	96
East Midlands	149.70	95
West Midlands	146.20	93
Wales	142.10	91
South West	141.60	90
Great Britain	156.80	100

Source: New Earnings Survey

Such images ignore the reality of the reasons for self-employment. Firms encourage self-employment in part to avoid the indirect costs of employment, which workers themselves then have to cover – pensions, sickness and holiday pay, and employment-related clerical and other administrative costs. These expenses reduce the comparative net earnings of the self-employed. Secondly, many self-employed workers will have periods without work, reducing further the benefit of high payments whilst in work (though partially compensated by extra leisure time). Finally, firms pay differential rates to the self-employed depending on how desperate they are to complete a particular task. In the jargon, they can more closely fix earnings to the marginal benefit they derive from hiring workers, whereas with direct employment and union-negotiated rates most workers receive roughly the same rate of pay. One result of self-employment for construction firms, therefore, is that it tends to lower their total wage bill, as unions are less able to use temporary conditions of high demand in certain localities to push up all workers' earnings. On the same reasoning, the highest rates are also highly unlikely to be earned by many self-employed workers; most will be paid far less. However, as there is no detailed information on self-employed earnings (and by their nature accurate ones are impossible to obtain), it is difficult to assess the overall consequence of self-employment on construction earnings and hours. Differentials are probably widened, but it is uncertain whether overall earnings are much higher than those actually recorded. No one is likely to become rich by being a building worker, though some reach that state by employing them.

Casual work and poor working conditions are not inevitable consequences of building work but of the way that the actual physical process of building is organised and executed. It could be claimed, for example, that the particular social psychology of building workers, with its emphasis on masculine bravado and individual risk-taking, leads to the high levels of accidents. A more plausible, if less romantic, alternative explanation would be that workers are given strong incentives to work fast which encourages them to dispense with safety precautions. Neither explanation, it should be noted, relies on some innate characteristic of building work.

PRODUCTIVITY AND COSTS

It is very difficult to produce accurate construction productivity and cost data, because of the heterogeneous nature of construction work and the widespread underrecording of output and employment within the industry (Fleming, 1966; Butler, 1978). Cost data obviously are needed to compare output information over time, and the Department of the Environment (DoE) has used increasingly sophisticated methods to derive cost indices.

Productivity data are more difficult. The growth of self-employment makes it impossible to measure employment change accurately. DoE-published data also refer only to gross output, which includes the value of materials as well as the productive efforts of the industry itself. If the value of materials alters, either because of price changes not accounted for in the price deflators or because more or less expensive materials are being used, any estimate of productivity will be correspondingly affected. National income accounts provided estimates of value added in the industry by calculating the total sum of incomes and profits minus the impact on profits of stock appreciation. Income estimates of national income are notoriously inaccurate, and they must be particularly bad for an industry like construction with its high levels of self-employment and income tax avoidance.

The data available to estimate productivity changes over time, in other words, are not very good. Their credibility vitally depends on whether the DoE's estimates of the rate of change of self-employment are accurate, and many believe them to be grossly low (e.g. Leopold, 1982). However the numbers are all we have, and although they might not be much use for calculating accurate annual rates of change they do give some impression of long-term trends.

Table 1.4 gives productivity estimates for 1973–85 based on both gross output and value-added data. Roughly the two series show a similar picture – a decline in productivity during the 1970s and a rapid improvement after 1981. The rate of change of productivity not surprisingly appears to be cyclical; sharp downturns in workloads adversely affect productivity, while upturns improve it. The decline in workloads through the 1970s had a disastrous impact on productivity. Hillebrandt (1984) reckons that 1973 itself was not a good year, and that overall from 1971 to 1981 gross output per worker fell by 16 per cent; a fall she partially attributes to the shift towards repair and maintenance, with its lower materials content, so that the value-added productivity decline was not so bad.

Table 1.4 *Estimates of construction productivity, 1973–85*

	£m at 1980 prices		Employment (000)	£ at 1980 prices	
	Gross output	Value added		Gross output productivity	Value added productivity
1973	26,100	14,312	1,911	13,660	7,489
1975	22,054	12,160	1,746	12,630	6,964
1977	21,617	11,958	1,592	13,580	7,511
1979	23,260	12,878	1,666	13,960	7,730
1981	19,947	11,801	1,606	12,420	7,348
1983	21,101	12,435	1,493	14,130	8,329
1984	21,842	13,243	1,519	14,380	8,718
1985	22,094	13,505	1,491	14,820	9,058

Notes
1 Gross output and employment from *Housing and Construction Statistics*; value added from *UK National Accounts*.
2 Employment includes DoE estimate of self employment.
3 Value added = income from employment and self-employment plus gross profits of companies minus stock appreciation, deflated to 1980 prices by using GDP deflator.

Productivity in the 1980s shows a very different picture – up 23 per cent between 1981 and 1985 on the value-added estimate. The rise could be accounted for by an underrecorded growth in self-employment, but the growth would have had to be exceedingly high as the DoE itself estimated a 21 per cent increase in self-employment over the period. The data do seem to indicate that during the 1980s there has been a substantial improvement in productivity, either because of the changing mix of types of work or because of changed methods of work, and most probably through a combination of the two factors.

Cost data show a similar difference between the 1970s and 1980s. During the 1970s real construction costs fluctuated considerably, but

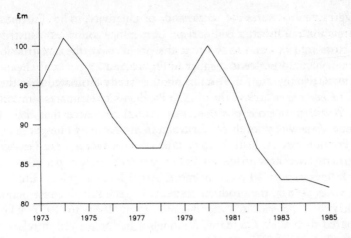

Figure 1.1 Index of real construction costs, 1973–85. Note: DoE all-new construction-output price index deflated to 1980 prices using GDP deflator. *Source: Housing and Construction Statistics.*

were virtually identical in 1974 and 1980 (see Figure 1.1). During the 1980s, on the other hand, costs consistently fell in real terms – average new construction costs fell by 18 per cent between 1980 and 1985. Even in nominal prices, construction costs in all new-build sectors apart from new private housing fell for at least a couple of years during the early 1980s.

Both the productivity and cost data seem to indicate that something substantial has happened in the construction industry during the 1980s, which seems to mark the period as a radical break with earlier patterns in the industry. It could be said that a 'successful' restructuring has gone on; undoubtedly a restructuring process has occurred, but what it has actually been about is not so obvious and will be considered in the following chapters.

INTERNATIONAL COMPARISONS
Little comparative work has been undertaken on construction industries, but the available information does not cast the British industry in a particularly attractive light. There is much anecdotal evidence, obtained by talking to experts and by reading the trade press, about slower building times in Britain and poorer construction quality than in other advanced industrial countries, but there is no systematic quantitative evidence to substantiate the claims.

One area where some statistical comparison has been undertaken is aggregate measures of cost and productivity. The European Commission published a comparison of member countries' construction costs in 1980 and found that the products of the construction industry were 34 per cent cheaper in France and 29 per cent cheaper in West Germany than in Britain; another study estimated that they were 27 per cent lower in the USA.[11] Productivity estimates similarly place Britain in a poor position. Roy (1982) estimated that the UK had one of the worst levels of construction productivity of eight major OECD countries in 1980 – only Japan had a worse one. German construction workers produced 80 per cent more output per year and French ones almost 40 per cent more. According to Smith, Hitchens and Davies (1982), the productivity record of the British construction industry had deteriorated significantly from 1968 to 1977 when compared with West Germany, although it had improved in relation to the USA. However, the US industry is not one of the world's leaders according to Roy's estimates; its construction workers lagged considerably behind their German and French counterparts, producing only 16 per cent a year more than those in the UK. Any improvement in the productivity record of the British industry during the 1980s, therefore, is unlikely to have brought it up to the level of the best of the other major EEC countries.

Approaching the construction industry

Amongst other things, this chapter so far has explained the object of this book – to elaborate the economic changes that have gone on in construction over the past decade and to understand their causes. In addition, it has put the construction industry in an initial context by considering some of its characteristics in relation to the rest of social life; some of the problems associated with construction quality and employment; and looked briefly at some aggregate indicators of change, namely labour productivity and construction costs. Such information is selective and descriptive, while the notion of change itself is vague. What must be specified more clearly are the elements of the industry in which change has a significant impact on its economic operation. To answer such a question requires a theoretical approach that outlines the key determinants of why construction is like it is and explains its patterns of development and change.

There has been little previous work looking at the economic operation of the industry as a whole. One reason could be that the industry is assumed to be essentially no different from any other. The next chapter, however, will argue that it *is* different in a number of crucial respects, ones that derive essentially from the ways in which distinct social agents combine in the physical act of construction. It is the combination of the social and physical nature of the construction process which simultaneously defines the boundaries of the industry and highlights its relative uniqueness, as later chapters will argue.

One theoretical avenue which seems of little use in studying the industry is to apply neoclassical economic theories of the firm that rely on the postulates derived from models of perfect competition. Construction in one respect would seem to be an industry that most closely approximates to one of the fundamental requirements of the perfectly competitive model – many firms. However closer inspection makes it clear that the firms are hierarchically, geographically and sectorally segmented, so models of oligopoly more closely correspond to the firm structure of the industry. In addition, rather than operating under the perfect competition assumption of full information, construction firms face considerable uncertainty in virtually every aspect of their activities.[12]

Such behavioural qualifications might suggest that modern neoclassical oligopoly theory offers a more fruitful avenue of enquiry, particularly the variants that rely on explicit assumptions of uncertainty in the context of game theory constructs. Two major problems limit the applicability of such approaches. The first is the way in which the relations between social agents are perceived. Economic agents are seen as essentially equal factors of production that voluntarily combine together to undertake specific tasks on the basis of their respective economic interests. In the market place itself, for one reason or another, one type of agent might be able to negotiate with another on the basis of some advantage, say because of an achieved monopolistic position, and such imbalances of power alter the market outcome. Yet, any such inequality is conjunctural and can be overturned without altering the basic economic workings of the market system, rather than structural and a necessary consequence of the forms of production and exchange that exist. In societies dominated by capitalist production, however, such fundamental structural imbalances do occur, as it is capitalist enterprises that instigate production, hire or purchase the other factors, decide which methods of production are preferable, and undertake the strategic decisions associated with investment and choosing the spheres of activity in which the enterprise operates. Other agencies, particularly the workforce, at best can only react and respond to those decisions. Their actions, in other words, are structured by the requirements of capital. This point is a standard Marxist critique of neoclassical theory, and it applies to the construction industry as much as to any other.

The second problem concerns the framework of the game analysis of oligopolies. Actors in some models may operate in contexts of uncertainty, but the parameters under which the games are played out are fixed or change in narrowly specified ways. This means that, while interesting scenarios may be explored within such a game-theory approach, there is little or no possibility of systematic analysis of the processes through which the constraints on any social agent change.[13]

It will be argued in this book that much of the conflict between different agents in the construction process is precisely over attempts to redraw the basis of the relations between them. What is required to elucidate those conflicts is a historical analysis of the evolution of the social relations of the modern British construction industry. Central to the analysis, it will be argued, is an examination of the 'Contracting System', the predominant form of building production in late 1960s and early 1970s. Under the Contracting System, specific and often ambiguous roles were assigned to contractors, design professionals and organised labour. A key question about the restructuring of the construction industry over the past fifteen years, therefore, is an analysis of the extent to which the Contracting System has changed or been undermined. The evidence points towards the latter, as later chapters will show.

Another theoretical approach which has been used extensively in the analysis of the construction industry in recent years has been that associated with Marxism.[14] Here historical development is placed at the forefront and, in doing so, many useful insights have been derived. There are problems, however, with some Marxist work of recent years. It is very easy for Marxists to adopt what can be called a fundamentalist approach to the analysis of an industry. Fundamentalism at its most extreme would regard capital as being all-powerful and having a single, unified interest. Empirical analysis of an industry under these assumptions follows an easy, if faulty, formula. First, the behaviour of capital must be elucidated; then the requirements of capital are deduced that follow from that behaviour; this finally leads to any empirical event being explained in terms of those requirements. Conflict, social differentiation and historical change as central analytical elements disappear.[15] A less mechanistic fundamentalist position places sole emphasis on the direct relation between capital and labour at the point of production, ignoring the wider social and economic contexts in which an industry develops.[16] Within its framework, any reasoning obviously can only be in terms of the development of the capital/labour relation because there is an initial presumption that other social agents, and developments such as shifting political and market contexts, do not matter. This book will argue that, at least in the case of Britain, the broader context matters considerably when looking at the construction industry.

This book will look at accumulation in the construction industry, in the context of how the broad social relations associated with it have emerged and are changing. Another way of stating the approach is to say that it will emphasise the institutional structures of construction, placing emphasis on their historical development and the pressures on each of them that lead to their reconstitution or dissolution.

Although the arguments made here will have extensive recourse to other literature in the field, there has been no previous work which takes a similar approach. This unfortunately places limits on the method of enquiry that can be adopted. Ideally, given the emphasis on social relations and their concomitant institutional structures, an international comparative analysis would have been useful. The enormous differences in labour productivity between countries noted earlier suggest that such an approach would have been instructive. Later it will also be argued that the social structure of the British construction industry in a number of key respects is unique. It would have been helpful to have been able to explore through comparative analysis the impact of that uniqueness, but hardly any published material exists on the distinct social structures of separate countries' construction industries. A comparative approach consequently was ruled out.

The arguments presented in the rest of the book and their order of presentation follow from the theoretical approach adopted. The next chapter surveys and criticises some previous theories of the construction industry, many of which start off from the presupposition that the construction industry is technologically backward. Chapter 2 also elaborates in greater detail the theoretical position adopted in this book.

The next three chapters then outline the basic social relations and institutional structures of the construction industry, placing most but not sole emphasis on the different types of construction firm and the ways they produce. Chapter 3 looks at the types of construction enterprise; Chapter 4 considers how Britain's unique Contracting System emerged; and Chapter 5 examines the ways firms organise production and accumulation and the constraints faced by them.

Having outlined the basic history and structure of the construction industry, the next five chapters consider what has happened to firms within the industry, and how their accumulation strategies have altered in the face of recent changes in the level and types of demand for construction work. Chapter 6 looks at the patterns of demand in the post-war era. Chapter 7 considers how the relationships between firms have been changing in the 1970s and 1980s, partially as a result of the shifting patterns of demand and partially because of the greatly increased use of subcontractors by firms of all sizes. Chapters 8–10 focus specifically on the fortunes of the larger firms. Chapter 8 considers how they managed to survive relatively unscathed the collapse in domestic workloads in the decade after 1972. Then Chapter 9 examines the key role played by mergers and acquisitions in attempts by firms to adapt their market strategies to the new environment of construction demand. Chapter 10 looks in detail at the restructuring of firms that has taken place within specific sectors over the past twenty years, concluding that the old framework of sectoral specialisation by enterprises has weakened considerably during the 1980s.

Chapter 11 draws on the previous analysis to present an assessment of the changes that have taken place in the relations between agents in the construction process in the 1980s. It argues that, although difficult to quantify, the changes have been considerable. Building firms, in particular, have managed to break out from some of the constraints imposed on them by the Contracting System, as a result of a weakening of the position of organised labour and of the management roles of the building professionals. The productivity 'revolution' of the 1980s noted earlier is one manifestation of their increased power. The changes have not been without their contradictions for the major building contractors, however, as they find themselves excluded from some of the major growth markets, especially those associated with repair and maintenance. The reorganisation of the construction process also contains inherent dangers in the greater indirect control that now exists over the inputs needed for production. Finally, it is not clear whether the reduced power of the other social agents in the construction process is a permanent or a temporary situation. A significant upturn in workloads might paradoxically lead to a weakening of the position of the building firm.

The final chapter attempts an assessment of the changes in the construction industry for the users of its products, and for contemporary debates over the role of construction in the reflation of the economy. On neither count, it is argued, are the prospects rosy.

CHAPTER 2

Is the construction industry backward?

It is easier to gather evidence about the problems of the building industry than it is to explain why those problems arise. Even interpretation of the data is often controversial. Such controversies perhaps are not surprising as associated with any explanation is, either implicitly or explicitly, a theory of how to study the construction industry. What this chapter will do is highlight the weaknesses of many traditional explanations of the construction industry, and then elaborate the theoretical approach that underlies the alternative explanation pieced together in subsequent chapters.

A diagnosis

One of the most common explanations of the nature of the construction industry is that it is backward (Clarke, 1985). Like the word 'crisis', 'backward' is derived from medical terminology. The backward thesis suggests that, unlike other capitalist industries, the infant construction industry failed to develop into a mature, technically-advanced, late-twentieth-century industry. It has, in terms of the backward metaphor, the mental age of an industrial child – living in the age of nineteenth-century handicraft technology (Lipietz, 1985). Something has either retarded its technological growth or prematurely brought it to a grinding halt, and the purpose of any explanation is to understand what inhibited the industry's development.

The backward diagnosis leads to a number of suggested remedies for the ailment. Yet all of them are unconvincing because, amongst other things, they put sole emphasis on one stage of the construction process, such as design or land acquisition.

The first remedy: design

One of the most famous proponents of the 'backward' construction industry thesis was the Modern Movement in architecture during the first half of the twentieth century. One of their central concerns was the high cost of working-class housing. Their explanation of the high cost partially centred on the activities of speculative housebuilders and landowners, who were said to raise prices in order to increase their profits. The distinctive analytical intervention of the Modern Movement, however, was in the field of design. They argued that the main reason why the construction industry had failed to advance at the same rate as other industries lay in the complexity of traditional building designs, which tended to emphasise the aesthetic individuality of buildings and clothed a building's basic structural features with intricate detailing. These design features, they claimed, were at odds with the standardised, mass-produced nature of commodities in modern industrial societies and ignored the beauty that could be derived from accepting the structural forms dictated by the functional requirements of mass production. Buildings should be designed on the same criteria as the other products of industrial societies and produced in essentially the same way. Designs which emphasised simplicity and function could be both beautiful and easy to build, they claimed (Banham, 1976). Others from academic or industrial backgrounds supported the idea of converting housing production into a factory-based technology (Bemis, 1936; White, 1965; Ball, 1988). However, it was the Modern Movement that formulated the design ideology which made possible such a convergence of ideas about the future of housing production. It was also an ideology amenable to other types of built structures and, in fact, it has been more successful in non-housing spheres, especially office development.

For the Modern Movement, the individual genius of the master architect is the key to cracking the fundamental design problems of the building industry. Le Corbusier's Domino House is perhaps the most famous of the Modern Movement's rationalised designs (Le Corbusier, 1970; Fishman, 1977). In the extreme version of the Modern Movements' dream, buildings would be produced like other consumer durables, rolling off the production line waiting for delivery, ready to be discarded when worn out or when the caprices of their owners dictated the need for new ones. 'Backward' is interpreted through an idealised model of the inevitability of a particular type of factory-based mass production and of the forms of consumerism needed to sustain it.

Clearly, there is much wrong with the Modern Movement's treatment of the building industry and its products. Design is given an unreasonably central place. Buildings are seen only through the eye of the beholder, ignoring the considerable foundation and other site work involved in any construction project, none of which comes within the architect's rationalising remit. Every other social agent involved in the construction process is idealised into a shadowy plasticity, prepared to do anything required of them by the designer.

Capitalist building firms, financial capital, landowners and building workers are ignored as active social agents. So, while talking in the language of economical building, Modern Movement architects' managed to ignore totally the economic context in which building takes place. This myopia led Le Corbusier, amongst others, to flirt with Fascism. Such authoritarian governments did claim they could create the submissiveness required for the master plans of a self-chosen elite (Fishman, 1977).

By ignoring the spatial fixity of buildings, the Modern Movement mispecified the path which technical development in construction would, and could, take. Even so, the Movement's emphasis on standardisation and functionalism in design has facilitated certain revolutions in building techniques. The most famous, and in Britain the least successful, Modern Movement experiments have been associated with housing. In office building and the prefabrication of concrete structures, like bridges, Modern Movement architects have facilitated, if not led, the rationalisation of building methods and their associated labour processes.

It cannot be said that the post-war success of the design ideology was solely the result of the efforts of its architectural proponents. Adopting the design criteria of the Modern Movement enabled property developers to maximise the floor space they could get out of a particular land site. Building such designs also meant that building contractors could cheapen costs, rationalise production methods and dispense with some building trades altogether. In the end, the Modern Movement had some effect on the building process because from the 1940s onwards it pandered solely to the needs of the dominant agencies in the construction industry, rather than attempting to go against them as its pioneers often claimed to be doing.

A few Western European Modern Movement architects worked in the Soviet Union during the 1930s. Their experience made them sensitive to the fact that rationalised design was only one potential element in the transformation of the building process, and not necessarily the most important one. Their experiences made them recognise the significance of cooperation in all stages of the building process, the utility of indigenous materials and the need to respond to housing consumers' wishes. However after their departure from the Soviet Union with the advent of Stalinism, they languished in obscurity, leaving the ideological field within the profession open to the champions of elitist individualism (Saint, 1983).

The state, particularly in Britain, saw the industrialised systems made fashionable by the Modern Movement as a way of cheapening the provision of working-class housing and a means of weakening the craft building unions. There was little concern over the effects on final users, who ended up paying the cost in poor-quality housing, characterless office blocks and a barren environment. Such end products did not make the Modern Movement popular. Widespread public disgust with the built environment that emerged in the 1950s and 1960s was pinned firmly on the architectural trend, while the Modern Movement's capitalist allies survived unscathed.

The second remedy: land rent

It has been argued, particularly by some French Marxists, that the construction industry is technically backward because of the way in which land rent is appropriated from the users of buildings, either through the continual need to pay a ground rent or through the price that developers have to pay to acquire building plots.

Marx's category of absolute rent, elaborated in *Theories of Surplus Value* and *Capital*, is used in the explanation. Absolute rent is said to exist because the low technical development of the construction industry means that it has a low organic composition of capital compared to the average for all industries (c.f. Ascher, 1974; Lipietz, 1974). Construction, in other words, employs a greater than average number of workers in proportion to the machines and raw materials used in production. Construction's low organic composition of capital means that landowners can extract absolute rent from the surplus value generated by workers in the building process. The appropriation of rent, in turn, limits the incentive for building capitalists to invest in new techniques and so hinders technical development. The result is that absolute rent is both a cause and an effect of the low organic composition of capital in construction.

Unfortunately, the argument about absolute rent does not specify the detailed mechanisms through which this rent is appropriated, nor does it explain precisely how investment is retarded. Instead, reference is made only to the circular explanation of the low organic composition, and to the authority of Marx, who, I feel, has been misunderstood and whose word anyway should not be seen as a viable substitute for theoretical consistency (see Ball, 1985a). As with design, the absolute rent theorists focus on only one social agent – the architect being replaced by that perennial radical target, the landowner.

There are many situations when rent cannot possibly have the effects claimed for it by the absolute rent theorists. A good example is when building firms contract to undertake a particular piece of building work and do not have to buy or rent land. Such cases are the norm in building contracting, where the client rather than the builder acquires the land. It is difficult to see why in those situations building capitalists should be bothered about land costs at all, and why therefore rent can have any direct effect on their profits and the production methods they use (Ball, 1985b).

Neglect of the other social agents in the building process becomes even more apparent when trying to evaluate the likely consequences of large sums of absolute rent being appropriated from the surplus value generated in building production. An enormous mass of surplus value must exist in construction if rent is to have the barrier effect claimed of it. Out of that surplus value must be paid the profit of the building capitalist, the revenue of building professionals, the interest of money-lending capitalists who finance projects, and landowners' rent. Such views about the production and distribution of surplus value in a capitalist society and its construction industry are theoretically simplistic and empirically unreasonable.

Rejection of the notion that absolute rent is the explanation of the contemporary nature of the building industry does not mean that land-ownership and rent have no influence on construction. Where there is a direct social relation between landowners and building capitalists, as there is for instance in speculative housebuilding, an antagonistic relation over the price of land is likely to arise between building capitalist and landowner. The result will probably influence the technical development of the industry, but that result can only be ascertained by detailed empirical analysis rather than by reference to some shaky generalisation about land rent.

Third: no remedy for a permanent affliction

Physical characteristics of the building process have been suggested to influence fundamentally the structure of the construction industry (e.g. Needleman, 1965).

According to the absolute physical constraint thesis, the technical advances associated with continuous or batch production in factories are impossible to achieve in construction because each building project is on a new site. Breaks in the flow of production are forced on construction by such spatial differentiation. The production process has to be organised over and over again with each new project. Both the workforce and the tools and equipment they use have to be mobile, moving from site to site to undertake a sequence of tasks that, to a degree at least, vary from project to project. The building industry does not correspond to the environment of a factory and, as a result, it is concluded that the building industry is doomed to relative technical stagnation. Only increasing the amount of off-site factory-based production will alleviate the problem, though never resolve it.

Empirically, it is difficult to say what proportion of construction work is inherently site-based. Changing techniques over time have considerably altered the sorts of construction work that have to be undertaken on-site. Many tasks have, over the years, been transformed into factory-based production. Bricks, for example, until the middle of the nineteenth century were generally made on-site by itinerant families of brickmakers, if the appropriate clay was available there (Hobhouse, 1971). Most woodworking activities have gone the same way. Modern materials – like plastics, plasterboard, steel and aluminium – advances in extrusion and moulding techniques, and the increasing importance of computer-controlled machines have resulted in dramatic increases in productivity in particular areas of the construction process which might once have seemed stubbornly resistant to technical change. Construction on-site is more and more an assembly operation of previously manufactured components. In comparison to the much slower change in the remaining on-site tasks, it is easy to see why the difference could be interpreted as indicating the problems of site-based production. However it is an argument which relies on a historically myopic view of what is physically essential in building work. Like the Modern Movement's ideas, however, the notion of inherent problems of site-based production was influential in setting the intellectual climate for the industrialised building programmes of the post-war decades.

It would be folly to ignore the special physical characteristics of building production, but to elevate them to a level where they are all-determining seems both logically and historically false. Technical change has a tendency to transform the physical content of production, making previously seemingly-insuperable physical barriers either non-existent or easy to overcome. Technological advance and physical constraints are mutually influencing processes. The question then becomes: What determines the form of technological change?

Developments in technique are not simply random processes subject to the skills and genius of individual inventors. Instead changes in production methods depend on the economic content of production and the social relations that underlie it. Thus the role played by the physical content of building production can only be understood in the context of the contemporary social relations of building production.

Many of the advances associated with modern factory production can, and have been, applied to building production. Machines have taken over much of the heavy manual tasks of lifting and digging, once done virtually unaided by human muscle. What is technically feasible, however, is not necessarily used. Railways and docks in Britain, for example, were still being made by navvies using picks and shovels at the end of the nineteenth century, over forty years after the widespread introduction of mechanical excavators in countries like the USA (Coleman, 1968). Similarly, a considerable amount of building work can be transformed from static, bespoke, on-site processes to factory production. However the shift of progressively more building work into factories should neither be regarded as inevitable nor the only means of mechanising the building process, as the widespread introduction of site-based machinery has shown. Even where the location of production is relevant, the extent of on- or off-site production is only partially a question of physical constraint; more important generally is the economic viability of such a transfer.

Taylorism and Fordism in the building industry

Many of the productivity gains of modern production lines come from reorganisations of the labour process which introduce progressively more complex divisions of labour and from the application of machines to tasks previously done manually. (Usually, of course, the two go hand in hand.) The simplification of tasks inherent in a more complex division of labour may mean that workers do not need the same level of skill as before, while the introduction of more standardised and repetitive tasks reduces the amount of productive time workers waste in switching from one activity to another and enables management more easily to control the pace at which workers do their jobs. The pace of work can be controlled either by direct supervision, by the speed at which machinery is set to operate, or by tying wage payments to work rates, as in piecework wage systems.

Such reformulations of the labour process began in the late nineteenth century to be key concerns of management theories. In particular, they were the central focus of *scientific management*, whose principles have become closely associated with one of its earliest proponents, F. W. Taylor, and so it is now generally known as *Taylorism* (Braverman, 1974; Wood, 1982).

Taylorism focuses on the physical actions of workers and how management can control and reformulate those actions through ever more complex divisions of labour. *Fordism* takes the process of control and reformulation a stage further by taking the determination of the speed of production out of the hands of a direct human agent; instead machines or production lines determine work rates (Littler and Salaman, 1984). Under Fordism, tasks are undertaken sequentially in a line. In the classic case of the line production of motor cars, workers have to undertake specified tasks at a speed dictated by the rate at which the product being assembled travels past them. From its introduction by Henry Ford in the assembly of his motor cars before the First World War, such assembly-line methods gradually spread throughout manufacturing industry (Burawoy, 1985). But have they influenced construction?

The extent to which Taylorism and Fordism can be applied to building production would seem to be the crux of the backward-because-of-physical-constraints thesis about the construction industry. Yet, as long as Taylorism and Fordism are applied in particular ways, it seems clear that both practices are applicable to building. Taylorism seems particularly easy to introduce, as the repetitive manual tasks of most building work make it possible, and highly profitable, to organise building work on such principles. Some of the earliest developments of scientific management were undertaken in studies of building trades (Braverman, 1974). Nowadays, most large construction projects, and many small ones, are operated on Taylorist principles, and building wages are often closely tied to Taylorist-style piece rates and bonuses (Campinos-Dubernet, 1986).

Fordism seems more intractable in building. The discrete-site nature of building projects seems to make the moving production line impossible. But that is only true if one has a narrow view of Fordism, with the product passing by fixed work-stations where workers and/or machines add components or alter those already there. Fordism is also possible in the reverse situation, where workers, machines and materials move round a static product (or products). Such an organisation of the labour process is very common in building.

In the application of Fordism to building work, two aspects need to be considered:

1 the organisation of work on one site; and
2 the flow of work between sites.

Fordist principles are easy to apply to individual sites by using them to determine the way in which the sequence of tasks is undertaken. A classic example would be a large housing estate, where each trade is organised so that workers move down the line of dwellings as previous tasks are completed. Building production would then be almost identical to the conveyor-belt model, except that it is the workers not the products which move down the line. This approach to building is frequently called the *horizontal* approach to building, as layers of construction are completed as a continuous whole. It contrasts with an alternative approach, where each house is completed in sequence (or in small batches), with secondary regard paid to continuous production within a well-organised division of labour – the *vertical* method of building (Ball, 1983). Vertical building is used because continuous production is uneconomic – firms would be left with stocks of unsold buildings with large and uncertain financing costs – rather than because continuous production is physically impossible. Even so, Taylorist principles can still be applied in the vertical method.

On construction sites there is no conveyor belt or line to fix the pace of work. In some cases, machines may set the pace. Concrete, for example, has to be spread as quickly as it is pumped. What fixes the pace of work more generally, however, is the overall plan of sequential tasks drawn up by management for a site. One task obviously has to be finished before another can start. The plan of work on a construction project, therefore, can take the place of the movement of the production line in determining the pace of work. Fordism is a central principle of modern site organisation and project management. Frequently, the complexity of modern building projects make such plans and work schedules complicated affairs, and management effort centres on their efficient formulation and implementation.

The application of Fordist production techniques would seem to be technically feasible on any individual building site, though, of course, this does not necessarily mean they are used. Similarly, it should be theoretically feasible to organise production between sites on a Fordist basis, with workers and machinery transferred from one workplace to another in accordance with some overall plan which aims at a continuity of repetitive tasks. For many building projects, and considerable parts of others, it would seem that the physical nature of building does not limit the application of modern capitalist production methods as the absolute-physical-constraint thesis would suggest. All that the physical nature of building can be said to do is to make their application different.

Backward or just different?

All of the analyses of the building process considered so far have started from the assumption that the building industry is technically backward. Backward is a relative term and so has to relate to something. The term implies that technological advance is a comparable process along which all productive activities can be ranked, with building seen as much lower down the scale than other industries. Such juxtapositions seem flawed both in practice and in principle.

Often the comparison is just an anecdotal one contrasting, say, the craft techniques of a skilled bricklayer with the capacities of a computer-controlled machine tool. Alternatively, the prevalence of handicraft techniques is noted, or comparison made between the long-term rate of productivity change in building and elsewhere (Ball, 1978). Yet it is wrong to say that production methods have not changed dramatically over the past 100 years in virtually every type of building work; furthermore these methods are continuing to change. Similarly, the degree of prefabrication, mechanisation and general technical sophistication varies considerably between different types of building work and different countries. All that can be said empirically is that building work is different from other productive activities and uses considerable amounts of labour, which is to say a lot and very little at the same time.

More worrying than poorly-formulated empirical comparisons are the theoretical implications of the backward view of the building industry. Why should the future technical development of construction necessarily be towards more and more factory production? An unwarranted idealisation of particular methods of production seems to be elided with a very essentialist view of technical change. Yet, without such a view of the perfect universal technology applicable to the production of everything, how can you compare technologies on a scale of backward and forward? Is the latest generation computer more technically advanced than the most recent piece of genetic engineering? Is an elephant more technically backward than a race horse? Outside riddles in the style of Lewis Carroll, such comparative exercises have no meaning. The backward view of the building industry is asking the wrong question.

The social determination of building techniques

Technical development is subordinated to the dynamics and constraints of particular societies and their social structures. Realising the importance of social organisation for technical change, a number of commentators on the construction industry have looked at the economic and social organisation of the industry to see the extent to which they have influenced its development. As with the backward thesis, there have been considerable variations in the rigour and sophistication of the arguments put forward.

One of the most popular conceptions of the building industry is that it is dominated by people who suffer from an excessive lack of moral scruple or too much elitist insensitivity. One or two social agencies are highlighted for condemnation: the get-rich-quick building speculator (e.g. Colclough, 1965); architects and planners for the

1960s and 1970s industrialised council-housing fiascos (e.g. Ravetz, 1980); corrupt builders and architects (like Poulson, and Maudsley, the chief architect of Birmingham who gave Bryant so much of the city's building work in the 1960s: see Direct Labour Collective, 1978; Gillard and Tomkinson, 1980); monopolies (e.g. Dunleavy, 1981); and, most commonly, 'cowboy' firms and building workers.

While cases of professional ignorance and insensitivity, and individual malpractice can be found, to explain structural problems by individual failings is both poor theory and false moralising. What conditions enable such practices to exist? And, if they are as endemic to the building industry as they are often claimed to be, why has not competition, pressure from consumers or state action eradicated them? 'Individual failings' type of explanations themselves fail as they confuse potential symptoms with their causes.

It is important to see individuals in their social context rather than to isolate them and exaggerate some of their individual characteristics, as the social-failings approach tends to do. The construction industry does have its own social structures. Landowners, quantity surveyors, architects, engineers, building firms, building workers, state agencies and others interlink in various ways depending on the type of work in question. Yet, traditionally, studies of how these social agents interrelate are rare.

One major exception is Bowley (1966). In an analysis of technical change in the building industry, she places strong emphasis on the unique historical evolution in Britain of the architectural and engineering design professions, their conservatism, and their formal separation from each other and from building firms. The institutional structure that emerged in the nineteenth and twentieth century in construction led to a separation of production and design which has been a major obstacle to technical change, she argues. Unfortunately, Bowley presents her argument in an empirical and pragmatic way and makes little attempt to theorise the existence of the social relations she elaborates. There is no explanation of the reasons why design and production have remained as rigidly separate as she argues they are. Only the historical origins of the professionalisation and exclusivity of design are presented. Institutional rigidity is given greater didactic force by classifying it, as Bowley does, as a building 'Establishment' with an inherent conservatism in technique. But, if it exists, the institutional rigidity has to be explained. Why, for example, has not competition from new, more efficient social relations broken the 'Establishment' down if it is such a barrier, as has happened in many other industries? Bowley's analysis, in other words, is one-sided. It examines a particular dimension of the social relations of the building industry in isolation from others. This does not mean that her argument about the deadening effects of the separation of design and production is necessarily wrong. It just means that, as the argument stands, there is insufficient evidence and explanation.

Towards a theoretical alternative: the centrality of the capitalist building enterprise

What is noticeable about all the explanations of the nature of the building industry described above is that none of them gives a central place to the agency that actually controls the process of building production. In Britain that role is overwhelmingly taken by capitalist building firms, either as speculative developers or contractors. Some of the theories above do incorporate the fact that modern industrial societies are capitalist societies, but somehow it is always something other than building capital which fixes the characteristics of the industry – landowners, architects, establishments, villains or the constraints of nature caused the problems of the building industry, but never capital. Here I want to put emphasis on the role of building capital in determining the present-day characteristics of the building industry. The argument will not be of the style of a radical polemic that always blames capitalism for the ills of society as a truism requiring little substantiation. Instead, I want to build up a framework in which the peculiarities of building capital can be explored. If the building industry is different from other industries that difference will be reflected in the enterprises that dominate it.

Many people recognise that the building industry is unlike any other and that this distinctiveness has something to do with the firms operating there. Building firms often seem unique in comparison to other types of enterprise. Yet, while the distinctiveness of construction firms may generally be known, there are few explanations or even categorisations of it going beyond the anecdotal. I shall argue that the development of capitalism in the British building industry has created a particular type of productive enterprise. Some of the peculiarities of construction firms arise from the characteristics of the industry suggested earlier (i.e. the physical nature of building work; the complexity of social relations, especially the separation between production and design; the role of land rent; the macroeconomic economic context; and, finally, the intricate patterns of subcontracting). However the significance of each of those factors can only be understood by examining the conditions under which building firms accumulate capital. A unique relation exists in the construction industry between production and exchange which leads firms to adopt a dual role as merchants and producers of buildings and other construction works. The role of merchant-producer helps to explain the building process, the employment of the workforce, and why the historical evolution of a specific institutional framework is so important to the understanding of individual countries' construction industries.

To examine the importance of the merchant-producer distinction and its particular effect in Britain, the general nature of building work under capitalist relations of production has to be considered first. The next chapter will then describe the broad characteristics of present-day construction firms and the environment in which they operate. Chapter 4 considers the historical development of construction in Britain in order to understand why the construction industry and its inputs have their particular current organisational forms. With these characteristics in mind, Chapter 5 examines how construction firms operate and the implications for the industry as a whole.

CAPITALISM AND CONSTRUCTION

Building firms are capitalist enterprises; they invest money to make a profit. Like other productive industries they profit from instigating a physical production process and selling the finished product. To do this they use money capital to purchase or hire the commodities necessary for production, namely plant, materials and a workforce. The workforce then uses its ability to labour in conjunction with the plant and equipment to transform a site and building materials into a new structure. Under capitalism, therefore, there are two aspects to building. First, there is a necessary set of physical processes required to produce a physical structure. At the same time, the firms controlling the building process must make a profit.

What has been said so far does not distinguish construction firms from any capitalist enterprise involved in a productive industry. This, in itself, is important, for it places the distinctiveness of construction in context. No matter what unique characteristics are ascribed to the construction industry, the extent of that uniqueness is limited by the economic pressures of profit-making through the production and exchange of commodities. Individual construction firms, for example, are subject to competition from other firms and to the general cyclical patterns and transformations of a capitalist economy. Construction firms consequently have very limited choice in deciding how they will go about making profits. They have to conform to the general pressures of accumulation and the market, as failure to do so means bankruptcy.

This closes off a number of ways of analysing firms in the industry.

It is not possible, for example, to attribute the nature of the industry simply to distinctive characteristics of construction firms (e.g. the importance of personal and family ownership in the industry), or of their managements (e.g. 'tough', 'hard-headed', 'Victorian mentality', etc.). Such characteristics may exist, but they are products of other aspects of the industry, not the cause of their own existence.

The next question is whether construction firms should initially be studied in the context of the world market for construction products or in the British context alone. One of the most striking developments since the early 1970s has been the rapid expansion of construction as an international industry, with firms from many nations competing for large turnkey projects.

New international markets have centred primarily around the development programmes of oil-producing countries, a feature which has helped to determine the characteristics of successful international contractors. The scale of profitability of these projects, for example, considerably increased the size of the largest international contracting firms, while the size of the market for international construction work is strongly influenced by the economic fortunes of the oil-producing states. A new international division of labour has also begun to emerge, with the growth of new large international construction firms from Third World countries, like India and South Korea, relying on vast reserves of potential labourers to undercut established firms from the advanced capitalist world.

Yet the new international construction market has shown why construction generally remains a domestic industry rather than a major component of international trade. Foreign firms only have a competitive advantage when there is a lack of indigenous construction technology and management skills; when there is a shortage of available building labour; when a firm's traditional (and usually domestic) markets have collapsed and the firm submits low bids in an attempt to win work elsewhere; or when governments can influence the rules of international competition in favour of their country's construction firms by direct subsidies, cheap project finance or diplomatic muscle. Without these factors foreign firms face only the disadvantages of international building work arising from a diversity across countries of the social framework in which construction takes place. Involvement in the local institutional framework of the building industry cannot be avoided, and there domestic producers tend to have an overwhelming advantage because of their prior knowledge of, and base in, the locality.

If the reasons for foreign firms having a competitive edge, as listed above, are considered geographically and historically, it can be seen that they are rare in advanced capitalist countries and hold only for specific types of building work and particular periods of time in the Third World. The apparent development of internationalised construction production in the 1970s, in retrospect, appears to have been primarily a short-lived result of the temporary success of OPEC and the end of the long post-war boom, with declining domestic rates of profit and recycled petrodollars encouraging financial capital in advanced capitalist countries to lend to the Third World and collapsing domestic markets inducing trans-national contractors to chase after any massive construction project that resulted. The only way building firms can buck these trends is to have long-established subsidiaries in particular countries, or to take over existing successful firms there. Those subsidiaries are then part of the domestic construction industry in question. Their capital and management might partially come from abroad but they will, in effect, be domestic-based capital. This is particularly true of the international presence of British contractors, much of which consists of long-established subsidiaries in the former 'white-dominated' colonies and dominions (i.e. Australia, Canada and South Africa). More recently, British contractors and materials producers have been acquiring firms in the booming regions of the USA. Elsewhere, British contractors rely heavily on diplomatic muscle and so are most successful in countries linked closely to Britain's imperial past.

In order to explain the development of the construction industry, it is necessary to examine the social relations that have evolved in individual countries rather than attempt to plot a path towards the emergence of a large-scale world market. This is one of the pecularities of the construction industry. Even between advanced capitalist countries there are wide variations in the social forces influencing the industry's development, producing quite distinctive organisations of the industry, which within broad limits are immune to overthrow by foreign competition.

THE SIGNIFICANCE OF THE MERCHANT AND PRODUCER ROLES
Construction firms are *merchant-producers*. As producers their role is obvious: they organise and control building production. Only under their instruction will the physical act of building take place. The merchant role is less obvious but vital to an understanding of the industry. Construction firms are dealers in construction outputs and inputs. They sell finished building products, or their ability to create them, and buy the inputs, like labour power, materials or land, necessary to build them. This buying and selling function is more significant in construction than in many other industries, and

production methods are subordinated to its requirements. British construction firms, for example, have been able to ride dramatic collapses in demand since 1970 because they have used their market power to reduce the cost of their inputs faster than the decline in price of their outputs (see Chapter 8). The workforce represents the most important input cost, so the mirror image of successful firms has been high unemployment, reduced wages and work speed-ups. Construction firms have only been able to do this because the organisation of production makes it possible.

In general, the extent to which the 'merchant' or the 'producer' roles of construction firms dominate depends on detailed institutional characteristics of the industry at a point in history. Institutional characteristics result from struggles between agencies involved in the construction process – between architects, building companies and building workers, for example, over matters like forms of building contract and conditions of employment. A component in such intra-industry struggles are the types of enterprises controlling building companies (e.g. independent building firms, financial institutions, property developers and hybrid conglomerates).

In Britain, since the development of capitalism in the building industry 200 years ago, the merchant role has always predominated because of the economic and political power of the independent building enterprise. Trade unions in the industry have remained divided and weak; there has been minimal integration of construction with branches of financial capital; and there has been a remarkable absence of direct state intervention in production. All three characteristics have contributed to the merchant-orientation of builders, while the long decline of construction output over the past twenty years has continued to heighten the significance of the merchant role.

In other countries, the constellation of influences on the industry has differed. Often financial institutions play a more direct role, as in France and the Netherlands. Elsewhere strong trade unions have influenced the conditions under which workers can be hired, for example in Australia and the USA (although the power of the American building unions has wilted with the general decline of trade-union power in the US (Davis, 1984)). In some circumstances unions have precipitated substantial state intervention in production, most notably in Sweden where a few huge, vertically-integrated industrialised firms have come to dominate the industry under state patronage (Dickens *et al.*, 1985). Such forces alter the conditions in which the merchant aspect of construction firms operates enabling, as in the Swedish case, significant advances to be made in levels of labour productivity. However, although a detailed comparative survey cannot be undertaken here, it is to be expected that variations between countries at most show only a weakening rather than the removal of the merchant role.

It is impossible to explain the nature of the construction industry by either a pure physical or social determinism. It is the way these two aspects of a mode of production interact which is important. Under capitalism it is the way capital uses the physical nature of a production process to expand accumulation that needs to be explored. For most industries, changes in production methods are of vital importance to individual firms – predominantly through attempts to increase labour productivity and heighten control over the workforce. Hence the general interest in Taylorism, Fordism and other means of transforming the labour process. In construction, the labour process may not be of such overriding concern to the building capitalist, not because the antagonisms between capital and labour are any less than elsewhere, nor because building capitalists are uninterested in reducing the costs of production. Instead, the weakening of focus arises from contradictions between the merchanting and productive aspects of builders' operations and from the complexity of class relations that building capitalists face.

The longevity and spatial specificity of built structures makes it impossible for the capitalist producers of buildings to appropriate most of the profit from their creation and existence. They try, but so do others – like landowners, land speculators and developers, building professionals, financiers and property owners. The class struggle in the provision of the built environment, therefore, is not a simple one between capitalist and worker. Building capital, moreover, does not necessarily play the determining role. In other words, the situation of industrial capital is weaker than in most other spheres of production. This does not mean that capitalist builders necessarily earn a lower-than-average rate of profit. The weakness instead relates to the options open to them to alter and transform the economic environment in which they operate, as the next few chapters will show.

So, whilst recognising that the distinctiveness of the production of the built environment is one of degree only, it must be recognised theoretically that the production of buildings cannot be treated in quite the same way as other capitalist industries. The accumulation of capital remains the focus of interest but careful attention must be paid to the social and physical constraints on accumulation in construction.

THE EFFECT OF PHYSICAL CONSTRAINTS

Unlike the output of most other industries, construction products are generally spatially fixed and immobile, and they last for a long time (or at least they should). The building industry is also distinguished by the physical nature of its production process. A large proportion of the work involved in building a structure takes place at the site where the product will be used. Even if building structures are totally factory-produced, they still have to be assembled on site and much preparatory groundwork is needed (site clearance, foundation work, connection of services, etc.).

Technically, the extent to which the spatially-fixed characteristic of buildings determines how much work has to be done on site depends on the nature of the structure being built and the level of technical development. Road building, for example, and much other civil engineering work, is highly site specific; at best only the materials and certain components (e.g. bridge sections) can be prepared off-site, for the task is essentially one of site clearance and assembly. At the other extreme, individual housing units offer considerable variation in the potential for on- or off-site production.

Building is the transformation of a pre-existing physical environment. Considerable variations in site conditions, rock structures and terrain exist. And, even with the best initial surveys and plans, unforeseen construction problems may arise. In addition, the changing seasons affect both climate and available daylight hours, added to which are the daily variations in the weather. So it can be seen that the natural elements with which building production has to deal hinder standardised production or uniform working conditions.

Together, the physical characteristics of the building product and its construction are central components distinguishing construction from other industries. Although other industries' production processes are site-based and subject to the vagaries of nature – particularly those which involve a physical transformation of land, like agriculture, forestry and mineral extraction – few combine a spatial fixity of production and product as occurs in construction. But to suggest that the products of the building industry are physically unique only implies that there are physical constraints, not that those physical characteristics alone determine the nature of the industry and its output. Technological developments and new products, moreover, change the boundaries imposed on working practices by the physical characteristics of nature. So physical constraints should not be seen as eternal, but subject to continual historical flux and transformation, as was argued at length earlier.

While the physical nature of building places limits on the types of products that can be produced and on the potential techniques used, it is the organisational structure of the industry which *fixes* within those limits, for particular historical moments, the nature of the product and how it is produced. Under capitalism, building is for profit, so those products will be constructed which yield the greatest profit, using techniques that do the same. Changes in the physical aspect of building only take place as part of a search for greater profit. The physical requirements of building production consequently are subordinated to the profitability needs of the firms controlling production. The next three chapters will explain how this general principle has operated in practice in the British construction industry.

CHAPTER 3

The different types of building enterprise

Building firms can be classified in a variety of ways, each of which presents a particular aspect of the structure of enterprises in the industry.

In the first place, enterprises can be classified in terms of the *physical type* of work they do. General builders, civil engineers, painters, electricians, roofers and electrical contractors are just some of the many work-based divisions that exist. Often official statistics on the structure of industry are presented in this way (see, for example, *Housing and Construction Statistics*).

Another obvious criterion is the *size of firm*, measured either by the number of workers employed or turnover. The extent of subcontracting in the industry, however, can give misleading impressions of size. Firms may have a much greater effective workforce than the number of workers directly employed when account is taken of the additional ones employed on a subcontract basis. Alternatively, the scale of a firm's operations may be undervalued when all, or part of, the work done by subcontractors is excluded from its total turnover.

Physical types of work and size classifications are extremely useful but, in isolation, they do not say much about how the industry functions because they do not describe how the different agencies in the construction process work together – in other words, they ignore the industry's social relations of production. Without an adequate understanding of the social relations of production, it is impossible to explain the economic forces determining the nature of the building industry. Two criteria are required to characterise the social structure of the industry. The first is the *economic organisation of the enterprise* in question; in particular, whether or not it operates on capitalist criteria, such as profit-making. The second relates to the *types of market structure* in which the enterprise operates; in particular, whether it builds speculatively and/or to contract. Once these aspects of the industry are clarified, it then becomes possible to examine the reasons for the contemporary hierarchy of firm sizes, and the causes of the current division of different types of building work between enterprises. A significant consequence of an initial analysis of the social relations of production is that it should highlight which aspects or sectors of the industry seem most important in influencing construction's present overall social structure. It will then be possible to concentrate subsequent analysis, at least for a while, on those sectors.

Economic forms of construction enterprise

Construction is different from many other industries in the variety of types of enterprise within it. Not all of them are capitalist, although all are influenced by the dominance of capitalism within the industry.

Non-capitalist enterprises predominantly are very small. Most are non-capitalist in the sense that they do not make profits and/or no-one is directly employed by the enterprise in question. Some are individual, or small gangs of, workers who sell their labour services, and share out the proceeds among themselves. Their labour services are either sold directly, as in small-time repair, maintenance and improvement (and frequently they operate in the informal economy), or as a form of employment contract with a capitalist building enterprise. Many self-employed building workers constitute themselves as companies for tax purposes, but frequently they work for larger firms (on a subcontract basis) rather than represent a distinct sphere of economic activity.

The direct sale of labour services to a building user does constitute a genuinely non-capitalist form of economic organisation, formally known as petty commodity production. It is common in private housing repair and maintenance. Though they are independent enterprises, their existence is still predicated on the overall economic structure of the industry. The industry's general employment practices and the lax legislative controls over building work make it possible for individuals to work as petty commodity producers, either on a full-time basis or part-time, by doing 'foreigners' jobs outside their normal employment.

The availability of such small-time building work for petty commodity producers is the result of its lack of profitability for capitalist enterprises. The nature of the work is small-scale, unstandardised and requires only a few workers, which makes it difficult to organise on a basis where capitalist forms of control bring clear productive advantages, and consequent lower costs. Only when such jobs are combined on a large scale are clear and repetitive divisions of labour possible. Local-authority housing offers such opportunities, as does work on standardised elements which need frequent replacement or repair, like central heating systems and the sale and fitting of proprietary double-glazing systems for private households. Petty commodity production relies on a pre-existing pool of skilled building labour. That pool has been made possible through the development of skills on the various training systems that have emerged to service other parts of the industry, or through an on-the-job learning of skills. Little or no machinery is used. Generally, there are just handicraft workers using relatively simple handtools, familiar to DIY practitioners, and possibly (subcontracted) scaffolding erected by specialist scaffolders.[1] There is control over neither the ability of workers in this sector nor the quality of the work they do. Bankruptcy, shoddy work and tax evasion are rife.

An extension of the petty commodity producer is the petty capitalist, who employs only a few workers and who directly does some of the work. Such firms may operate in the same spheres as petty commodity producers and use similar practices, but they can operate at a larger scale and, because a certain amount of capital is advanced, can undertake different sorts of activity. Petty capitalists, for instance, are common in speculative housebuilding, buying up small land plots and building one or two houses. They build something less than 10 per cent of total private housing output in Britain (Ball, 1983). The working proprietors of such firms obviously want to make a profit on the capital they have advanced or borrowed, but they do not need continuously to turn over a mass of capital as do genuinely capitalist enterprises. When one job is finished, another can be started. Ambitious proprietors might try to expand until they join the ranks of capital, but most, if they make a windfall, just take the excess profit as revenue, possibly using it to withdraw from work for a time. Again, these enterprises rely on the spaces made available by the competitive situation of larger firms in the industry.

All other enterprises in construction in one way or another are capitalist ones, operating under profit-making criteria as described in the previous chapter. Publicly-owned building enterprises, like local-authority direct-labour departments, are legislatively required to operate on capitalist criteria. They have to make a rate of return on capital, and to use the standard accounting criteria of private firms. In effect, they constitute a form of state capital. They do have some leeway, however, in substituting politically-determined objectives, like extensive training schemes, for all-out profit maximisation.

Type of market structure

There are two principal markets for building firms. They either build to contract, where a particular structure is ordered by a client, or they build speculatively for a general market in which the actual purchaser is not known until after the structure is underway or complete. The economic forces operating on speculative builders are different from those on contractors. Generally, the former have to worry about land acquisition whereas, for the contractor, land assembly and its cost is the client's problem not their own.

Speculative builders and building contractors (who are called subcontractors when the client is another builder) are the two main types of capitalist builder in Britain. Usually firms concentrate on either one sphere or the other, although in a growing number of cases speculative and contracting subsidiaries are owned by one parent firm.[2]

It is important to distinguish the content of speculative and contract building in order to be able to understand their respective influences on the development of the industry as a whole.

SPECULATIVE BUILDING

The most common present-day form of speculative building is owner-occupied housing, although industrial and commercial developments may also be undertaken in this way. Speculative building, amongst other things, involves selling the finished product and at some stage purchasing the land on which it is built or the right-to-build on that land. The significance of the merchanting function is clear for speculative builders, with product sales, land acquisition and building input purchases all necessary. In the USA speculative builders are actually called merchant builders (Eichler, 1982).

In Britain, speculative builders generally control all of the development functions involved in converting a land site from its previous to its new use. There is rarely an intermediate land dealer or developer who sells serviced plots with planning permission to builders. Instead, when acquiring land, builders deal directly with landowners, sometimes making joint applications with them to the relevant planning authority. One of the objectives of a speculative housebuilder is to minimise the conversion of the potential profit made on development into land rent, as represented by the land price paid to the landowner. In this sense, speculative builders are akin to capitalist tenant farmers who also try to minimise the appropriation by landowners of ground rent. However speculative builders differ from farmers in terms of their product and its market, so the mechanisms used to resist the appropriation of rent differ (Ball, 1985b). The actions taken by speculative builders over the conversion of potential profit into rent are important in understanding the nature of this section of the construction industry, because they affect the production methods used and the way the workforce is employed – as can be seen if the economic pressures on a speculative builder are examined a little further.

Speculative builders are a type of commercial capital, buying cheap and selling dear, and they profit from getting the timing of those operations right. A much better price obviously can be obtained during an office- or house-buying boom than when those markets are depressed. Timing obviously is also important in land purchase, and there is no necessary reason why the best time to sell completed developments coincides with the best time to buy land. Speculative builders as a result tend to hold land banks. Stocks of development land enable them to produce at the best times, to cutback during market slumps, and to acquire attractive sites when they come on the market.

Land banks give builders a degree of market power over landowners as they are not forced to buy land at specific times or locations in order to build. Instead, they can, if necessary, run down their land banks until market conditions swing in their favour. The land-use planning system may play a role in this process because builders may be able to buy land without planning permission cheaply, and then take time over winning planning approval, going through successive planning appeals when the initial attempt fails (Economist Intelligence Unit, 1975; Ball, 1983; Short *et al.*, 1986).

The turnover of capital for a speculative builder, in short, does not depend on steady production rates, but on the successful manipulation of land purchases, development programmes and building sales. Given the volatile market for speculative buildings it is highly unlikely that steady output levels can be achieved, so the production methods used have to facilitate variable output levels. The increasing volatility of property markets since the end of the long post-war boom in the early 1970s has heightened the need for such flexibility in production. As a result, small runs of standardised units based on simple, repetitive building tasks carried out by a casualised workforce characterise this sector, and vertical building is the norm (Ball, 1983).

The types of project undertaken by speculative builders depend on the amount of capital that has to be invested, the time period of production and sources of credit. Large-scale speculative office-developments by builders are rare and only undertaken by the largest construction companies, because of the amount of capital that has to be invested and the length of time building takes. Generally, construction of major office developments is only undertaken on a contract basis by a building company for a separate developer. Because, historically, financial capital in Britain has been reluctant to be involved directly in production (Coakley and Harris, 1983), even in the case of property development, most large-scale post-war speculative developments have been undertaken by independent property developers using short-term loan finance. The growing instability of this sector, however, has forced financial institutions who want to invest in completed office schemes to become more involved in the development process (cf. Massey and Catalano, 1978; Smyth, 1985).

Speculative small-scale industrial development by building firms is common. Frequently firms rent out completed estates, retaining ownership as an investment asset. Some building firms have been transformed in this way into being primarily property companies. Percy Bilton, a large metropolitan speculative housebuilder in the 1930s, is a classic instance of such a transformation.[3] Small shopping and office developments may also be builder-led, but large shopping and office schemes are only undertaken by the largest contractors. Office developments by building companies specifically represent only a small proportion of total shop and office development activity in Britain. Unfortunately, however, no aggregate statistics are available to distinguish accurately the different types of commercial developer.

The area where speculative builders do have an overwhelming advantage is owner-occupied housing. The time to build is quite short, the capital tied up in building work-in-progress is limited, and commercial banks are willing to extend credit on the security of land holdings. Land banking, small production runs and easy credit have enabled speculative builders to squeeze out virtually all other forms of building organisation, whereas in other countries the role of pure developers or the direct intervention of financial institutions is more common (Martens, 1985; NAHB, 1985).

In the absence of a detailed comparative analysis, no adequate explanation can be given for the phenomenal success of the speculative housebuilder in British private housebuilding. A key element must be the relative weakness of the building workforce. In speculative housebuilding, it is almost completely non-unionised and employed on a casual basis. Labour relations in speculative building, however, depend on those existing in contracting. The major struggles between building workers and their employers, which have been such a significant influence on the development of the industry, have all taken place in contracting rather than speculative building.

In general, the contracting side of construction has played the leading role in the industry's development, as speculative building tends to follow trends set elsewhere in the industry. Technical change and methods of organisation, for example, tend to be adopted in speculative building once they have proved their worth for contractors. Local-authority housing, for instance, was used in the mid-1970s as the test-bed for the timber-frame building systems that are now common in speculative housebuilding (Cullen, 1982). Moreover, speculative builders contract out most of their building work, so they represent potential clients for some contractors. They tend, however, to use smaller non-capitalist contractors, epitomised by the labour-only subcontracting (Ball, 1983).

THE CONTRACTING SYSTEM

Contracting differs sharply from speculative building because of its place in the development process. Contractors do not instigate development but only build projects for clients. This creates two crucial distinctions with speculative building. First, building production becomes the means through which profits are made rather than a prerequisite for realising a development gain. Second, there is a division of control between the conception of a project and its productive implementation. The client is the developer, the contractor is the producer, and generally some professional designers will draw up the client's plans. These divisions create potential antagonisms between the two aspects of the building process.

Such antagonisms make the conditions of market exchange under which the building contract is drawn up crucial. Elaborate legal frameworks and forms of contract have developed in this exchange relation. There are complex procedures for tendering, for the determination of acceptable cost additions above the initial tender price, for setting project completion times and penalties for delay, and for clients to be able to inspect and check the work done. Where the project is large and many subcontractors are involved these exchange relations can get extremely complicated. Each part of them has to be seen as a component of conflicts between the divergent interests of the parties involved. They are one aspect of the social relations associated with contracting. The institutional form those relations have taken in Britain has come to be known as the *Contracting System*.

With speculative building, the potential social antagonisms are primarily between landowners, building firms and building workers; in the Contracting System, they are between clients, design and other professionals, building firms and building workers. The social antagonism between capitalists and workers in construction therefore has never been a simple two-way conflict. It has always been structured by simultaneous conflicts with other agencies.

What is interesting about the relations of building firms to most of the other social agents is that they tend to take a market form, in that the relationships are predominantly contractual, either directly or in terms of distinct contractual agreements with a client. Even the production-centred relation between building capitalist and worker has increasingly over the years been transposed from one of a combination of market relations (such as hiring and firing) and hierarchical control at the point of production through management direction of the worker's tasks, to one of greater use of the discipline of the market through forms of building contract at the expense of direct management control. Such a shift is a direct concomitant of the shift away from direct employment towards subcontracting, a trend which is so prevalent in the modern British construction industry. These market exchange locations help to explain the importance of the merchanting function for building firms; much of a contractor's profit depends on taking full advantage of the contemporary institutional structures, rules and practices of the various markets in which they deal.

The state has played an important part in the development of the Contracting System. Two aspects of its role are particularly significant. The first is that the state fixes the legal framework in which building to contract operates. The second is that the state has always been a major client of the building industry, thereby acting as an important catalyst for new forms of social organisation. Most political pressure exerted by the building industry on the state has come from the participants in the building process itself; that is, landowners, building capital professionals and workers. Each has made alliances with other social forces to influence state policy, yet there has been little general political concern over the nature of the industry. Special pleading rather than campaigns mobilising mass support have characterised the political practices of all the social agents associated with construction, unlike, say, agriculture, coal-mining and the railways.

Despite political neglect of the industry itself, intense political activity has centred on the products of construction (e.g. housing, office development and planning), yet rarely has political interest in the products of the construction industry excited interest as to how they are produced. Capitalist building enterprises have been remarkably successful in containing and diverting general political criticism of the costs and consequences of the built environment they create.

In what sense is there a construction industry?

This chapter has considered the different types of construction enterprise, and has argued that there are important differences between them. Firms have to be distinguished not only in terms of their size and the type of work in which they operate, but also in terms of their economic structure and the nature of the markets in which they operate. Such differences are not merely descriptive but fundamentally affect the way firms go about making profits and the relations they have with other agencies in the construction process. So, why is it possible to analyse something called the construction industry if its constituent parts are so different?

There are two reasons for holding to the notion of a construction industry, and both refer to its dynamic change. First, there is a movement of capital between construction sectors in search of profit opportunities in a continually-changing economic environment. The largest firms, to varying degrees, straddle virtually all sectors of the industry, putting emphasis on particular sectors in accordance with current management strategies as guided by senior management's assessments of future profit potentials (which are often determined by contemporary fashion in an industry beset by substantial uncertainty). The movement of capital between sectors, of course, is not limited to companies with existing presences in a variety of sectors. Firms whose current specialisms limit profitable openings will often diversify into new construction sectors, either by setting up divisions from scratch or more commonly through takeover. As Chapter 9 will show, construction firms put high emphasis on diversification when restructuring their operations.

Time profiles are important when considering the movement of capital between sectors of the industry. Such trends are medium- to long- rather than short-term, as it takes time to build up a presence in a new sector. Hence, the movement of capital should be seen in terms of evolving management strategies rather than a day-to-day option open to all enterprises. As a result, it is particularly feasible and important for the larger firms in the industry. As consideration moves down the firm-size scale in the industry, the movement of capital is more likely to be characterised by the birth and death of firms, as construction is an industry in which the life of small enterprises can be very short.

The second, and more important reason, for considering the construction industry as a unity is the mutual influence of its sector's social relations on each other. Though the distinct sectors may involve separate combinations of social agents, as exemplified in the differences between speculative and contract housebuilding, there are clear linkages between sectors which influence the nature of potential change within each of them. An obvious instance occurs with respect to political lobbying and influence, where the actions of one type of building enterprise may help all private builders, as, say, against the threat of nationalisation which was perceived to exist by the employers' organisations in the mid-1970s. Most important are the economic interlinkages. All construction firms buy roughly the same inputs, so input purchase practices in one sphere have spillover effects on others. Here, labour relations are particularly significant. As speculative housebuilding has a long tradition of the dominance of labour-only subcontracting, for example, contractors have not had to invent a new category of employment in their switch towards greater use of this form of employment. Instead, they could use and extend already-existing practices.

The example just used was of the influence of the speculative sector on the Contracting System. However, in the development of the British building industry, it has been primarily the evolution of building to contract that has determined the principal characteristics of construction. The next chapter consequently looks at the history of the Contracting System from the early years of the nineteenth century.

Construction in context

This chapter and the previous one have given a broad outline of the social relations under which construction activity takes place. In doing so, they enable the parameters of the industry to be delimited.

Construction cannot be seen solely as a production process because the market contexts in which construction firms operate have significant effects on the organisation of production and the respective strengths and roles of the social agents involved. The whole construction process, in other words, is not limited to the point of production alone. Instead, it encompasses a variety of other production activities – like design and certain elements of off-site production – and a series of exchange, evaluation and legal activities – such as the way in which work is obtained, the drawing up of bills of quantities, specification of contracts and the settlement of disputes over those contracts.

A considerable variety of construction processes exist, each one depending on the precise way in which the various elements of production and exchange are brought together. Speculative house-building, for instance, has a very different history from council house-building. It uses different methods of production and technologies and distinct social agents are involved, despite the fact that ostensibly a similar product is being produced – mass housing.

As historical products, the nature of specific construction processes cannot be read off from some grand theory of the construction industry. It is not even possible to define the physical content of production without understanding the specific social context in which production takes place. Difficulties arise, in particular, over deciding whether the production of building materials is a part of construction or just a set of intermediate-goods producers whose principal client is the construction industry.

A good example of the problem is the production of common bricks. When produced on site, as they were up to the middle of the nineteenth century in Britain, brick production may be said to be an integral part of the construction processes in question. The existence of on-site brick production influenced both the sequence of activities involved in building and the financial calculations of the instigators of building work. Modern factory-production of bricks has broken those links. Physically, the production of bricks has gone the way of continuous mass-production, involving plants at a limited number of locations. And the economics of mass brick-production differ considerably from either those of contract or speculative building. It is not surprising, therefore, that there has been virtually no integration between the mass-producers of building materials, like bricks, cement, tiles and ceramics, and construction firms (Bowley, 1960).

For some materials, the situation may be different. One example is when the monopolisation of key sources of raw material supply is more important than continuous-production technology. Hence, aggregates and block-making have been one of the main areas of integration between construction and building-materials producers; the profits from one sphere have frequently enabled further investment in the other. The investment strategies of Tarmac are a well-known example. Yet the integration is only at the level of ownership by one firm, rather than integration of production processes. Laing's sale of its Thermalite block-making subsidiary in 1982 illustrates the point. The new chief executive complained of years of underinvestment and poor strategic management when the company was under Laing's control – 'there was just no investment in the company because Laing only understood building' (quoted in *Financial Times* 4 May 1983).

In certain situations, none the less, the separation of materials production and construction is not clear cut. Timber-frame housebuilding systems, for instance, although mass-produced in computer-controlled factories, could quite reasonably be argued to be a part of construction, as the form and fortunes of their manufacture are intimately linked to those of the speculative builder (Cullen, 1982). Alternatively, a number of materials producers operate as specialist subcontractors, supplying and fixing their own proprietary products.

Asking the question 'What is the construction process' is not simply a scholastic exercise in classification. The answer has a considerable influence on the way in which analysis of the construction industry is approached. What is being suggested here is that the industry has to be divided into separate construction processes based on differences in the activities directly associated with either the implementation or execution of building projects. It is a classification that mainly excludes building-materials producers, but not the professionals associated with construction. Once the industry has been broken down into its process sub-branches, common influences on all or some of them can then be examined.

One consequence of the need to break down the industry into distinct construction processes is that there is no single way that firms organise production. Organisation will depend on the sphere in question, even though, as we have seen, there are common features. Lessons drawn from one sector of the industry cannot be assumed to apply in others; the different consequences of speculative and contract building, even for the same product such as housing, are a good illustration of the point.

CHAPTER 4

The development of class relations in the building industry

Building contractors and the social agents associated with them in the contracting system have been the driving forces behind the development of the industry's current class relations. The last chapter argued that speculative builders with their concern for development rather than building profits have tended to play a subordinate role, taking advantage of the contemporary state of affairs in contracting rather than forcing through changes themselves.

The framework of the present-day Contracting System can only be understood in terms of the length of time capitalism has dominated construction in Britain, and by realising how quickly the principal class relations were established. The Contracting System emerged during the early years of the nineteenth century, and its social structure has remained broadly the same ever since. This, of course, does not mean there has been no social change in the building industry for over 150 years. Obviously developments have taken place for each type of social agency involved – firms, workers, professions, etc. Yet those developments have been structured by the basic form of the Contracting System. The longevity and resilience of this form of building organisation needs to be explained.

The genesis of the Contracting System

The importance of the early introduction of industrial capitalism to the subsequent development of Britain's industries is widely recognised (cf. Gamble, 1981). It led to the development of unique social divisions, one of the most widely cited being the divergent interests of the City and industrial capital (Ingham, 1984). The building industry has its own long-established traditions and beliefs, but as significant has been the subsequent inability of any major group until recently to challenge the basic structure of the industry.

The history of the Contracting System is one of the substantial and ossifying political strengths of an unsteady alliance between building contractors (especially the largest ones) and building professionals, particularly architects, civil engineers and surveyors. Capitalist contracting spawned the need for the modern types of architect, engineer and surveyor. Once in existence, capital and professions combined to protect the system that is their economic rationale. Defence is principally against the demands of the workforce in an industry where capital relies on extensive exploitation.

Being the first country dominated by capitalism, feudal building guilds and petty commodity building producers disappeared early in Britain. The breakthrough to capitalist forms of contracting occurred when firms undertook building projects in their entirety instead of individual trades being assembled by clients. A key change was the negative but vital one of dismantling the legal controls which had sustained feudal building guilds and the power of the independent craft worker (Leeson, 1979). As important was the catalytic effect of public building contracts during and after the Napoleonic wars. The practice of public building procurement and contemporary Commissions of Enquiry into the best ways of letting public-sector contracts helped to promote a system based on fixed-price contracts and main contractors (Cooney, 1955). These state-led developments, plus large-scale projects associated with canal and, later, railway building, helped to establish the economic superiority of the capitalist contractor. The change was principally in the organisation of building work rather than in the techniques used. Contractors still gained economies over previous forms of building organisation, however, through the ways they supervised and executed building tasks (Ball, 1981; Price, 1980).

By the middle of the nineteenth century there was a significant number of large contractors. Such contractors in the main did not get involved in the risky, and frequently disreputable, speculative side of the construction industry, so a division arose within construction (Cooney, 1955; Kingsford, 1973; Hobhouse, 1971; Dyos, 1961).[1] In terms of the volume of work, contracting always tended to be greater than speculative building. This can be seen for the years 1865–1913 in Figure 4.1, if the data are interpreted on the reasonable assumption that the speculative/contracting divide was the same as the housing/non-housing one. Contracting, in fact, was distinguished by the size of its leading enterprises, while speculative housebuilders were extremely small. According to Cooney:

> Firms of such a size and character were quite large by the standards of industrial Britain in the mid-nineteenth century. In the space of half a century an industry which had been organised primarily on a craft basis had, without the stimulus of any important technological advances, thrown up a group of large, complex, and markedly capitalist enterprises. (Cooney, 1955, p. 173)

55

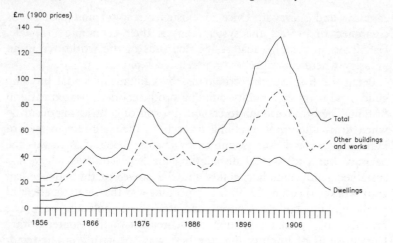

Figure 4.1 Construction output, 1856–1913. *Source:* Feinstein (1972).

Taking advantage of the organisational advances of the new capitalist main contractor and Britain's technological lead in railway building, some nineteenth-century contractors even began to operate on a world scale, building railways in Europe, the Americas and Asia (Middlemas, 1963). As with the international markets of today, the role lasted only as long as British contractors were in advance of others, so the initial world market penetration gradually subsided during the second half of the nineteenth century, even though some firms, like S. Pearson & Co., could still demonstrate technical advantages (when tunnelling under the Hudson River in New York) and political acumen (in Mexico) in the late nineteenth and early twentieth centuries (Spender, 1930; Jeremy, 1985).

The timing of the introduction of capitalist contracting in Britain is important. The basic organisational form of the Contracting System predates the advent of large institutions external to the industry which could act as major sources of credit, either in the form of the modern banking system, which grew up in the second half of the nineteenth century, or the state, which has in the twentieth century come to be a major source of industrial finance. Such sources of finance have played an important role in the development of the organisation of the building industry in other European countries where industrial development came much later; in Britain, however, they have had to contend with a strong pre-existing organisation of the industry, and so financial capital has been able to make few inroads into the building industry.

The emergence of the building professions

The early development of capitalism in the building industry also helped to create a rigid formalisation of building professions and their separation from building contractors, not as a necessary consequence of the advent of capitalism in building but as a product of the struggles associated with its emergence in early nineteenth-century Britain. Professionals in construction are involved, first, in the design of buildings – architects, civil engineers and structural engineers – and, second, in measurement and costing – surveyors. These professionals intervene in the exchange relation between contractor and client, helping to determine the precise form exchange takes. Architects, engineers and surveyors have been able to influence the form of the contractor–client exchange relation through their control over the specification of the content of the contract; the architect draws up the design and the quantity surveyor measures up the work required in a bill of quantities, and then costs it.

Control over the specification of the contract provides a means by which the work of the contractor can be checked in the interests of the client. Alternatively, the same professional authority can be used to justify additional claims by the contractor for extra work done. The role of architects and surveyors is therefore ambiguous with respect to client and contractor, as they can operate in either's interest (Bowley, 1966). Architects and surveyors have taken advantage of this ambiguity to avoid being drawn under the subordination of building capital. The evolution of the present-day standard form of building contract, for example, is principally one of disagreements and compromises between architects and building contractors over the obligations of the latter in the face of an independent architectural profession.[2]

Architects have maintained the independence of their position by restricting the conditions under which their services are sold. Registered architects, for example, are a professional closed shop and traditionally they were not allowed to work in the modern form of capitalist enterprise, the limited liability company. The restrictions on entrance to the architects' profession and on architects' work practices were gradually extended after the formation of the Institute of British Architects in 1834, later to become the Royal Institute of British Architects (RIBA). Present-day architects have to be registered with the Architects' Registration Council of the UK, a body set up by Parliamentary legislation in 1931 (Saint, 1983).

The advantages of restrictions on entry to a profession are frequently couched in terms of competence and integrity. In practice, they ensure that entry to the profession is limited and that architectural services are independently sold, rather than the profession being transformed to a body in which most architects are salaried members of building companies' or developers' design teams. Such a transformation to wage labour would most probably have happened to architects, judging from the earlier experience of craft workers who lost their independence and became wage labourers. However, architects, through their professionalisation, have generally remained petty commodity producers working alongside, but not subordinated to, capitalist building firms.

Registered architects can work for other architects in their architectural practices, as most do, carrying out the detailed execution of the outline schemes of leading members of the profession. In this way the largest architectural practices undoubtedly constitute capitalist enterprises. However the product of even these large practices is still only that of a division of labour within architecture, rather than part of a wider division of construction labour under the control of a building firm.

As a profession, architects are not subject to the same disciplines as the capitalist builder. Their product is sold on the basis of its physical qualities as a design, rather than for either its ease of construction or its cost effectiveness. Competition between architects is generally on the basis of ephemeral aesthetic criteria, with economic considerations only of secondary importance. This characteristic is heightened by the ideology of professionalism in Britain, which stresses the importance of vocational merit rather than pure economic interest which might encourage architects to work more closely with contractors or developers.

RIBA's role in British architecture today bears a close resemblance to Rubinstein's description of the typical nineteenth-century profession:

> The process of incorporation, acquisition of an expensive and palatial headquarters in Central London, establishment of an apprenticeship system, limitations on entries, and scheduling of fees, are all manifestly designed to 'gentrify' the profession and make it acceptable to society. This aspect of professionalism is profoundly anti-capitalist. (Rubinstein, 1977)

The role of the architect in the British construction industry is a peculiarly ambiguous one. It is as though, for example, firms in the car industry had no control over the design of their cars, but just produced models conceived, possibly within quite rigorous cost constraints, by others who are oblivious of the effect of their designs on methods of production – not necessarily through ignorance but because their own success depends on totally different (and primarily aesthetic) criteria. Added to which the designer may interfere in the actual production process by nominating suppliers and changing the working drawings and work schedule, even while production proceeds. If the car industry had been faced with such an artificial division of labour, it is unlikely that the Fordism of mass line-production would ever have been economically viable.

In Britain, little merging of the labour of building design and production has been possible because of the social constraints imposed by the Contracting System. This has limited the ability of building contractors to initiate changes in technique and organisation that may arise from a breakdown of that social division. The application of new building technologies, moreover, frequently depends on their acceptability to designers and only secondarily on their implications for production. The social division of labour between architect and building contractor in the Contracting System, consequently, has often been cited as inhibiting the introduction of new technologies and encouraging inefficient building practice (cf. Bowley, 1966; Leopold and Bishop, 1981). Until recently, builders have only been able to control the design process in the limited cases of 'package deal' standardised industrialised systems, and in the standardised products of the speculative housebuilder (see Chapter 5).

The modern architect is a product of the development of the Contracting System in the early nineteenth century and, once established, formed a crucial element in its subsequent evolution. Yet the ambiguity of the design role between client and contractor quickly threatened to eclipse the fledgling architect. With no professional constraints over self-nominated architects, early nineteenth-century clients had little guarantee of their efficiency or probity. The temptation of fraud was strong for architects, particularly when they also doubled as builders. The public reputation of the architect consequently was low, yet clients needed some means of getting adequate building designs and knowledgeable supervision of their execution by the builder. A small group of well-connected architects managed to turn this need of the client to their advantage by creating a professionalism which defined and limited the position of the architect, even if during the nineteenth century many architects chose to remain outside the RIBA fold (Saint, 1983).

In architecture, like other Victorian professions, ideological emphasis was placed on service rather than quick profits and on quality rather than the scale economies that could be derived from standardised high-volume turnover. The training requirements to gain recognition as a professional architect and the limits imposed on what a professional architect could do undoubtedly encouraged the idea of architecture as pure art, in opposition to the money-grubbing of the building capitalist. Although itself a product of industrial capitalism in Britain, design in its institutionalised form and practices was an anti-capitalist activity harking back to a bygone age of noble patrons, with an organisational structure that was hierarchical and stultifying.

The attempt at professionalisation quickly received legal status and royal sanction in the 1830s. Again, the timing of the development of the Contracting System seems to be an important consideration in explaining the success. Leading architects had close contact with the landed aristocracy and gentry, who had been their main patrons for over a hundred years; thus architects could count on the political support of the leading strata in British political life at the time. Moreover, they could also find ideological allies amongst the rising bourgeoisie, with its nineteenth-century penchant for the formal insti-tutionalisation of the learned/artistic professions. The newly-emergent building contractors could not count on such connections, so they had to work with architects rather than against them.

So the evolution of the architectural profession in the form it took should be regarded more as a remarkable political coup than a necessary division of the building process. If circumstances in the early nineteenth century had been different, the capitalist way of doing things might have had greater success. For instance, design might have continued to merge with building (and come under the sole control of capital), while regulation could have centred on the refinement and policing of the building contract (trends which are re-emerging in the 1980s).

Another potential alternative form of organisation of the building process would have placed another profession, that of the surveyor, in the key role of the client's agent, downgrading the architect. This did in fact occur when work involved little architectural input. Surveyors took on the role even more frequently before the emergence of general contracting, when, as measurers, they tended to look after the interests of the client (Thompson, 1968). But professionalism came late to the surveyor. The first Institute of Surveyors was founded in 1868, and its successor, the Royal Institute of Chartered Surveyors, only received its charter in 1881, over forty years after RIBA. Prior to its professionalisation, surveying suffered from the same problems of fraud and disrepute as architecture had. It therefore could not challenge the role of the architect at the time when it mattered, and has ever since had to be content with a subordinate place.

Interestingly, the Royal Institute of Chartered Surveyors (RICS) also adopted the same criteria of professionalism adopted previously by architects, namely that registered surveyors could not be employed by limited liability enterprises. RICS members cover the whole spectrum of surveying disciplines, from building and valuation to auctioneering and estate management (many estate agents, for instance, are RICS members). Quantity surveyors are of key importance to the Contracting System, as they are the construction industry's measurers and valuers of quantities. In the late 1970s 15,000 RICS' members were quantity surveyors, out of a total membership of around 51,000 (Dolan, 1979). Contractors have to employ quantity surveyors, so RICS' unlimited liability stipulation created tension within the surveying trade as it effectively barred contractors' surveyors from membership. The conflict led finally, in 1938, to the founding of the Institute of Quantity Surveyors by quantity surveyors excluded from RICS.

Dolan (1979, p. 31) describes the differences between quantity surveyors employed by contractors and in independent consultancies:

(They) share some of their activities such as site measurement, valuation preparation and final account production, but other duties vary considerably according to the specific needs of their respective employer, whether client or contractor.

The contractor's quantity surveyor, for instance, may be called on to perform several jobs, which his (sic) private counterpart is not. Some examples of this are the computation of prices and rates for tender submission, cost reconciliation between income and expenditure, formulation and implementation of bonus schemes and the negotiation and agreement of subcontractors' accounts.

The consultant quantity surveyor on the other hand is more than ever involved in the financial implications of a project prior to the tender period. Clients increasingly approach him to check a proposed scheme's economic viability and advise on the type, size and quality of structure which would conform to their budget and cash flow requirements. During the design stages he continually monitors the proposals and applies financial checks on the developing scheme. Finally, his pre-contract services end with advice and guidance on the most advantageous contractual arrangements and the preparation of tender and contract documentation.

The only time these duties would extend to a contractor's quantity surveyor is in the case of those whose building firm offers a package deal contract to clients. This system is a relatively modern phenomenon by which a commercial organisation undertakes the provision of all services from design to construction stage.

The differences outlined by Dolan, as well as highlighting the division of interests between contractor and client, also bring out some of the distinctions between the consequences of professionalisation and of incorporation into a building firm's labour force. When quantity surveyors perform independent advisory roles they take on few management functions, because of the potential contradictions between the objectives of a profession and the needs of a productive enterprise. Conversely, contractors' quantity surveyors undertake technical and managerial roles associated with control over the process of production and the labour force because their activities are under the direction of the productive enterprise. The physical division of labour between the two types of surveyor, in other words, is very much a product of their place in the social division of labour in the British construction industry.

Change has been forced on both the architectural and surveying professions in the 1980s. Rapidly declining workloads from the mid-1970s, combined with the increased complexity of many large building projects and a gradual shift away from the traditional form of building contract, have forced a dilution of the professional exclusivity of architects and chartered surveyors. RIBA, with some prodding from the state, was forced to abandon its rule forbidding architects to compete on the fees charged for their services; from mid-1982, mandatory fee scales were abandoned. The introduction of price competition between RICS' quantity surveyors followed in March 1983 (Hillebrandt, 1984).

Even more far reaching in its long-term effect has been a weakening of the constraints on the activities of the two professions. Since 1981 restrictions on architects holding directorships in construction firms and working for limited liability companies have been watered down or removed. Similar trends have occurred in surveying. Limited liability *and* RICS membership, for example, were finally made possible in 1986 (*Financial Times*, 5 November 1986). RICS had earlier abandoned its restriction on quantity surveyors working for contractors, in an attempt to win back control over a profession which had expanded rapidly with the post-war boom in building work, albeit under the aegis of the contractor. The principal rationale for the two separate professional surveying bodies was thereby removed. However it took the slump in workloads of the late 1970s and early 1980s to force a merger of the two in 1983. A new phase of jockeying for power between the building professionals, and between them and the contractors, has opened up in the 1980s, a theme that will be taken up again later in Chapter 11.

The growth and limitations of trades unionism

The relations between components of the Contracting System described so far have concerned the conditions of contract exchange; in other words, the forms in which the building product is conceived and purchased. The other key component for an understanding of the workings of the Contracting System concerns the conditions under which the workforce is employed. Here, again, the early historical existence of capitalism is important because the initial development of contracting in Britain helped to set the future pattern for building workers.

In the early years of the nineteenth century, trade unionism in general was weak and the state active in limiting its power (Pelling, 1976). Trades unionism, nevertheless, developed early roots amongst the skilled building trades. The tradition of the craft guild, whose final demise had been comparatively recent, helped reproduce an ideology of mutual help and solidarity. This craft-based ideology of trade unionism has persisted since then. Building workers, for example, were one of the main proponents of guild socialism during the 1920s (Kingsford, 1973).

Craft unionism has been one of the great strengths, and also a major weakness, of trade unionism in the building trade. Its strength derives from the solidarity created within skilled trades, and from the ability of workers to force general improvements in conditions as a result of one strong trade winning them first, perhaps only in one locality, the benefits then slowly being spread through the rest of the workforce on the basis of fairness and hallowed differentials. The weakness of craft unionism stems from its exclusivity and lack of concern for fellow workers outside the craft or its accepted rules of behaviour. These contradictory strands of craft unionism have had two distinct effects: the first concerns the direct struggle between workers and capital in the building industry; and the second relates to the ability of building workers to force state intervention to improve their situation.

Building industry trade unionism has gone through four major phases since the early nineteenth century. Early years of fragmented, temporary unions and intense struggles were superseded in the 1860s by a formalisation of industrial relations in the industry. From the early years of the twentieth century to the 1940s, building unionism was reformulated through amalgamations of craft unions and the growth of union membership outside traditional craft boundaries. The final phase, from the 1950s onwards, has been dominated by the decline of craft-based unionism. Interpretations of the four stages vary, depending on the labour historian in question, but themes can be drawn from each which illustrate the significance and evolution of building trades unionism.[3]

At a general level, it is important to be aware that, since the inception of capitalism, struggles by building workers have played an important part in the industry's development. The varied forms of worker action are central to understanding the directions taken by labour relations in the industry. Historically, building trades unionism has generally been effective, despite low proportions of unionised workers and its almost total exclusion from speculative housebuilding. Union successes have been achieved through organising key sections of workers and gaining significant influence on major projects. Struggles won or lost there have then permeated the rest of the industry.

Building unions have also had considerable influence on the general development of the British labour movement, though their role has been substantially reduced since the Second World War. Throughout the nineteenth century, in particular, the building industry was an important base for the development of trades unionism in general, with the building unions being central, for instance, to the formation of the Trades Union Congress (TUC) in 1868. Yet in the industry itself, trade unions gained roots amongst only certain sections of craft workers employed by particular types of firm (master builders) in a limited number of cities and towns, reflecting sharp divisions amongst the workforce which have characterised construction ever since.

THE EARLY YEARS
During the first period up to the 1860s, many historians have argued that action by workers was mainly against the new Contracting System and based on idealisations of previous forms of organisation, or variations on them, influenced by Owenite socialism. The fights were primarily by craft workers organised into a wide variety of local unions, the existence of which could often be short lived or whose membership fluctuated widely. Frequently craft workers were themselves employers of labourers, so a harking back to the old craft guild system would seem to be the easiest interpretation of their actions. Price (1980), however, points out that what workers were doing was exercising a power that the new site-based Contracting System gave them: an ability to hold up work in order to realise local demands over pay and working conditions at times when it was most financially embarrassing for a contractor. They were attempting, amongst other things, to resist the debilitating effects of the instability of employment within the new form of contracting.

Strikes would be instantaneous and would be over issues ranging from those associated with wages and hours through to the organisation and control of the labour process in terms of matters such as subcontracting, piecework and 'driving' foremen. Struggles would be spontaneous and based on work groups rather than union members, who were generally a minority anyway, even within a particular trade on a site. Although strikes were over local issues, often they would reflect wider developments within the industry, particularly over levels of remuneration and employers' attempts to increase labour productivity in an industry whose economics did not facilitate large-scale changes in productive techniques. Once one trade on a site had achieved a victory, 'custom and practice' and time-honoured differentials would then facilitate its achievement by others in the industry. In this way, craft fragmentation was a benefit, in that the costs of a dispute to the workforce were minimised and borne by the strongest trades at that time.

Forms of wage payment were, and are, central to the struggle between employers and workers over control of the building labour process. The switch from day to hourly payment in the industry during the 1860s was strongly resisted by the workforce, primarily as Price (1980, pp. 111–15) argues, because it considerably weakened workers' traditional means of control over production. The notion of a 'normal' day was destroyed, leading to long hours in summer and consequent unemployment in winter; overtime could not be regulated so effectively in the hours' system; trade 'customs' were based on a generally-accepted regular working day; hourly pay opened the door to incentive payments rather than standard rates of pay; job insecurity was increased and with it the power of the driving foreman; conditions were made worse, including no payment during inclement weather; and, finally, the cohesion of the work group was weakened. The extent to which all these 'losses' were actually experienced is debatable, but the example illustrates clearly that, formally or informally, accepted working rules are vital to workers in the building industry and are inextricably tied up with forms of wage payment. The point at issue concerns not just a given level of pay and working conditions, but also the forms of power open to either management or workers to change them.

THE FORMALISATION OF INDUSTRIAL RELATIONS
In the 1860s Postgate (1923) notes a major shift in craft unionism. The Contracting System was accepted and the unions were reconstituted to reap the benefits of a 'labour aristocracy'. The period was characterised by comparative harmony between craft workers and their

employers, based on the principles of relatively high wages, limited strikes and unions as friendly societies providing a range of benefits for members. The trend towards the new unionism of unskilled workers in the 1890s was actively resisted by craft unions, both directly and in the TUC (Kingsford, 1973).

Although there is little doubt that there was a substantial shift in the content of building trades unionism after the middle of the nineteenth century, there is disagreement over the class harmony implied by Postgate's acceptance of the labour aristocracy thesis, and the validity of the general notion of a labour aristocracy itself has been questioned (Stedman Jones, 1983). Price (1980) suggests that there was considerable conflict between employers and workers during the second half of the nineteenth century over control of the labour process. One reason was that the procedures of the new unionism had added another layer to the power of workers to win benefits during booms and to resist wage reductions and speed-ups during slumps. National permanent unions at the same time changed the content of what was being bargained over. Locally-based struggles over 'fair' working practices were replaced by negotiations and disputes over nationally-fixed rates and rules. National union organisations, with their own bureaucracy, rules, procedures and personalities, partially, though not entirely as Price claims, replaced local spontaneity.[4]

Once established, independent craft unions had strong inertia against amalgamation, partly through reasons of craft pride and rivalry and partly because of the privileges enjoyed by the union bureaucracies. Periods of stringency associated with dramatic losses of membership have been a major cause of union amalgamations; otherwise loose and fairly ineffectual federations have been tried, such as the National Federation of Building Trades Operatives (NFBTO) which was formed in 1918 and lasted until the foundation of UCATT, the main present-day craft union, in 1971 (Hilton, 1968; Price, 1980; Wood, 1979).

Subsequent to the development of the craft unions' new bureaucracies, shop stewards emerged, and in the years prior to the First World War began to take on their modern-day role (Hinton, 1973). Stewards were the collectors of union dues and the organisers of plant or site union activity, the elected representatives of union members in the workforce and the direct means of communication between the higher echelons of a union and its membership. Increasingly in building, moreover, union subscriptions were deducted from wage packets by employers on behalf of the union, weakening the traditional role of the branch and focusing more local union power on site (though many have argued that it has also increased worker apathy towards their unions). This potential conflict between work group power to disrupt site activity in attempts to win grievances, and nationally-negotiated rules, wages and conditions became, and remains, embodied in the role of the shop steward. The situations in which they are placed can lead to contradictorary pressures, particularly in their roles as work-group representative, site-based link with stewards from other unions and in their relations with their own local officials. As many disputes are of a localised nature, often strikes will be called on site and only later made official, provided they are not condemned for going against official union policy.

Since the First World War, there have been only three major national strikes in building over issues related to the industry – 1924, 1963 and 1972 (Hilton, 1968; Wood, 1979). Locally, the situation is very different. Though not one of the most strike-prone industries, stewards have considerable power to disrupt sites and ruin contractors' financial projections. Employers' periodic complaints voiced from the early 1870s about the inability of unions to control their memberships became centred around the role of the steward (with heavy doses of 'red-baiting' frequently associated with them).

A classic instance of a groundswell of local union activity not officially sanctioned by the relevant unions were the strikes in London in the years prior to 1914 against subcontracting, especially in its labour-only form (Price, 1980). In London after 1896, non-union subcontractors were formally recognised and accepted in the working rules, but there was substantial rank-and-file resistance to the rule, including strike activity, forcing some London unions to take a stronger stance against the practice (Price, 1980). Fights, like the one just described, show that labour-only subcontracting (LOSC) is not just a modern phenomena; instead, it has been the bane of trade unionists in building since the early years of the nineteenth century. No data seem to exist on the size of LOSC prior to 1914, but it seems to have been very large, dominating speculative building and being used by contractors whenever they could get away with it. Price (1980) suggests that by the turn of the century non-union and subcontract labour had virtually become synonymous. McKenna and Rodger (1985) estimate that in 1901 union membership had doubled in three years to reach 20 per cent of the industry's workers. They claim that this level of membership made the unions extremely strong, yet, given Price's statement, LOSC could have been as high or even higher than it is today. So considerable rank-and-file concern over its existence at the turn of the century is not surprising.

THE RESTRUCTURING OF BUILDING TRADES UNIONISM

The third phase of building trade unionism lasts from the early years of the twentieth century until after the Second World War, during which time the strength of traditional craft unions was slowly undermined – by technical change, dilution and economic crisis. Both World Wars, however, enhanced the power of the craft unions because of the key roles their skills played during the wars and the subsequent phases of reconstruction, when labour supply was severely depleted and demand was at record highs. Building unions in the main were able to resist dilution and the weakening of apprenticeship rules, and strengthen their members' situations, as laid down in the working rules. The post-war defeats for the unions, therefore, followed two periods, both almost a decade long, when official union activity operated from positions of exceptional strength.

Divisions between the traditional craft unions, newly-emerging building skills and the growing organisational ability of unskilled labourers had arisen in the late nineteenth century, but the inter-war years saw their formalisation into distinct union structures. Though mergers between craft unions have taken place throughout the twentieth century, the craft unions have tended to shun other building workers, or treat them as secondary. Technical developments such as the introduction of reinforced concrete created new skills to which the old unions could not respond. Motor-driven machines like bulldozers and trench-diggers also required new skills, yet their operatives were classified as labourers. Workers in the new skills therefore combined with ordinary labourers during the inter-war period under the aegis of the Transport and General Workers Union (TGWU). Thus was created the classic trade union divide between traditionally-recognised skilled craft unionism, and general unionism – a divide which still can be seen today.

THE DECLINE OF CRAFT UNIONISM

The last phase starts in 1947 with the introduction, for the first time outside wartime, of officially recognised incentive payments. The switch to incentive payments was a considerable weakening of workers' control over their pace of work, and was only conceded after intense political pressure (Foot, 1975). It is perhaps for that reason that, LOSC apart, incentive payments were only in limited use until the late 1960s, when unemployment in the industry started to rise (Hilton, 1968).

Trends within wage payments in the building industry have generally been towards attempts by employers to tie pay as closely as possible to the pace of work. This pattern, however, should not be seen as inevitable, a natural consequence, say, of employers' Taylorist strategies. The nature of wage payments will always be one of the central concerns of employer/trade union disputes. Changing the form of wage payment may be one way of tipping the contemporary balance of power, or of trying to eradicate causes of grievance. The drift of private-sector building employers away from detailed, work-study based, wage payments systems in the mid-1970s is an example of such a shift.

The post-war years have seen a dramatic decline in the power of craft unionism, despite the unprecedented levels of construction activity that persisted for twenty-five years until the early 1970s. The decline occurred because of the growth of self-employment outside normal trade union influence (Austrin, 1980). Many of the craft unions were forced to amalgamate into one union (UCATT) at the end of the 1960s because of their individual weakness; others are locked in periodically unsatisfactory arrangements with trades in other industries (particularly constructional engineers in the AUEW).

At the same time as the craft unions saw dramatic declines in their memberships, shop-steward-led unofficial strikes became a major weapon of building workers to improve local pay and conditions, to control work speeds, and to fight against the introduction of self-employed 'Lump' workers. Table 4.1 documents the level of strike activity (as measured by working days lost) in construction and the economy as a whole from 1961 to 1975. The trend of strike activity in construction appears to be cyclical and, excluding the monumental dispute over wages in 1972, does not follow the general upward trend in days lost for the economy as a whole. What is noticeable is the very large number of unofficial strikes in the industry (100 per cent in 1964), the bulk of which were limited to a number of large, predominantly public-sector, projects in areas of high labour-demand (Hilton, 1968). Two of the most famous, those at the Barbican and Horseferry Road in London in the mid-1960s, received such publicity that they led to an official Court of Inquiry (Cameron Report, 1967). That report condemned 'politically motivated' unofficial action by shop stewards and their liaising body, the London Joint Sites Committee, for obstructing official negotiations between employers and unions.

Table 4.1 Construction industry disputes: official and unofficial, 1961–75

	Construction, working days lost			All industries and services, working days lost		
	Total	Official	% official	Total	Official	% official
1961	285	44	15	3,046	861	28
1962	222	61	27	5,798	4,109	71
1963	356	279	78	1,755	527	30
1964	125	—	0	2,277	690	30
1965	135	16	12	2,925	607	21
1966	145	6	4	2,398	1,172	49
1967	201	17	8	2,787	394	14
1968	233	31	13	4,690	2,199	47
1969	278	12	4	6,846	1,613	24
1970	242	10	4	10,980	3,320	30
1971	255	21	8	13,551	10,050	74
1972	4,188	3,842	92	23,909	18,228	76
1973	176	15	9	7,197	2,009	28
1974	252	22	9	14,750	7,040	48
1975	258	nk	nk	5,957	nk	nk

nk = not known
Source: Department of Employment Gazette, April, 1976.

Tensions between the power and grievances of the work group, the ambiguous role of the shop steward, and the desire of employers only to negotiate with 'responsible' union officials was to reach its peak in the 1960s and 1970s.[5] For employers, the effect of labour-only subcontracting in industrial-relations terms was to remove both stewards and officials from the scene, and to reconstitute the power of the work group into a market-related form. The industrial relations results for employers of the shift to subcontracting, however, have been ambiguous, as Chapter 11 will discuss.

One attempt was made in the 1960s by the unions to deal with the growth of self-employment by negotiating changes in the industry's working rules to incorporate labour-only subcontractors within them. The new rules also made main contractors responsible for their subcontractors' actions. The attempt failed, as subsequent legal judgments showed, and was felt by many trade unionists to have helped vindicate LOSC rather than hinder abuses of it. A similar charge was made later against the P714 certificates introduced in the mid-1970s in an attempt to stamp out the tax evasion associated with multiple subcontracting. The Phelps Brown Report (1968), commissioned by the 1960s Labour government, was another milestone in the defeat of the unions' position on subcontracting, as subcontracting and labour only were held by the Report to be useful in a volatile industry like construction.

Employers' organisations

At the same time as the unions were organising on a national footing at the end of the nineteenth century, so were the employers (Hilton, 1968; McKenna and Rodgers, 1985). Employers' organisations are not as central to the analysis of the development of the construction industry as trade unions, because of the unequal power relation between individual workers and employers (which unions attempt to redress). Large employers find their representative organisations useful rather than central to their accumulation and industrial relations strategies; some of the largest building firms have not even bothered to join the relevant organisation, while others play a passive role.

The Building Employers Confederation (BEC) is the principal organisation representing building contractors. It is party to all the major contemporary construction-industry organisations, such as the National Joint Council for the Building Industry (NJCBI), where wages and conditions are nationally negotiated, the Joint Contracts Tribunal (JCT), the Building and Civil Engineering Economic Development Committee, the Construction Industry Training Board (CITB). Civil engineering firms have their organisation, the Federation of Civil Engineering Contractors (FCEC). The smaller builders' organisation is the Federation of Master Builders (FMB) and there are various other specialist organisations. The prime roles of these bodies are in the industrial relations sphere and in political lobbying, via the public, politicians or directly to various governmental bodies and agencies.[6]

The state and construction

During the first half of the twentieth century the state became the principal client of the construction industry, and many local authorities set up their own direct-labour building departments. In addition, politics at the local and the national levels has played an important role in the development of the industry.

The early role of the state in the formation of the Contracting System has already been considered. One of the most significant changes brought about by the state in the twentieth century was the introduction of central-government-subsidised local-authority housing after 1919. This shifted the balance in the building industry, bringing large-scale general contracting for the first time to the housing sphere. As a consequence, local politics started to have a significant impact on the building industry. With the growth of the Labour Party in local government, building workers and trades unions were to benefit from the implementation of fair wages legislation, client-stipulated employment practices such as the non-use of labour-only subcontracting, and from the meteoric growth of local-authority direct labour, which at its inter-war peak employed 21 per cent of the total building labour force and produced 14 per cent of total output.[7]

Contractors and architects also gained from the introduction of local-authority housing. With the Contracting System now in the housing sphere, traditional modes of organisation were reinforced with local-authority clients that had little alternative but to go along with contemporary industry practices, bearing whatever costs they imposed. Both architects and builders were able to use local-authority housing as a means of experimenting with design ideologies and practices, and with new building techniques like industrialised building systems (some of whose principles were useful in the commercial sector) and timber-framed housing (Cullen, 1982). Corruption has also periodically scarred the building of local-authority housing, both within the private and public sectors (Direct Labour Collective, 1978).

Central government has always been a major client of the construction industry, but construction-related state expenditure expanded rapidly with the post-1945 switch away from rail to road transportation, the nationalisation of key public utilities and industries, and the growth of health and education programmes. During the years of the mid-twentieth century the balance between private and public construction expenditure was fundamentally altered from that of the nineteenth century, with the proportion of public-sector work reaching a peak in the mid-1970s (see Figures 4.2 and 4.3 and Chapter 6).

Apart from the greatly increased importance of the state as a client, there have also been a series of significant political developments affecting construction since 1914.

The dominance in building of craft-based unionism has been influential in minimising the political impact of workers' struggles and demands. The site-based, individual trade nature of craft unionism has made it very difficult to get sustained national-level collective political action by organised building workers. This has reduced the possibility of alliances with wider forces in the Labour movement. Such alliances would have been particularly useful in mobilising political action over employment practices in the industry or with

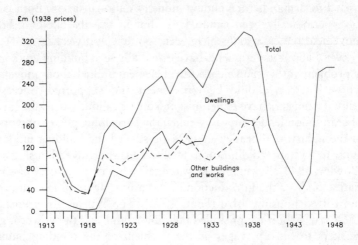

Figure 4.2 Construction output, 1913–48. *Source:* Feinstein (1972).

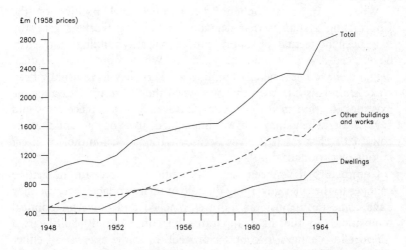

Figure 4.3 Construction output, 1948–65. *Source:* Feinstein (1972).

regard to demands for building industry nationalisation. Both issues have periodically been agitated for, but in the absence of a broad movement the campaigns have been sporadic and weak.

Even Labour governments have essentially seen building workers as a 'problem' rather than a constituent element of the Labour movement whose interests should be represented and supported. Successive Labour ministers have either misguidedly or callously used the loyalty of craft union leaderships to weaken the bargaining power of workers in the industry. Wheatley in 1924 persuaded the building unions to agree to widespread dilution to facilitate his short-lived housing drive (Bowley, 1944). Bevan in 1947 was against building industry national-isation and for the introduction of incentives, again in the name of a short-lived housing drive (Foot, 1975). The Wilson government of 1964 saw a shortage of skilled building labour and the power it gave workers to bid up wages as the problem of the building industry (National Plan, 1966). Subsidies to industrialised building and official condonation of LOSC (through acceptance of the recommendations of the Phelps Brown Report in 1968) were tried as a means to break that power. Finally, the 1974–9 Labour government legitimated LOSC through the introduction of the P714 tax-certification scheme, whilst ignoring demands for decasualisation of the industry and its partial nationalisation.

What is important about the national-level politics of the Contracting System is that demands of building workers generally have been ineffectual, or simply ignored, whereas building contractors have faced divergent political reactions. When contractors' political demands have been against building workers they have usually been successful. This has been the case when they have tried to alter the existing situation in their favour (e.g. over dilution, piece rates and LOSC) or when they have campaigned to stop potential anti-contractor changes (e.g. over decasualisation, local-authority direct labour or nationalisation).

Contractors have been far less politically successful in getting changes to the rules governing the sale of their products, because they have come up against far more entrenched and powerful political opposition. So the state apparatus has offered only half-hearted support for changes in contract procedures at the expense of either clients or the building professions (cf. the Simon Report, 1944; the Banwell Report, 1964; the Wood Report, 1975). The only major changes accepted by public-sector clients at the behest of central government have been the introduction of select-list tendering in the 1960s, price index-linked contracts in the early 1970s, and an ever-increasing series of constraints on the operations of local-authority direct labour.

Abandonment of competitive tendering – where any firm can tender for a project and the public client is generally obliged to accept the lowest bid – by itself did not offend the interests of the professionals. But to replace it, a variety of new contract forms have been proposed and opposed. Three principal, post-1945, innovations in public-sector contract procedures have been mooted and tried: *select tendering*, where in theory firms are invited to tender only if the client is satisfied with their competence and financial probity; *negotiated contracts*, with negotiations with one contractor only; and *serial contracts*, where one contractor is offered a series of negotiated contracts subject to the successful completion of an initial select-list-tendered contract. Each of them has been viable within the constraints of the Contracting System as they do not offend the interests of the building professionals. If anything, such developments have increased the power of the architectural profession, as it is generally senior architects that draw up or approve a public client's select list of building contractors and who negotiate with building firms.

Two clear instances exist in the twentieth century of the relative political weakness of contractors in the crucial sphere of their relation to building professionals. They concern the disagreements contractors have had (and still have) with architects over the terms and conditions of building contracts, and the means by which public-sector work is awarded to specific firms. The comparative failure stems from the fact that contractors have had to deal with equal (architect and other professions) or stronger political forces (a 'public client' faced with pressures on state expenditure and a prevailing ideology of economic liberalism).

Running disputes between architects and contractors over standard forms of building contract have existed since the beginnings of the Contracting System. The years from 1900 to 1937 were especially fraught, with periods when contractors and architects refused to recognise each others' forms of contract with their different obligations on the contractor and procedures of resolving contract disputes. Only careful negotiation and compromise over many years led to establishment of the Joint Contracts Tribunal, a body on which contractor, architect, surveyor and public-sector clients were represented. The JCT form of contract was finally officially approved in 1937, and revisions and amendments to it since then have reflected the careful political balance between the professions and contractors which the latter have had to accept (Dolan, 1979). However, even late in 1986 contract procedural disputes still raged. Specialist subcontractors threatened to block the workings of the Joint Contracts Tribunal because of dissatisfaction over a new Standard Method of Measurement. The new method was worked out as a compromise by the other parties without reflecting the interests of the specialists, claimed their representatives (*Building*, 19 December 1986).

Similarly, in the post-war era contractors have had little political success in getting steady high levels of public-sector orders, despite intensive lobbying and propaganda about their importance to the industry. Some success has been achieved in improving the terms on which individual firms win public-sector work through the switching from competitive to select and serial forms of tendering, but even here progress has been limited, despite numerous official reports by committees packed with establishment members of the building fraternity. Even the inflation indexing of public-sector contracts was won only after some spectacular bankruptcies in the early 1970s, most notably of Cubitt.

State-orchestrated change in the British construction industry, in other words, has taken a peculiarly unidirectional form. Building firms have faced a fairly rigid framework in which they sell their products, yet conversely a fairly flexible one for the input of labour-power. The conditions under which they can win contracts, furthermore, has limited the boundaries of their production processes to exclude, in particular, design, restricting the potential for changes in the products produced and the production methods used.

The outcome in terms of output and input exchange relations has not arisen as a necessary result of the capitalist nature of the industry but from the balance (or, more accurately, imbalance) of social forces in the industry. Few other advanced capitalist countries have the social and power relations that exist in the British building industry, especially where they have had such a well-developed social democratic tradition as Britain did from the 1940s to the 1980s. During economic crises in the industry, consequently, it is not surprising that the workforce has usually had to bear the brunt of those crises.

Up until the 1980s the Contracting System survived, despite considerable changes in building technology. Over the years there have been substantial changes in methods of production and in the way in which building processes are organised, but revolutions in production which might have threatened the Contracting System have not taken place. This is because of the importance of merchanting for building firms. It encourages them to keep their productive capital in the most liquid form possible whilst engaged in building production; new methods are only adopted by firms when they enable that liquidity to be sustained. This places severe limitations on potential changes in technique, which in turn has helped to sustain the Contracting System. Put another way, it can be said that keeping productive capital liquid is an economic means by which building firms have been able to take advantage of the Contracting System, and changes in the social structure of the building industry during the 1980s have not altered those imperatives. The next chapter examines the way in which this is done.

CHAPTER 5

How construction firms organise production

The position of building firms in the construction process

The role played by building firms in the construction process depends very much on their relationship to the other agencies involved. So, in this chapter, the place of contractors in the overall construction process is examined first. Some general features of accumulation in the industry are then considered, highlighting the dual role of construction firms as merchant-producers. Focusing on the merchanting side, discussion moves on to tendering procedures and input purchases. Then aspects of the process of production itself are considered.

With *speculative building* the role of building companies is straight-forward. The building firm is the instigator of the construction process, with the object of selling the completed product on the general market. They control the whole of the construction process, usually independently of the influence of a financial institution. Differences occur between speculative builders over whether they retain direct management control of production. Most prefer to have control over detailed site supervision in order to have maximum influence over the speed, quality and cost of building, even though virtually all of the actual building work may be subcontracted. A few opt out of such management demands, preferring the easier, if riskier route, of letting out all the work to a main contractor or a series of subcontractors.

Contracting is far more complex. The complexity arises from the different relationships and obligations that arise between those involved in the construction process. Figure 5.1 describes three common divisions of management structure in contracting – traditional, project management and management contracting.

The genesis of contracting in the traditional form was described in the previous chapter. As Figure 5.1 shows it in, building professionals intervene between the client and the building contractor, taking over some of the functions of planning and control; local-authority sites would include a clerk of works acting on the client's behalf. The architect may also nominate specialist subcontractors. In contractual terms, the client makes separate contracts with each of the building

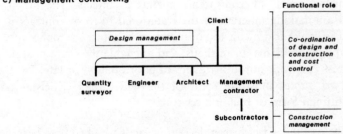

Figure 5.1 Management structures in contracting a) Traditional b) Project management c) Management contracting. Notes: Management and contractual structure are identical. Functional roles in italics. *Source: CIOB* 1982.

professions (which may take the form of direct permanent employment) and with the main contractor. Each of the subcontractors then makes a separate contract with the main contractor. The subcontractors may, in turn, make contracts with others to undertake part of their assigned tasks.

Traditional forms of contracting have considerable advantages for clients. Clients can exercise direct control over, or intervene at, various stages of the construction process. They can take and weigh up advice from different sources; are able within limits to change the specifications of the project; and there are a variety of interests that police each other's activities, especially the contractor's work and charges. Even though the traditional form of contract is specifically designed to circumscribe the areas of action open to building contractors and to limit their freedoms within them, actual control of the production process is still overwhelmingly under the control of the main contractor, with all the cost advantages to the client over earlier non-capitalist building forms.

Yet, despite those client advantages, many of the problems of the building industry are said to stem from the traditional contractual form (cf. Direct Labour Collective, 1978; Wood Report, 1975). Two examples illustrate the claim. The division into separate contracts inherent in the form makes continuity of work across projects for a unified 'team' of management, workers and equipment impossible. Thus the inherent physical spatial discontinuity of building work is reproduced and heightened in this form of contract. The second problem relates to the division between contractual obligations and management design, planning and control functions. Some agencies have management powers with little or no ultimate responsibility. If things go wrong no costs are imposed on them; such a situation is a frequent grouse by contractors against architects. The division of decision-making inherent in the traditional form of contract is also said to make it difficult to coordinate and control complex projects, to apportion blame for mishaps, and to enable the client to seek legal redress for work not undertaken, of poor quality, or late.

Two quotes illustrate some of the widespread criticisms of the traditional form of building contract:

> The conditions which then develop on-site have often been likened to a jungle. Indeed, the average jungle may well be more orderly. At worst, site operations may be nothing less than anarchy. While it would be wrong to suggest that all building operations are conducted in such conditions the possibility of their developing is far from remote in some circumstances. (Hilton, 1968, pp. 16–17).

At the present time the roles in the building industry are in a state of considerable confusion. The implications of this for the experience of any individual in the building team are, firstly, he (sic) finds that there is no settled and stable definition of what his job actually is, and secondly, nobody else can be clear about exactly what he does and what he is responsible for without finding out a lot more about the sort of building team he is in. (Higgin and Jessop, 1965, p. 61)

Other forms of contract have emerged as a result of the inherent problems of the traditional contract. Only a few will be described here, but hopefully it will become clear that the different forms of contract represent distinct power relations between design professionals and building contractors and between the main or managing contractor and the other contractors working on the project.

Project management overcomes some of the problems arising from a division of management responsibilities by placing a project manager in overall control of a project (Figure 5.1). Control over and coordination between the building professions and the on-site production process then become the central functions of project management, and the notion of a main contractor, with whom all the other building enterprises make subcontracts, is made irrelevant. The client has to put considerable faith in the skills, efficiency and honesty of the project manager, as there are few independent means of checking, but when the client has little professional building expertise, or when the project is complex, dispersed or novel, project management avoids some of the pitfalls of the traditional system. Overall management responsibility lies with the project manager, but even so there is no guarantee that the approach avoids all the problems associated with management pitfalls, contract disputes, poor coordination between subcontractors and failures to meet deadlines.

Being a project manager is not the exclusive task of one particular agent in the construction process. The manager may be an individual, a company from one of the building professions, a contractor, or a firm from outside the industry altogether. Contractors have the advantage over others of knowing how contractors operate and, hence, how to control them, yet that need not necessarily give them an overriding superiority over others in the role of project manager. In much repair and maintenance work, for example, particularly when it is relatively small-scale, surveyors will have the advantage of being able to assess and plan the work required, as well as orchestrate and manage the repair tasks. So, much of this work has always been under the management control of surveyors – even if they were not called 'project managers'.

Management contracting is the other contractual form illustrated in Figure 5.1. Here design remains independent of construction but the role of main contractor is replaced by management by a building contractor on a fee basis; hence, many contractors call it the 'fee system'. The management contractor then makes a series of contracts with subcontractors, either directly or on behalf of the client (the ambiguity is often deliberate). The role of the management contractor bears similarities with the pre-capitalist role of the architect/surveyor in making contracts with petty commodity producers from the separate building trades (a practice that only recently disappeared in Scotland: see Wallis, 1945; Thompson, 1968). Again, the management contractor does not have to be a building firm, although their building management and tendering skills give them a strong advantage over building professionals and non-construction enterprises. Management contracting has been growing rapidly in recent years, especially in private commercial building. Most large contractors have a division specialising in it, and some firms, like Bovis, concentrate almost entirely on it.

Management contracting has been pushed strongly by building contractors in recent years, and for them it can be seen as the ultimate extension of subcontracting to all work. Although generally limited to the execution of the project rather than including its design (but the management contractor may be called in for consultations at the project formulation and implementation stages), ambiguities and divisions of management responsibility still arise, as they can with project management. For instance, it has been suggested that management contractors can abuse their position and take bribes from successful subcontractors, the cost and inefficiencies of which are born by the client. In both project management and management contracting the temptation to indulge in such practices must be considerable for individual managers and firms. A firm, for example, could put in a low fee to win the job and then make their profits up through illicit payments from subcontractors (and blame the latter for the higher costs!).

Building unions do not like management contracting because its status with regard to the industry's working-rule agreements is unclear. Problems with management contracting are illustrated in the confused situation of a building strike in London in the mid-1980s. In September 1984 one of the largest building projects then being carried out in Britain, the £120 million London Bridge City project, was strike bound. Management contractor John Laing claimed to be powerless to resolve the problem, which stemmed from the client demanding bank-guaranteed performance bonds from a subcontractor as insurance against inadequate or non-existent work. The subcontractor claimed to have been able to produce the bond and said he was dismissed for other reasons. Whatever the reason, twenty bricklayers were made redundant and the TGWU declared an official strike, bringing the project to a halt (*Construction News* 6 September 1984). Subcontractor, management contractor and client could blame each other. The dismissal of the subcontractor could have been an elaborate ploy to weaken union organisation on the site, yet it looks like a classic case of one management hand not knowing what the other was doing – a problem project management is said to avoid in comparison to traditional contracting.

Another interesting development is a technique imported from the USA in the mid-1980s called *fast-tracking*. Fast-tracking is the design equivalent of 'just in time' inventory-control techniques pioneered in Japan, where materials are delivered to the factory just before they are used (Sayer, 1986). With fast-tracking, the design stage is not completed prior to tendering and construction; instead the contract is let on the basis of rough drawings and quantities, and construction starts once the conception of the building is sufficiently advanced to enable the initial stages to begin. Only later will all the detailed working drawings become available for subsequent parts of the construction process. Detailed design of, say, the upper floors of a large office block do not have to be ready before foundation work commences. The developer of the Broadgate office scheme in the City of London (1984–6) who used the approach claimed it saved £40 per sq. ft in construction costs out of the usual £120 per sq. ft cost, that rents could be received a year earlier and that substantial interest charges on work in progress were avoided (*Financial Times*, 2 October 1986). The idea of the simultaneous production of drawings and the final building not only requires the use of modern sophisticated planning techniques, but also a considerable rejigging of the relationship between design professionals and builders implicit in the traditional Contracting System.

The final variation on contractual relationships worth considering is where the building firm takes on both the design and building of a project. The building part may involve direct employment of a workforce, a project-management style of scheme or a management contract one. *Design-and-build* schemes arise where a building contractor can reproduce a standardised or proprietary product. Small factories and warehouses fall within its aspect. Industrialised systems enable the mass reproduction of a building technique over which the building firm has monopoly rights. Most industrialised concrete-housing systems of the 1960s and 1970s were of this type, including the now infamous Bison Wall-Frame system. Timber-frame housing systems are also usually proprietary designs. Rarely, however, have individual construction firms been able to devise a clearly differentiable, structurally viable and successful building technology. Wimpey's No Fines system was perhaps one of the most successful in Britain. In certain ancillary processes construction firms have been more successful in establishing differentiable products based on patented technologies; good examples are the blossoming of scaffolding systems, like Costain's 'Quik-Fit'.

One of the few areas of construction-related activity where firms do compete on the basis of technique is process engineering (not officially classified as part of the construction industry in Britain). Firms building process plant are able temporarily to monopolise advances in plant design. The firms – like Kellogg and Fluor from the USA, and Davy International and Drake and Scull from the UK – compete on a world scale on the basis of their unique design and construction capabilities. The converse of such success, however, is the extent of the specialisation required and its associated high fixed costs; both make the firms vulnerable to fluctuations in the world economy and the demand for new industrial plant.

One likely reason for the limited extent of proprietary designs in construction is the socially-created division between design and building associated with the professionalisation of design (see Chapter 4 and Bowley, 1966). Where independent designers have control over the detailed conception of a product, as they often do in building, they are unlikely to favour standardised systems. In part, the aversion will stem from an attempt to provide the design which satisfies the client's needs most closely; in part, from a desire to put their own stamp on the design for personal and career reasons; and in part, because the choice of a standardised design is an implicit admission of the redundancy of the designer's rarified role in the building process. It is interesting to note that even for the limited number of proprietary concrete and timber housing systems adopted in Britain over the past thirty years, most have been technologies bought on licence from their European or North American originators. Even so, contractors who adopted 1950s and 1960s concrete systems complained that much of the potentially-derivable advantages of scale were lost through the need to respond to variations required by the architects appointed for each project (Bowley, 1966; Cooney, 1974; Wood Report, 1975). The success of Wimpey's No Fines system was aided by its flexibility, which meant it could respond to design variations.

The rapid growth of forms like management contracting indicates that the social relations in the building industry are currently in a

state of flux. However, many of the economic principles
building contractors operate have not been substantially
of the effects of those principles can therefore now
without the need to differentiate between particular typ
contract, assuming for simplicity that main contracting is in operatiо..
(though the difference between building to contract and building
speculatively must still be borne in mind).

Accumulation and construction

The flow of profit to a building firm, as with all capitalist enterprises,
depends on the difference between total revenues and costs. The
problem is that both revenues and costs are highly variable in
construction, so it is imperative for firms to organise production in
ways which avoid periods when outgoings are greater than income.
The imperative creates one overriding principle for success: turnover
of capital invested in production must be continuous and rapid, even
if the result is sharp breaks in production.

For speculative housebuilders the variability of revenue is clear, as
a firm's income depends on being able to sell houses. On each site
firms usually find that only one or two houses are sold each week,
creating sharp variations in revenues. The situation is compounded
by the general instability of the owner-occupied housing market.
Meanwhile, site and ancillary costs are incurred whose variability is
not directly related to revenue. Land-banks must be held, while the
development of individual sites involves a bunching of costs during the
initial stages of site clearance and service provision. Not surprisingly,
therefore, speculative housebuilders try to minimise working capital
tied up in site production. Production methods and the nature of
employment of the workforce have to facilitate that flexibility of
working capital. Simple production techniques, using little fixed
capital and a casualised workforce, are the result (Ball, 1983).

Contractors' cash flows vary for different reasons associated with
the flow of income and costs from projects as they proceed and the
success of subsequent claims for unforeseen work that had to be
undertaken. During the early stage of a project cash flow is negative,
due to set-up costs and initial site work. Monthly progress payments
from the client then should gradually raise project revenue above
costs. Where there are a large number of disputed claims, or a serious
miscalculation of the work required, cash flow might again be negative, with a profit made only when disputed claims are finally settled.

The obvious way for builders to avoid long periods when costs
outweigh revenues is to spread their productive activity by having a

ries of projects at different stages of completion. Profitability for a builder depends on achieving a balanced mix of projects under way and new ones being bid for. An ability to diversify to achieve such an array of current and future work is one of the principal advantages of scale in the industry.

Variable costs and revenues are common to all productive industries. With such variations in mind, firms hold stocks, diversify their products, operate in different markets and adopt particular investment strategies. What distinguishes construction is that each new sale involves a new point of production. Cash-flow variability in construction cannot be absorbed in the sphere of market exchange alone, or by relying on credit and loans to finance temporary cash outflows. The production process itself must vary by switching from site to site, and by operating at differing degress of intensity on one site as a project is constructed. The combination of exchange and production variability means it is difficult for individual firms to gain a market advantage over competitors through technical innovation, especially where innovation requires large amounts of fixed capital. Innovations still occur, of course, and three specific areas can be highlighted – production techniques, materials and site management. The point is that their form is structured by the peculiar requirements of market relations in construction.

One of the principal means by which contracting firms avoid the pitfalls of having too high a variance in cash flow is by operating specific strategies concerning the main aspects of their activities – tendering, production and input purchase.

TENDERING

Profitability depends on the number, spread and pricing of the building contracts undertaken by a firm. Firms try to choose the most profitable array of contracts available in the contemporary economic situation. Contractors, therefore, speculate on getting a *portfolio of contracts* right.

Specific strategies are adopted on tender bids and cost claims depending on the state of the market and the firm's position within it. The relative profitability of different types of work varies over time, for instance, and firms can decide which types of work to bid for and the profit mark-up included in the bid, based on their assessment of market conditions. The final price paid to the contractor depends not only on the accepted tender price, but also additional cost claims submitted. It is not uncommon for these additional payments to be far greater than the initial tender price. Final claims are not generally assessed on the actual costs incurred, but on a valuation of the extra work done. Such claims for additional work can easily be made, as the work required often is unclearly specified in the original contract and changes in specifications are frequently made while the project is underway. There is thus considerable potential variability and leeway in the additional claims a contractor can submit and in their timing. Initial tender prices, for example, can be set low in the hope of winning the contract and succeeding in subsequent cost claims.[1]

Such pricing strategies do not mean that contractors never lose. It is precisely because substantial losses can be incurred on particular projects that such strategies are so important. Little is known empirically about the profitability of contracts; some spectacular losses have sent well-known large contractors into liquidation, but they can hardly be said to be representative. Losses for firms on one in six contracts has been suggested as typical (Chartered Institute of Public Finance and Accounting, 1975); others have suggested one in ten (Lea, Lansley and Spencer, 1974).

It has been suggested that some losses are anticipated because firms sometimes deliberately make unprofitable bids. When firms are desperate for work, for instance, they may put in bids that are unrealistically low in order to gain a temporary cash-inflow to offset the cash drain in other parts of the business. Medium-sized firms are said to be prone to this practice during downturns. Another situation in which firms might deliberately put in a loss-making tender bid is when they want to enter a market or when the project has prestige that helps the firm's image. It is difficult to know either how prevalent is the practice of 'cut-price' tendering or whether the claims that it exists are the disgruntled justifications of failed bidders. As with farmers and the weather, tender prices are never right in the eyes of the contractor.

Firms have a great incentive to tender for a large number of contracts in order to maintain an adequate inflow of revenue, even if this means over-committing capacity. It is not often realised how small are the number of major contracts let each year. Even during the second half of the 1960s, for example, when construction activity was at a much higher level than in the 1980s, the number of contracts let nationally averaged less than three per main contractor per year (Lea, Lansley and Spencer, 1974). Once variations in the size of contracts, and sectoral, regional and local differences are taken account of, the contracts effectively open to bids from any one firm are often few. Contracts lasting a year or more are particularly hard to come by (see Table 6.2, page 106).

Because of the ever-present fear of insufficient work, contractors prefer to over-commit themselves whenever possible in order to insure against periods when no new contracts are available. Projects are extended beyond contract dates if necessary. Extensions have become such an accepted part of the Contracting System that penalty costs are rarely incurred. As Bishop argues, 'This is a remarkably successful tactic for coping with variability, especially as the industry's clients have become conditioned to relatively slow progress, and meet most of the cost of funding by way of interim payments' (Bishop, 1975, p. 63). If every enterprise in the Contracting System adopts this tactic – architect, main contractor and subcontractors – the cumulative effect of disruption and delay is substantial. The probability of over-commitment obviously varies with the cycle of construction activity. When work is scarce, overcommitment is difficult and remarkable improvements in contract completion times occur, as happened in the early 1980s. During upturns, however, overcommitment is easier, so long construction times and high-priced tender bids result rather than more actual building work.

Firms that can undertake different types and sizes of contract, and work across a large geographical area, increase their likelihood of winning contracts. The extensive use of subcontracting aids this approach, as skills and know-how can be hired temporarily when required. The widespread use of subcontracting, in turn, increases the range of work for which specialist subcontractors can tender. Many techniques used in construction are relatively simple, and can be easily transferred from one type of work to another, but there are constraints on the potential spread of contracts. Even with well-known, fairly simple and easily transferable techniques there are advantages in specialisation. This is perhaps most clearly seen in particular sectors of civil engineering, but it extends across most types of work. A knowledge of particular designs and structures, for example, is likely to reduce the possibility of unexpected snags and holdups. Different types of work, similarly, might require common techniques but in different proportions, creating distinct management problems. Wide geographical spread can result in a loss of managerial control over infrequently-visited outlying sites. Building firms consequently tend to specialise by function (e.g. civil engineer) or broad product range (e.g. housebuilder).

The relative balance of the increased spread of contracts and concomitant decreased control over production depends obviously on the initial specialisation of the firm and its size. The largest firms get the greatest advantage because they can gain both a wide spread of contracts and the advantages of specialisation, through setting up functional and regional divisions whose individual workloads vary more than the company's as a whole. Emphasis can then be placed on the divisions with the strongest current market positions. A corollary of the advantage of size is that smaller firms have less chance to spread contracts. For the smallest, this is unlikely to be a great loss as they can undertake only a few contracts at a time and, with small overheads, can be highly flexible. The impact is likely to be far greater on medium-sized firms with more substantial overheads, so they are likely to be the most prone to collapse in economic crises.

The notion of a portfolio extends beyond building contracts. Each time a contractor's invested money capital becomes liquid again, for example when payment is received for work done, a choice has to be made on the future use of that capital. The most profitable option might be switching to other types of work or holding off from building contracting altogether when expected profit margins fall below other options. Other options could include temporary investment in the stock and money markets until the demand for building work picks up, investing in land and property, or moving out of construction-related fields altogether.

PRODUCTION AND INPUT PURCHASE

Contractors try to gain the maximum advantage out of the conditions of commodity exchange in the purchase of the inputs for production as well as in the sale of their product. The Contracting System places them in a good position to take advantage. Production methods are affected accordingly.

Construction is a labour-intensive industry; plant and equipment is used far less than in manufacturing. This situation, of course, did not just happen but arose precisely from the long-term effect of a need to avoid techniques which require a substantial investment in machinery. However, machines reduce costs, so firms are placed in a contradictory position with regard to investing in them. Costs on any individual project are reduced, but fixed overheads increase, threatening the firm's overall profitability and chances of survival. This dilemma means that investment by construction firms tends to be concentrated in equipment that is highly mobile. Within the traditional construction process some of the most spectacular productivity gains made from the use of machinery have been in earth-moving and materials transportation (hauling, lifting, pumping, etc.). Most of the equipment can be used on many different projects, is self-moving, or can be erected in a few days (like tower-cranes).

Investment in mobile machinery solves some of the problems of fixed capital for contractors, but it does not overcome the costs imposed by the large amount of idle time of equipment when owned.

Each project requires specific types of plant for limited time periods. The amount of idle time for equipment is staggeringly high; it can be as large as 90 per cent of time on site (Stone, 1976). The hire of plant can reduce idle time. The contractor only pays for the equipment when it is required and hirers can utilise the equipment more intensively; for sophisticated machinery trained operatives are also provided by the hire firm, reducing the skilled workforce the contractor has to retain. In this way, the use of expensive equipment is possible, even for small firms.

A separate plant-hire industry has grown up to cater for construction firms' equipment demands, and it accounts for more than half the total construction plant investment in Britain. As plant is only hired when a firm cannot utilise bought equipment adequately, there are sharp variations in any individual contractors' plant hire. The aggregate demand for plant hire is less variable, however, as individual firms' demands tend to balance each other out.

The picture is different, however, for peaks and troughs in the construction cycle. Plant for hire gets short during upturns, as firms gear up for work. This generates rising hire rates, equipment bottlenecks and resultant project delays. In sharp downturns hire firms bear the brunt of excess plant capacity. If the slump is short most can survive by cutting back on new investment and maintenance programmes. On average, the plant for hire gets older and less well maintained as a result. In long-lasting severe slumps, these tactics are insufficient and plant-hire firms go to the wall.

Resorting to plant-hire and the consequent growth of the plant-hire industry is an obvious rational response to the nature of building production and exchange for an individual building firm. A potential problem for the builder of having fixed capital tied up in production is resolved through plant-hire. This is another illustration of how the nature of the Contracting System creates a dominance of a building firm's merchant role over its producer role. The effect on the productive efficiency of the industry as a whole is less clear-cut. When half of the industry's investment in plant is by non-producers, the coercive force of competition on technical innovation in production is further weakened. Contractors cannot gain much of an advantage over competitors by investing in innovatory equipment as those competitors can hire the same. Similarly, during downturns contractors have little incentive to restructure their production processes as the coercive effect of large amounts of fixed capital is not there.

Some, but not all, of the economic pressures are transferred to the plant-hire industry. Plant hirers have a commercial incentive to offer for hire the most modern equipment, on the best terms. Their profits depend on trying to beat the competition, and the less efficient fold during slumps, leading to a restructuring of the industry (see Chapter 10). But the economics of the hire industry mean that its firms are in a particularly poor position to reinvest for an upturn. Moreover, technical innovation is divorced from the production process as a whole; it is therefore piecemeal, through an incremental improvement of individual pieces of equipment, limiting the potential for major changes in production methods. The separation of the plant-hire industry is likely, as a result, to weaken pressures for technical change in construction.

Subcontracting extends the economic principles and problems associated with plant-hire to all aspects of the construction process. There is a considerable variety in what is subcontracted: it can just be the hiring of the workforce, as in labour-only subcontracting; the workforce, equipment and materials ('supply-and-fix'); the workforce plus plant, as with groundwork; or alternatively whole aspects of the building project, including much of the workforce, the plant and the purchase and assembly of materials. In part, subcontracting is the product of the increasing technical complexity of large building projects, where particular tasks are sub-let to specialists. Under the Contracting System the architect also has the right to appoint specialist subcontractors, irrespective of the wishes of the main contractor. The general economic advantages of subcontracting under the Contracting System, however, mean that far more than specialist tasks are subcontracted. The clearest example is labour-only subcontracting, which is associated with general building trades (bricklaying, carpentry, etc.) rather than specialist ones who supply-and-fix. Any large site has an array of subcontractors under the formal control of the main contractor. Subcontractors can also subcontract part of their work, so a hierarchy of subcontracting exists. The hierarchy does not reflect firms' size or status since subcontractors may be larger firms than the main contractor; this is particularly the case with specialist trades.

Subcontracting work adds considerably to a building firm's ability to adjust to variations in workloads and to undertake different types of work. Whole aspects of the construction process can be contracted out for a known price, whilst overheads associated with employment, plant and management become the responsibility of the subcontractor. Moreover, in so far as subcontracting increases the productive time of specialists by enabling them to work for more than one main contractor by moving from project to project, their overall cost can be reduced.

Building firms are not the only companies to use subcontractors.

Subcontracting is a feature of most industries, for similar reasons; it facilitates specialisation and a flexible response to varying workloads. Like construction, its use is growing in other industries.[2] What is distinctive about the construction industry is the extent of its use and, most importantly, that it takes place at one point of production, the building site, with workers employed by different subcontractors or the main contractor working side by side. In contrast, subcontracting in other industries is generally of particular components or of peak orders and so is spatially differentiated.

On site, there are a multitude of worker/employer relations. Unity across workers over site-based struggles is made difficult as the terms and conditions of employment vary amongst them, and their conflicts are with different employers. As the site is the basis of trade union activity in the British building industry, subcontracting weakens the power of the workforce to fight for improved conditions; the antipathy between trades unionism and labour-only subcontracting shows the effect at its most extreme. This disadvantage to workers, of course, is an advantage to employers. Subcontracting in construction transforms worker resistance at the point of production.

Contractors have strong incentives to create employment conditions that make total wage costs flexible. And the weakness of worker resistance under the Contracting System makes this an easy possibility in Britain. Workers are employed on the basis of required tasks on a particular project. If the contractor has no further work available on other projects the operative is dismissed. Labour turnover is therefore high, and manual employment overwhelmingly casual in nature.[3]

Wage payments and other employment conditions are also used to increase the flexibility of wage costs. Flat-rate bonus and piecework incentive schemes, for example, make up a large proportion of construction workers' wages. From the point of view of the employer, such incentive schemes mean that maximum wage payments are only incurred when maximum output is required. As work tails off so do bonuses and, therefore, wage costs. A high proportion of bonus payments has the added benefit for the employer of minimising the need to supervise the work of operatives. The site location and bespoke nature of building work makes it difficult for management to control the intensity of work by the non-pecuniary methods associated with factory production (e.g. via detailed supervision and the speed of the production line). Work-study-based incentive schemes partially overcome the problem, although often bonuses are haphazard or not related to specific tasks but to attracting labour to a site; incentive payments certainly seemed to grow rapidly in the construction industry during the 1970s (see Table 5.1). Another advantage for contractors of bonus payments is that the variability of bonus induces operatives to leave sites as bonuses tail off. In this way, levels of employment can be adjusted to the contractor's requirements without the need for large severance, or statutory redundancy, payments.

Table 5.1 *Bonus and piece-rates in construction workers' wages, 1975–85, for full-time male manual workers, aged 21 and over*

Year	% of total pay		% of employees who received	
	Overtime	PBR*, etc., payments	Overtime	PBR, etc., payments
1975	14	13	61	59
1980	11	15	53	52
1985	12	13	51	54

* PBR = payment by results, bonuses, commission and other incentive payments.
Hilton (1968, p. 154) says that a Ministry of Labour survey in the late 1960s shows only 16–18 per cent of construction workforce on genuine incentive schemes, though more were paid undifferentiated site, etc., bonuses.
Source: Housing and Construction Statistics

The sphere of market exchange, this time between workers and employers, is here once again being used to overcome a potential contradiction between a rapid turnover of capital and the needs of production. The resulting situation, however, creates problems for contractors. Skilled workforces are disbanded and can be difficult to recruit again when needed. Disputes over site bonuses can be highly disruptive, and control by management over operatives' speed and quality of work might be ineffective. However the whole strategy is virtually impossible with non-manual employees who represent a fairly unavoidable overhead for the building firm.

Table 5.2 gives a breakdown of types of building employment from 1970–85. Overall, estimated employment fell by 17 per cent, but there are considerable variations between the categories, indicating shifts in employer/employee relations as building firms tried to increase their flexibility and to win new areas of public-sector work from local-authority direct labour. Public-sector employment fell the most, the number of manual workers by 44 per cent and administrative staff by a much smaller 18 per cent between 1970 and 1985. Contractors' employees show similar magnitudes of decline, 39 per cent and 7 per cent for manual and APTCs (administrative, professional, technical and clerical staff) respectively. The big growth area for employment has been self-employment, up by 56 per cent over the fifteen-year period, and many would regard the official

Department of Employment estimates as unrealistically low. Leopold (1982), for example, argues that Inland Revenue data show a 40 per cent higher number of self-employed in construction. Even if the latter estimate is on the high side, as not everyone holding an Inland Revenue P714 tax certificate may be a full-time active building operative, it is reasonable to assume that at least half of all manual workers in the building industry are self-employed; many, of course, will be hired in that capacity by contractors and speculative housebuilders.

Table 5.2 *Employment (in thousands) in the construction industry, 1970–85*

	Contractors		Public authorities				Self-employed†		Total employment
	Operatives	% APTC*	% Operatives	%	APTC	%	Operatives	%	
1970	912	51 230	13 258	14	103	6	300	17	1802
1975	806	46 234	13 232	13	112	6	362	21	1746
1980	767	45 235	14 212	13	110	7	365	22	1689
1985	556	37 213	14 169	11	84	6	469	31	1491

* APTC = administrative, professional, technical and clerical staff.
† Self-employed are Department of Employment estimates, 1980 average of 1979 and 1981 estimates.
Percentages are of total employment.
Source: Housing and Construction Statistics

It seems reasonable to surmise from the employment data that the trends in types of employment are interlinked. The switch, within the overall decline of employment, from the use of directly-employed to self-employed workers, is an obvious one. However the much smaller fall in APTCs is also likely to be closely linked to the new patterns of employment. APTCs now represent a far higher proportion of contractors' employees; in 1970 the ratio of contractors' operatives to APTCs was 4 to 1, but by 1985 it was almost down to 2 to 1. Contractors have retained APTCs despite falling workloads for a number of reasons. In part, it is because of the increasing technical sophistication of some types of construction work, but other reasons associated with the organisation and control of the workforce seem to be more significant: the growing importance of bonus payments (requiring bonus estimators, work-study experts, etc.); the increase in sophistication of tendering strategies and the extra experts needed to implement them (estimators, operations researchers and legal specialists, to name a few); and, finally, the growth of subcontracting and the additional administrative staff it requires.

Data in Table 5.3 on changes in the types of APTCs employed in the private building industry give credence to the control rather than technology explanation. Only managerial staff increased in number from 1975–84 (albeit by a mere 2 per cent). The most clearly technically-related staff experienced falls – quite sharp ones for architects, surveyors and engineers (−18 per cent) and small ones for technical staff (−2 per cent). Computerisation is likely to account for the falls in clerical and sales staff (−12 per cent) and the decimation of draughtsmen and tracers (−30 per cent), while the growth in subcontracting could account for the fall-off in foremen no longer required to supervise direct-labour gangs.

Table 5.3 *Administrative, professional, technical and clerical staff (in thousands) by type, 1975–85*

	Managerial	Architects, surveyors, engineers	Technical	Draughtsmen and tracers	Foremen	Clerical and sales	Total
1975	58.4	19.9	25.1	4.0	38.4	94.2	240.0
1980	61.3	18.3	27.6	3.2	38.1	90.7	239.2
1984	59.3	17.3	24.7	2.8	33.8	82.6	220.5

Trainees and public-sector employees excluded.
Source: Housing and Construction Statistics

Financial controls and site organisation

One of the major developments in the construction industry over the past decade has been argued to be much greater managerial controls over financial flows and site-level activity (Bartlett Summer School, 1979, *passim*). The reasons for the greater emphasis on these aspects of a construction firm's operations become apparent in the light of the discussion in this chapter. Financial and site control are two of the areas where building firms have the greatest degrees of freedom in controlling their operations, given the imperative of maintaining the maximum flexibility of their capital resources. During an era like that from the early 1970s, when building firms have faced potentially disastrous falls in profitability resulting from declining and uncertain workloads, it is not surprising that the major innovations in the industry have taken a managerial and financial form. Increasing financial control and sophistication, moreover, will probably improve the flexibility of a firm's capital, while the greater emphasis on site planning and management partially reflects the changed social relations on a building site, especially the greater use of subcontractors.

Subcontracting requires greater degrees of careful timing and control, as they cannot be redirected to alternative site tasks in the

same way as a directly-employed workforce. Adaptive and instantaneous site-management strategies have to be replaced by more
careful pre-site planning of work flows. In other words, a corollary
of lower and flexible working capital implied by a switch from direct
employment to subcontracting is *less* flexibility in day-to-day site-
management operations. In addition, with subcontracting, the lowest
level of management control is raised to a level above the old one of
foreman. The foreman's immediate supervisory role over work gangs
implied a close knowledge of the labourers and their tasks and
provided an immediate vehicle for management directives and control.
With subcontracting the foreman's role is lost. A ganger or foreman
in the subcontract gang might perform similar tasks, but they will
reflect the interests of the subcontractor and not necessarily those of
the contractor. Again, improving the site-planning process and higher
levels of site-management is a way that the contractor can try to win
back some of the lost information and control.

The consequences of competition in the contracting system

Earlier sections of this chapter have shown how important is the
merchanting role of the British building contractor. Dealing in portfolios of contracts and using the sphere of exchange to speed up the
turnover of productive capital focus a contractor's operations, to
which the production process must be subordinated. These exchange
relations even provide, in the form of credit, much of the contractor's
working capital via monthly progress payments from the client and
delays in payments to building-materials merchants, plant-hire firms
and subcontractors.

The primacy of the merchanting role is an inevitable outcome of
the historical development of the Contracting System in Britain. One
result is a weakening of the coercive pressure of accumulation in
revolutionising the productive methods of the industry and forcing
producers towards the known limits of productive efficiency. The
fragmentation of the building process between different enterprises
involved in design, surveying, contracting, plant-hire and materials
creates a minefield of dispute, delay, avoided responsibilities, and
missed opportunities for innovation. It is hardly surprising that, faced
with such divisions, construction management manuals and studies
of the construction process place so much emphasis on 'teamwork'.[4]
The most profitable building contractor is the one that achieves the
best portfolio of contracts rather than being the least-cost producer.
The vagaries of tendering and tendering strategies enable firms of

widely varying productive efficiencies to co-exist, either as main contractors or as subcontractors. Larger firms, for example, often are better placed to gain a profitable portfolio of contracts and so they can push smaller ones out of business by competition, simply because of that trading advantage rather than because of lower costs.

This does not mean, of course, that competition never occurs; it is simply a statement about the way in which competition operates when it takes place. The portfolio effect, for instance, can easily create the paradox of the least-cost producer being forced out of business because it is not the one with the most favourable portfolio. If the lowest-cost producer is not necessarily the most profitable, the incentive to innovate is weakened. With the overriding importance of adequately-structured portfolios, innovation is, moreover, as likely to be in financial manipulation as productive efficiency.

CHAPTER 6

Construction output: a thirty-year view

In Britain, during the 1970s, there was a dramatic collapse in the demand for new construction work. By the early 1980s, new construction output in real terms was barely half the peak post-war levels achieved slightly over a decade earlier, although more recently workloads have recovered. Similar collapses in workloads were experienced during the late 1970s/early 1980s in other advanced capitalist countries, though with different relative declines and temporal patterns. Such declines show how dependent construction and related industries are on the wider economic environments in which they exist. This chapter explores the changing pattern of demand for construction work, while subsequent chapters will examine the resultant effects on the industry itself.

One common argument about the problems of the construction industry suggests that construction's dependence on extremely volatile demand explains the characteristics of the industry. The claim of a peculiarly volatile nature of construction demand is examined in this chapter, and shown empirically not to be true, at least at the aggregate national level.

The long building cycle from the 1950s to the 1980s

The existence of long waves in building activity has been empirically recognised for many years (e.g. Parry Lewis, 1965; Gottlieb, 1976). The late 1940s to the early 1980s seems to be such a classic long cycle. As Figure 6.1 shows, output in real terms rose rapidly until the mid-1960s then, after a five-year plateau, dropped sharply. The decline shows a stepped formation; several years of rapid decline associated with periods of general economic crisis, occurring in 1974–5 and 1980–1, with intervening periods of relative stability from 1976–8 and 1982–5. Output in the early 1980s was back to low levels not experienced since the 1950s. Subsequent years showed partial recovery of output from the depths reached in 1981, but the path of construction output over the next few years, if construction forecasts are to be believed, is for at best a plateau at around the 1985 level, rather than continued expansion (National Economic

Development Office, 1986; forecasts later in 1987 were more optimistic following unexpectedly strong construction demand in that year).

What distinguishes the post-1945 building cycle from earlier ones is the central role played by the state. The significance of state expenditure since 1945 has brought construction activity firmly into line with the overall pace of accumulation, whereas some earlier building booms had been counter-cyclical, as in the 1930s (Richardson and Aldcroft, 1968). Since 1945 not only has the role of the state operated directly via its own expenditure on construction work, but also indirectly via its influence on macroeconomic factors such as the rate of growth of incomes and the availability and cost of credit.

There are two prime indicators of construction workloads – output and new orders. It is to be expected that output reflects in a smoothed fashion the magnitude of earlier orders, though in practice orders tend to under-represent the scale of subsequent output. Care must be taken in comparing the orders and output series, partly because of technical problems over the correct indices to use for deflating both series to comparable constant price terms (Butler, 1978), but principally because the orders data are for contractors only whereas the output data are for all agencies undertaking construction work. As well as contractors, the latter includes the output of public-building agencies, like local-authority direct-labour departments (although their new building output is relatively small), and estimates of the unrecorded output of small firms and self-employed workers (who might be working as subcontractors for firms covered by the output surveys). Such differences, particularly the estimates of unrecorded output, explain the peculiarity of the relationship between the orders and output series, where for fifteen years from 1967–82 orders are always shown below output. Nevertheless, orders for new construction work do exhibit a similar, if more volatile, pattern to the output series. The volatility of the order series, interestingly, is greatest during the 'high plateau' demand years from 1964–74 (cf. Figures 6.4 and 6.5).

Repair and maintenance

New building work is overwhelmingly dominated by capitalist building contractors and speculative builders. This is not true of repair and maintenance (R&M), so output data tend not to be very accurate for this sector.

In repair and maintenance, public building agencies and small-time jobbing firms predominate. Output estimates for the latter are poor, whilst do-it-yourself work by occupiers is entirely absent, by defi-

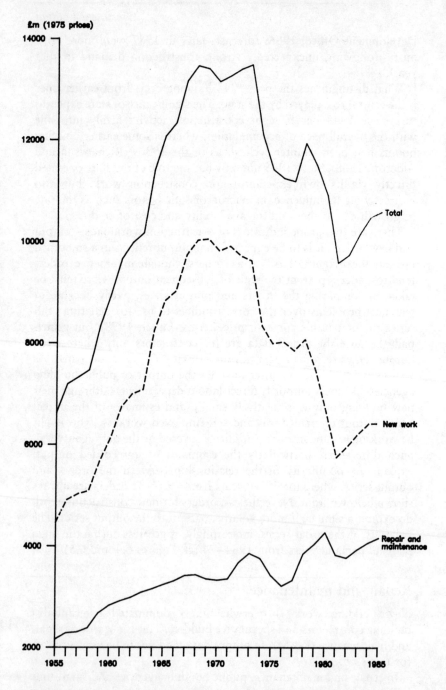

Figure 6.1 Construction output: new work and repair and maintenance, 1955–85. *Source: Housing and Construction Statistics.*

nition, from the industry. The data given in Figure 6.1 (page 100) show a distinct pattern of change for R&M work. The long post-war cycle for new building work is not repeated with R&M. Instead, its long-term trend is one of a steady but significant increase; 1980 R& M output was almost double that of 1955. By the 1980s, construction work had become far more repair-orientated; in 1985, 46 per cent of construction output was R&M, while in 1972 it was only 29 per cent. The data omissions in the official statistics imply that the real current percentage could be even higher. Forecasts suggest that any sustained real growth in total construction output is likely to be in the R&M sector, especially housing (National Economic Development Office, 1986).

In part, such a marked increase in R&M is the simple arithmetical consequence of years of high rates of new building; more buildings need more repair and maintenance, the importance of which increases as structures age. This feature has been reinforced by trends in certain construction sectors, like housing, towards maintaining existing structures longer rather than rehabilitating or renewing them. Fashion and the changing economics of housing provision encouraged this shift. Housing R&M is now greater than all new housing output, and has been since 1981; by 1988, housing R&M is expected to be more than 25 per cent greater than new housebuilding.

What has become clear since the late 1960s is that repair and maintenance has become subject to a marked short-term cycle around its trend, unlike new construction. The cause of these fluctuations is not hard to find. They are closely associated with the general short-term cycle of activity in the British economy; squeezed incomes of private and public agencies during recessions lead to less building maintenance (and vice versa).

Sectoral changes in new building work

Figures 6.2–6.4 disaggregate new construction output and orders since the 1950s: first, by whether it was for the public or private sectors (Figures 6.2 and 6.3); second, there is a division of output into the standard categories of public-sector housing and non-housing output, and private-sector housing, industrial and commercial output. The figures show that there are important differences in the trends of demand for each type of work.

Although each of the five sectors of work roughly follows the trend of the overall building cycle, what is most striking about the data in Figure 6.2 is the difference between public and private work. Much of the decline in construction output since the late 1960s can be

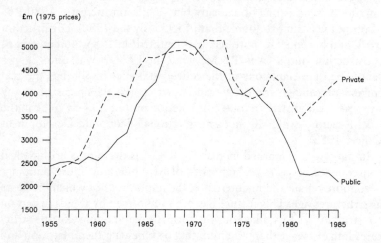

Figure 6.2 Construction output: public and private sectors, 1955–85. *Source: Housing and Construction Statistics.*

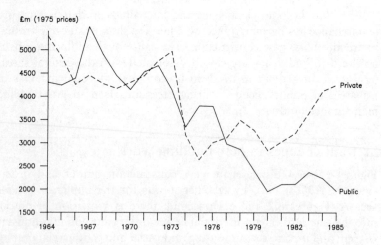

Figure 6.3 Construction: new orders, public and private sectors, 1964–85. *Source: Housing and Construction Statistics.*

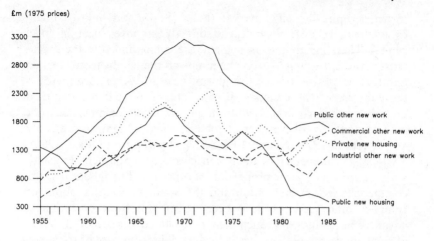

£m (1975 prices)

Public other new work
Commercial other new work
Private new housing
Industrial other new work

Public new housing

Figure 6.4 Construction output by type of work, 1955–85. *Source: Housing and Construction Statistics.*

attributed to the collapse of public-sector demand. Public-sector construction work in the early 1980s was only 40 per cent of that achieved in the peak years at the end of the 1960s; 1980 levels were even less than those of the 1950s. Private-sector work, on the other hand, has held up much better, even experiencing a boom in the mid-1980s, although there have been marked short-term cycles since the early 1970s (Figures 6.2 and 6.3). Construction work for the public sector can be interpreted in terms of the long-term trends, whereas the private sector exhibits more short-term variability.

Looking in more detail at the public sector, the trajectory of public non-housing work is the most dramatic and symmetrical (Figure 6.4). Like a rocket, it shoots up – trebling in real terms in fourteen years, a feat unmatched by any other sphere – only to fall rapidly again, dropping by half between 1969 and 1981. Public housing shows more variability around a similar stark trend of rise and fall. Housing even manages to rally during the mid-1970s when other sectors are showing dramatic declines, a rare case of counter-cyclical government construction expenditure. The overall pattern of public-housing output changes is a complex amalgam of reaction to rising working-class militancy, public-expenditure crises, party political ideology and response to the expansion of owner occupation (Ball, 1983; Merrett, 1979). By 1985, output was less than a fifth of its 1968 peak, and still falling.

Turning to the private sector, both housing and non-housing work shows greater volatility: housing, because of the instability of the owner-occupied housing market (Ball, 1986); and industrial and commercial, because they depend directly on investment in fixed capital. These instabilities in demand are compounded in the speculative nature of supply – everyone jumps on the bandwagon when an upturn is in prospect, even if a glut of new offices, factories, etc., is the end result. The commercial sector has exhibited the strongest growth, particularly in the 1980s. In the late 1980s, commercial work may account for 30 per cent of total new work, compared to only 16 per cent in 1979 (National Economic Development Office, 1986). Regionally, commercial work is concentrated in Southern England, with a particularly large proportion of office building (about half the commercial sector) in London and the South East. Installations of complex office services have been at the forefront of technical advances in the industry. Such high value-added work, half the value of some modern buildings, has helped to change the face of some key construction sectors.

Looking at all new work as a whole, it can be seen that, to an extent, sectors of work counter-balance each other. Aggregate changes in workloads, therefore, at times are the sum of opposing movements in sectors of the industry. Such divergent demand patterns have obvious implications for firms specialising in particular sectors; their sector may be short of work whilst the industry as a whole is not. Alternatively, increased workloads for one type of work may not, at least in the short-run, lead to many new firms entering the sector because of barriers to entry associated with: a lack of technical expertise or knowledge of local market conditions; the need for personal contact with clients, building professions and subcontractors; and the firm's acceptability for invitation to select-tender lists. So, short-run upturns in demand within a sector can easily lead to tender-price escalation, and subsequent higher profit margins for those firms winning contracts, despite general excess capacity in the industry.

Sectoral variations in demand and short-run barriers to entry help to explain the tender-price explosion in Britain from 1972–3 – when the public-sector housebuilding tender-index rose by 39 per cent in one year and the non-housing index by a staggering 41 per cent, at a time when general price inflation was only 7 per cent a year. Although total construction demand had begun to falter by 1971, strong demand in three sectors (public non-housing, private housing and private commercial) resulted in high margins, which spilt over into other sectors via knock-on effects on the general costs and availability of construction inputs.

New-orders data by sector provide additional information on what

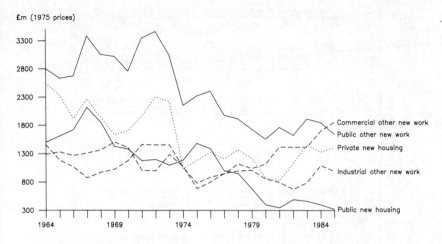

Figure 6.5 Construction orders by type of work, 1964–85. *Source: Housing and Construction Statistics.*

has been happening to construction demand over the past twenty years (see Figure 6.5). Again, orders data for each sector tend, as would be expected, to fluctuate more than output. An important feature to notice is the points in time when the direction of change for two or more sectors coincides. The 'plateau period' of oscillations in aggregate orders from 1964–73 can be seen to result from a coincidence of peak orders for public-sector work and for private housing in 1967, and of public non-housing, private housing and private commercial in 1973, with quite sharp intervening troughs. Similarly, between 1974 and 1976, public-sector orders offset declines in private ones, whereas, from 1977 to 1979 and again 1981–2, two or more of the private sectors were moving against the general overall downward trend. In 1981 and 1982, for instance, despite the overall trough in construction work, as much office building and other commercial work was ordered from contractors as in the more well-known office-building boom of the early 1970s.

The shift away from the public sector

Sectoral variations in construction demand partly reflect long-term structural changes in the composition of construction work. The long-term trend towards repair and maintenance has already been noted. In new building, however, there has been a shift away from public-sector work. In 1969, for example, 51 per cent of new output was

Table 6.1 *The changing composition of new construction orders, 1972–83: new orders (£ million at 1980 prices)*

Type of work	1972	1973	1974	1975	1976	1977	1978	1979	1980	1981	1982	1983
Public												
Housing	2,210	2,073	2,277	2,848	2,664	1,892	1,816	1,288	758	672	955	895
Gas, electricity and coal	397	473	388	527	357	386	367	346	390	459	295	299
Rail and air	138	138	104	177	147	212	179	93	173	293	86	142
Education	1,313	912	612	710	604	482	384	394	330	299	264	375
Health	560	519	335	438	371	354	390	342	320	509	492	463
Offices, factories, etc.	560	586	453	613	612	573	873	693	589	552	615	720
Roads	1,704	1,586	997	886	876	784	684	605	562	858	819	832
Harbours	137	95	151	175	104	172	161	132	97	101	100	127
Water and sewerage	1,063	840	453	617	602	418	391	331	294	362	348	450
Miscellaneous	987	781	706	615	668	554	528	592	487	520	604	943
Private												
Housing	4,380	4,046	2,082	2,513	2,484	2,643	3,062	2,729	1,964	1,899	2,711	3,398
Industrial	1,923	2,507	2,100	1,425	1,832	2,084	2,160	2,219	1,803	1,653	1,397	1,607
Offices	1,280	1,302	1,039	633	977	919	1,012	977	1,045	1,544	1,488	1,259
Shops	607	648	386	383	438	474	567	493	536	565	548	572
Entertainment	430	393	265	192	277	282	370	367	342	413	402	378
Garages	117	100	65	46	71	96	148	136	125	104	141	173
Schools and colleges	37	43	31	19	25	51	52	71	44	51	51	70
Miscellaneous	340	329	280	352	252	246	285	240	270	295	287	400

Price deflators used: public housing, index of public-sector housebuilding; private housing, house-price index; private housing, house-price index; rest, public-sector building tender-price index; roads, road-construction tender-price index; rest, public-sector building tender-price index *Source: Housing and Construction Statistics.*

for the public sector; by 1985, the proportion had fallen to only 32 per cent; and for orders, the fall was even more dramatic (Figure 6.3). Within the reduced public-sector workloads, certain types of work have suffered disproportionately (Table 6.1). Education, and particularly school building, has had the biggest proportionate decline (education work fell from £1,313 million in 1972 to only £264 million in 1982). Similar large falls have been experienced in housing, roads, nationalised industries, and water and sewerage. Privatisation has also moved some previous public-sector work into the private sector, like that for British Telecom.

The shift away from public-sector work has also altered the size and duration of construction projects. Table 6.2 shows the duration and value of new orders obtained by contractors in 1985. It can be seen that, with the partial exception of commercial work, the public sector provides most long-lasting, high-value projects. The situation was even more dramatic before public-expenditure cuts began to bite heavily, particularly in council housing, where virtually no large schemes are now under way. In 1982, for instance, though only 1 per cent of public non-housing orders were over two years in duration, they represented 23 per cent of the total value of all public other work in that year. Most private housing work is over within six months, and much industrial work within a year. Only large office projects and energy-related ventures match the value and time scale of public-sector work, and they are a quite small proportion of private-sector work.

Table 6.2 *Distribution of new orders obtained by contractors by duration and value, 1985: percentage of total value*

	Public housing	Private housing	Other public	Private	
				Industrial	Commercial
Duration in months					
0–6	5.3	59.8	27.0	43.2	33.3
7–12	41.8	30.8	25.0	32.6	29.1
13–24	50.8	8.3	30.6	11.2	26.7
25+	2.1	1.1	17.4	12.9	10.9
Value in £ thousand					
25 and under 50	0.7	11.1	4.8	6.4	4.4
50 and under 100	3.3	17.2	7.8	7.5	7.2
100 and under 200	5.6	19.0	7.4	11.3	10.1
200 and under 500	18.0	26.5	14.8	14.9	11.8
500 and under 2,000	56.4	22.5	26.4	27.2	22.7
2,000 and over	14.0	2.7	38.8	32.7	43.8

Source: Housing and Construction Statistics

gional changes in demand

lifts in regional patterns of demand are the last demand item that needs consideration; Table 6.3 shows the changing shares of total orders for the regions of Britain from 1970–85. Not surprisingly, it has been the economically dynamic regions which have increased their shares of construction work, particularly the South East, whose share rose from 31 per cent to 40 per cent from 1970 to 1985, while the North and Wales lost most heavily. The importance of Southern England for private builders is now almost overwhelming. Taking account of the different sizes of the regions by calculating new orders on a per capita basis, the South East in the 1980s (using the 1981–5 average) generates almost 75 per cent more new orders than the lowest region, the North West; the ratio for East Anglia is not much different, and the South West is not far behind either.[1]

Table 6.3 *New orders obtained by contractors by region, 1970–85: percentage of value of total new orders in Britain*

Region	1970	1975	1980	1985
North	7	7	5	4
Yorks and Humberside	9	8	8	6
E. Midlands	6	7	7	6
E. Anglia	3	4	4	4
South East	31	31	35	40
South West	7	7	8	9
W. Midlands	8	8	7	8
North West	11	10	9	9
Wales	6	7	6	3
Scotland	11	13	11	9
Great Britain	100	100	100	100

Source: Housing and Construction Statistics

The impact of the changes in construction output on construction firms

Changes in the demand for construction have had a dramatic impact on the markets in which builders operate. The scale of the collapse in new work has been the most traumatic change for building firms. Although the growth of repair and maintenance has partly offset the decline in new work, this has been of little help to all but the smallest of firms because larger ones tend to be uncompetitive in such small-scale work.

The drift away from public-sector work and the changing nature

of what remains has had a number of consequences for
In the first place, the number of big public-sector turnkey
slumped disproportionately and has not been replaced b
private-sector ones. Schools, large housing estates, road
and hospitals constitute large building projects with a
degree of standardised work processes; the loss to firms specialising
in those sectors, and the need for them to restructure, has been
considerable. In addition, the shorter duration of projects leads to
the time horizon of a contractors' assured future work shrinking
dramatically. Firms have to tender for more projects, and more
frequently, to gain an equivalent workload.

The shift towards the private sector has also meant that proportionately far more building work is speculative (and involves land
assembly) than fifteen to twenty years ago. The increasing significance
of private housebuilding is a clear example, but much factory and
warehouse building is also speculative and requires the initial
assembly of land, possibly in conjunction with a developer or financial
institution. One implication of the greater speculative nature of
demand is that profits become more variable for a given level of
output. It is also likely that the decline of the public-sector work has
had a detrimental effect on profits because of the impact on tendering
practices, time overruns and additional claims procedures. Public-
sector clients may easily be viewed by contractors as soft options; the
public sector, after all, has been a bastion of the traditional contract
and the Contracting System.

It has not been easy for many construction firms to switch between
different types of work to take advantages of the changing sectoral
composition of work. Large firms with diversified presences across
many types of construction work can take advantage of inter-sectoral
variations by changing the emphasis they put on their particular
specialist subsidiaries. On the other hand, firms that do not have an
established sectoral base from which to expand, or a presence in a
specific geographic area if the upturn is localised, face considerable
difficulties in switching their attentions to new areas. The attempts
by firms to break into new areas of work will be explored in greater
detail in later chapters.

What is clear from this analysis of construction output is that
medium-sized firms, particularly in economically depressed regions,
have been worst hit by the changes in demand. Public-sector housing
work was a good market for the medium-sized regional contractor.
Firms specialising in non-housing public-sector work have also taken
a pounding. Unfortunately, it is very difficult from the available stat-

...ics to discover what has happened to the traditional medium-sized producer. Changes in larger firms will be considered in a later chapter.

Is the construction industry like it is because governments use it as an economic regulator?

Many official reports on the construction industry, plus a number of academic commentators, have suggested that sharp variations in construction workloads have been a major cause of inefficiencies in the industry. The state has been highlighted as the prime creator of instability. Since the Second World War the role of the public sector as a source of construction demand has increased dramatically, even if it has declined in significance over the past decade. It is claimed that rather than attempting to smooth out destabilising variations, successive governments have exacerbated them by using construction as a regulator of the overall level of demand in the economy, or as a means of reducing the share of state expenditure in national income, or both (cf. Emmerson Report, 1962; Wood Report, 1975; NEDO, 1978; Parry Lewis and Singh, 1966). The argument focuses in particular on the use of construction demand as a short-run regulator of aggregate demand, rather than on long-term shifts in the size and composition of construction output. And it is widely believed that construction is subject to far more short-term variation in workloads than other industries. However the data show a different story.

A brief look at the aggregate output data for construction over the past thirty years casts considerable doubt on the short-run destabilising-demand thesis. Looking at Figure 6.1, it can be seen that there are dramatic long-term changes in orders and output but relatively little variation around those trends. The new orders series, which is likely to be more volatile, exhibits noticeable short-run instability only during the output peak 'plateau' years from 1965–72, and even during the plateau period orders fluctuated by less than 10 per cent around the trend – hardly a disruptive variation that generally could not be smoothed out in the process of transforming orders for work into actual production and output. It may be the case that individual sectors exhibit greater variability (see Figure 6.4), but they tend to offset each other and the destabilising thesis is directed principally at the total level of demand.

Comparisons between construction and manufacturing industry outputs do not support the view that construction suffers unduly from short-run variations in demand. Sugden (1975) found this using annual data from 1950–71. In a later paper, Sugden (1980), a longer-term historical comparison was undertaken. Coefficients of variation around output trends were calculated for construction and manufacturing from 1900 to the 1970s. From 1901–15, construction's was higher than manufacturing's (3.85 compared to 3.09 for manufacturing). During the inter-war years the difference widens considerably – 7.70 for construction compared to 2.70 for manufacturing. However the post-war years from 1950–71 show a completely different picture; the coefficient of variation for construction drops dramatically to 2.02, compared to 2.04 for manufacturing. Sugden, not surprisingly, concludes that:

> these figures give no support to the contention that the construction industry suffers unduly from fluctuations of demand. Rather they demonstrate that it has benefited relatively more than others from post-war Keynesian policies. This is not to say that construction demand is not cyclical, merely that the demand for the products of most industries is cyclical, so unique features of construction industry structure and performance cannot be explained in these terms. (Sugden, 1980, p. 3)

A report from a non-building Economic Development Committee study undertaken by NEDO in the mid-1970s came to similar conclusions (National Economic Development Office, 1976a). Using quarterly data from 1958–73, it was found that there was less variation around the output trend in construction than manufacturing industry as a whole, and even than for every individual manufacturing Standard Industrial Classification (SIC) apart from one – food, drink and tobacco. However, the variation in employment in construction was much higher than any other sector of the economy. It concluded: 'Construction is a different matter: here there seems to be a genuine tendency for given output fluctuations to generate larger changes in employment in a way that is unique among the sectors it has been possible to measure' (National Economic Development Office, 1976a, p. 36). It is difficult to think of a better statistical demonstration of the fact that the success of capital in the construction industry has been won at considerable expense to the workforce.

Demand does play an important part in determining the nature of the construction industry, but its effects operate principally in terms of long-term shifts between sectors. Long-term variations in demand help to encourage adjustments in work processes, social relations and firm structures. Short-run fluctuations, on the other hand, cannot explain very much, particularly when their uniqueness to construction is exaggerated.

Persistence of the unduly-severe-demand-fluctuations thesis can perhaps be explained by the political motivations of its proponents.

The building Economic Development Committee of NEDO, like the other sector working parties, is a corporatist political forum bringing together government and representatives of capital and labour in the building industry. Its expert committees are dominated by representatives of the interests of the major contractors in the industry, so the emphasis on demand can be seen as a piece of special pleading, supported by the unions who are concerned to increase the security of employment of their members.

There is no denying the significance of periodic state expenditure cuts and subsequent reflations on the demand for construction work. 'Stop-go' policies adopted by successive British governments since the Second World War have placed emphasis on cutting state construction expenditure during the 'stop' periods of deflation. This item of public expenditure is cut the hardest because it is politically more palatable than laying off public-sector workers, reducing welfare benefits or military expenditure, or reneging on the National Debt. The sharp deflation induced by Conservative governments in the 1980s continues this trend.

What is not clear is whether demand-management policies have had a devastating short-run impact on construction workloads. Public expenditure cuts may have been a major contributor to the dramatic decline in workloads since the early 1970s, just as it was a major contributor to the increases of the 1950s and 1960s, but the data do not show a short-run effect of demand management. The riddle can perhaps be explained by reversing the direction of causality. The construction industry is not like it is because governments use it as an economic regulator; instead, governments use it as an economic regulator because construction is like it is.

Construction can be used as an economic regulator as firms are geared up to variations in workloads. Operating in the Contracting System is the cause, where each new piece of work generally has to be won on an individual basis no matter the overall level of demand, rather than aggregate fluctuations in the public-sector orders. The construction industry has proved, therefore, a good instrument for transmitting short-term deflation through the economy without creating widespread political upheaval, economic disruption or closure of productive capacity. Instead, building workers can be quietly laid-off, helping to create the desired slack in the labour market. Deflationary macroeconomic policies might not work as hoped for, but this particular chosen instrument does. 'Stop-go' policies did not change the nature of the Contracting System, but took advantage of it. Criticism of the long-term consequences for the construction industry of the need for productive flexibility is actually a criticism of the contemporary nature of the industry itself.

CHAPTER 7

A hierarchical industry

Emphasis so far has been placed on mapping out the relations between all the agents involved in the construction process and the resultant effects on the ways in which construction firms organise production. This chapter will explore the relation between building enterprises in the industry. Firms of widely differing size coexist in construction. Frequently, size is a consequence of the types of activity undertaken and the specific relations of production (e.g. capitalist or petty commodity production), as well as an indicator of the relative success of a particular enterprise.

Two general features can be discerned about the relations between building firms. First, many are closely linked through complex chains of subcontracting. And, second, certain types of firm dominate particular sectors of work because their specific organisational structure makes it difficult for others to operate profitably there. Thus there are aspects of both complementarity and competition in the relations between firms.

Declining workloads have stimulated substantial changes in the relationships between firms. Subcontracting has increased considerably over the past fifteen years, while the increased role of repair and maintenance has put many of the larger firms at a disadvantage. The changing relationships between different types of firm are part of the restructuring of the construction industry that has gone on over the past decade.

This chapter looks at the distribution of firms' sizes within construction, and how this has changed over the past twenty years. In the light of the evidence, conjectures are made about the current hierarchical structure of relationships between firms.

Changing numbers of construction firms

Construction is an industry with thousands of firms. Most of the firms are very small, just a working proprietor or a working proprietor and one or two workers; of the 168,000 construction firms in existence in 1985, 151,000 firms employed less than eight people.

Little information is specifically available on the tens of thousands

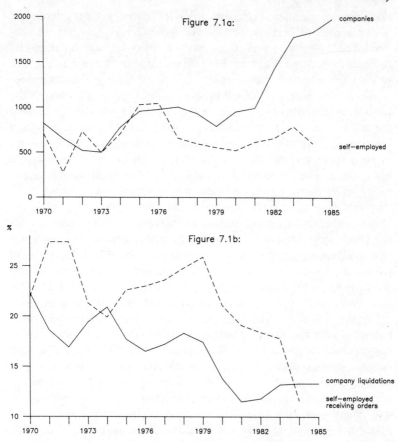

Figure 7.1 (a) Insolvencies of construction firms, 197085. (b) Percentage of all receiving orders and liquidations, 1970–85. Note: data for self-employed not available for 1985. *Source: Housing and Construction Statistics.*

of small companies in the construction industry.[1] Nevertheless, two useful sources of data are available. The first concerns insolvencies, while the second is the number of firms existing in the industry. A reasonable presumption is that during the long decline of output from the early 1970s onwards the number of construction insolvencies rose as progressively more firms ran out of work, while the number of firms operating in the industry might be expected to have fallen because of those insolvencies plus a voluntary net outflow of firms from the industry. The insolvency and firm-number data enable these two hypotheses to be evaluated.

Figure 7.1(a) shows the number of insolvencies amongst construction firms from 1969 through to the 1980s. A 'firm' in the construc-

115

tion industry frequently consists solely of a working proprietor – it is one means of being self-employed – so receiving orders on self-employed workers as well as liquidations of construction companies must be considered (Figure 7.1(b)). The confusion created by the lack of distinction between self-employed workers' firms and firms proper highlights the blurred distinction in the official statistics between the impact of the construction output collapse on workers (including the self-employed) and on capitalist enterprises. Moreover, although insolvency is usually regarded as the ultimate in corporate failure, in construction it can be a successful means of avoiding financial obligations. The 'cowboy' firm which declares itself insolvent can easily set up again elsewhere under a new name. Some caution must therefore be used in interpreting the statistics.

While there was not an enormous increase in insolvencies during the 1970s, nevertheless the general pattern is consistent with the trend of overall construction output. The four years from 1974 to 1977, in particular, indicate a shake-out of the weaker enterprises caught by the collapse of the high-profit years. The self-employed were particularly badly hit; receiving orders on them almost quadrupled between 1971 and 1976. Few of the insolvencies, however, were of major enterprises in the industry (although there were some spectacular bankruptcies of medium and large firms during 1974–5, as the next chapter shows). What the pattern of insolvencies is likely to be indicating primarily is one manifestation of the squeeze on subcontractors by main contractors during the early stages of sharp downswings in workloads. The fear of insolvency worked in another way to the major firms' advantage by encouraging clients to place work with them in order to avoid costly delays caused by the failure of a cheaper, but financially weaker, smaller competitor.

It is important to put the absolute level of construction-firm failures in perspective. As a proportion of all company liquidations in Britain, construction actually declined over the 1970s, despite the severity of the collapse of the construction market. The steady increase in the share of all receiving orders for construction self-employed (also shown in Figure 7.1(b)), moreover, could indicate the growth of self-employment as much as an increasing risk of insolvency within the industry itself. In terms of the total number of firms operating in the industry, the number of insolvencies is very small. In the peak year of 1976 in Figure 7.1, insolvencies represented only 3 per cent of 84,000 firms active in the industry in that year.

Insolvencies and voluntary moves by firms out of construction should reduce the total number of firms left in the industry, but data on firm numbers show a more complex picture. The number of firms

Table 7.1 *The changing composition of construction firms, 1973–85*

Size of firm: no. of employees	Number of firms*				
	1973	1977	1980	1983	1985
1	29,563	24,915	36,549	64,585	72,896
2–7	43,962	34,148	55,108	78,859	78,576
8–13	9,311	7,584	10,052	7,129	7,164
14–24	6,315	5,070	5,849	4,949	4,582
25–34	2,364	1,811	2,002	1,684	1,519
35–59	2,298	1,836	1,985	1,604	1,480
60–79	743	596	595	541	441
80–114	697	563	484	418	409
115–299	872	730	663	563	512
300–599	246	217	208	154	141
600–1,199	125	116	92	72	66
1,200 and over	80	56	48	39	39
Total	96,576	77,642	113,632	160,596	167,825

Trade of firm	Number of firms*				
	1973	1977	1980	1983	1985
General builders	39,659	31,889	44,790	64,276	67,475
Building and civil engineering contractors	2,364	2,054	2,910	3,561	3,623
Civil engineers	2,114	1,633	2,191	2,510	2,662
Plumbers	8,432	6,565	9,595	14,671	14,934
Carpenters and joiners	6,533	4,749	6,994	10,359	10,949
Painters	15,375	11,356	13,341	15,107	14,662
Roofers	1,974	1,837	3,374	5,103	5,818
Plasterers	3,480	2,547	3,010	3,836	4,019
Glaziers	494	460	1,926	3,758	4,387
Demolition contractors	474	376	483	573	559
Scaffolding specialists	212	228	478	779	966
Reinforced concrete specialists	347	278	388	482	515
Heating and ventilating engineers	3,284	2,906	5,510	8,335	8,461
Electrical contractors	6,550	5,618	8,938	14,616	15,449
Asphalt and tar sprayers	430	422	632	822	856
Plant hirers	2,017	2,059	3,545	3,619	3,664
Flooring contractors	743	636	923	1,391	1,400
Constructional engineers	520	407	1,096	1,396	1,560

Table 7.1—continued

Insulating specialists	192	261	770	1,348	1,308
Suspended ceiling specialists	184	231	455	772	842
Floor and wall tiling specialists	485	413	712	1,079	1,167
Miscellaneous	713	707	1,571	2,203	2,549
All trades	96,576	77,642	113,632	160,596	167,825

Trade of firm	1985 percent of total employment
General builders	34
Building and civil engineering contractors	15
Civil engineers	6
All main trades	55
Plumbers	4
Carpenters and joiners	3
Painters	5
Roofers	3
Plasterers	1
Glaziers	2
Scaffolding specialists	2
Reinforced concrete specialists	1
Heating and ventilating engineers	6
Electrical contractors	9
Asphalt and tar sprayers	1
Plant hirers	2
Flooring contractors	1
Constructional engineers	1
Insulating specialists	1
Miscellaneous	2
All trades	100

* Change in industry definition in data from 1982.
Source: Housing and Construction Statistics

operating in construction did change considerably during the 1970s as Table 7.1 shows. At first sight the changes look very strange. The number of firms fell rapidly, as would be expected, from 1973 to a low point in 1977, with an overall 20 per cent firm decline. Yet between 1977 and 1985 the number of firms rose again to well above the 1973 figure. In only three years, from 1977 to 1980, the number of firms registered on the DoE's annual Private Contractors Construction

Census shot up again by an incredible 46 per cent. The answer to this riddle is twofold.

The first reason is the variable quality of the statistics, which, because of changes in data collection methods, led to a sharp increase in the number of firms reporting, as the official statisticians explain:

> The Department of the Environment maintains a statistical register of private contracting 'firms', from which samples are drawn for regular enquiries into orders, output and employment. These 'firms' are strictly 'reporting units' as some large firms instead of reporting as single units, prefer to report separately the operations of parts of their companies, e.g. regional divisions, while, in other cases, a single return may be made covering associated companies each of which are legally separate firms. In 1972 there were about 70,000 reporting units on the register, but in 1973, as a result of special enquiries, 25,000 others (mostly very small) were added. By late 1977 the number on the register had declined to about 85,000: this was partly a reflection of the fall in construction activity, but partly was a result of the difficulty experienced in picking up new entrants to the industry. Arrangements have been made to obtain names and addresses of firms newly registered for VAT purposes as construction firms: with this additional source of information, the statistical register had expanded by early 1981 to about 120,000. Most of the new additions are, of course, small firms, but the register will still not include some very small firms and self-employed workers. (*Housing and Construction Statistics 1970–1980*, p. 175)

The second reason lies in new Inland Revenue regulations governing self-employment introduced in 1978. They had the effect of legitimising previous labour-only subcontracting and other self-employment work practices. 'Firms' sprang up on the basis of the new P714 and other certificates issued to individual workers and labour-gangs. The dramatic increase in firms, therefore, reflects statistical quirks and legislative change with respect to pre-existing employment practices, rather than a flowering of small business enterprise. What has happened beneath the smog of statistical confusion is that the number of capitalist enterprises active in construction has fallen as output has declined while, at the same time, self-employment has increased.

A long-term decline in the number of capitalist enterprises and the growth of very small firms, which often consist of small groups of self-employed, can be seen by looking at changes in the number of firms of different sizes. The increase in firms between 1977 to 1980 is limited entirely to those employing less than sixty employees, and it is particularly marked in the lowest employment categories, as Table 7.1 shows. After 1980, all size categories above those with seven employees fell. A working proprietor is classified as an employee, so most of the 73,000 single-employee firms in 1985 actually employ no-one at all. For all but the smallest size categories, there does, therefore, seem to have been a shake-out of the industry, with many firms not surviving the slump. The falls shown in Table 7.1, in part, result from firm losses from the industry, but they are also caused by still-active firms laying off workers and hence moving down the size categories. Such workforce reductions partly represent genuine declines in workloads, but also shifts in employment practices towards greater subcontracting. Consequently, there is a link between the decline of firms in the higher size ranges and the growth of small ones.

The trade of firms (also shown in Table 7.1) unfortunately provides little additional information on the linkages between firms. One available statistic is that over 60 per cent classify themselves as specialists of one sort or another. For most types of work, therefore, they are subcontractors for other firms. All trades show substantial increases in firm numbers, except, surprisingly, the traditional subcontract specialism of painting. Electrical contractors rose almost threefold in eight years.

Employment and value of work by size of firm

Employment in construction has an hour-glass shaped distribution, rather than a pyramid one like that of firm numbers. Roughly a third of employees work for very small enterprises (employing less than eight), but 20 per cent work for big firms that employ 300 or more (Table 7.2). The majority of building workers (55 per cent) work for general builders and contractors, though a surprisingly large proportion work for specialists. Electrical contractors, heating and ventilation engineers, painters and plumbers are the main specialist employers.

Value-of-work-done data (Table 7.3) show an even greater weighting towards the larger firms and less for the smallest in comparison with the employment data. The difference is presumably mainly accounted for by the greater use of materials in the work undertaken by larger firms. In the aggregate-value-of-work data, there is a dramatic shift between 1975 and 1985 in work shares towards the smallest. Most of the shift appears to reflect the growing importance of repair and maintenance in total construction workloads, because once total work is disaggregated into new work and repair and maintenance it can be seen that small firms dominate R&M. The profile of work shares for new work is little different from that of the total in 1975, when R&M was a much smaller proportion of all work, but the data do indicate how difficult it has been for large builders to diversify into R&M work.

Table 7.2 *Private contractors' total employment by size of firm, 1985*

Size of firm (no. of employees)	1985	
	Number	Percent of total employment
1	67,800	7
2–3	120,500	13
4–7	108,000	12
8–11	71,800	8
14–24	82,200	9
25–34	43,600	5
35–59	65,700	7
60–79	29,000	3
80–114	38,800	4
115–299	89,300	9
300–599	59,300	6
600–1,199	55,200	6
1,200 and over	108,600	12
All firms	941,000	100

Source: Housing and Construction Statistics

Table 7.3 *Private contractors: value of work by size of firm, 1975 and 1985, percent*

Size of firm (no. of employees)	1975	1985	Of which	
			New work	R&M
1	1	6	3	11
2–3	8	9	5	16
4–7		10	6	15
8–13	6	7	5	10
14–24	7	9	7	11
25–34	4	5	4	5
35–59	7	8	8	7
60–79	4	4	4	3
80–114	5	5	5	3
115–299	13	11	13	7
300–599	11	8	10	4
600–1,199	11	7	9	4
1,200 and over	22	13	19	4
All firms	100	100	100	100

Source: Housing and Construction Statistics

What the firm-size statistics by value do not show is a collapse in the position of medium-sized firms (taken as those employing between 60 and 300). Their share of the value of work is remarkably constant between 1975 and 1985, and they do not even seem to be adversely affected by the growing role of R&M. The data, however, do not indicate the changes that might have taken place within any of the size categories. Medium-sized firms could have changed entirely, but the data would not show it. There could, for instance, have been a total collapse of medium-sized contractors and a growth of speculative housebuilders to replace them, and the latter would have large turnovers relative to their direct employees, given their employment practices. So it is uncertain from the available data whether or not the claimed crisis of the independent medium-sized contractor is a myth.

One sphere where there has clearly been a crisis for the medium-sized producer is in speculative housebuilding (as classified by the number of houses built, rather than by number of employees). From being a sector dominated by small- to medium-sized producers in the mid-1960s, speculative housebuilding is now dominated by a handful of giant national concerns (Ball, 1983).

Subcontracting

It is notoriously difficult to get accurate information on the total amount of subcontracted work in construction. The DoE do provide some statistics which can be regarded as a minimum estimate. The smallest firms are less likely to subcontract, so the amount of subcontracted work done for larger firms is the best indicator of the prevalence of subcontracting in the industry. Data in *Housing and Construction Statistics 1970–1980* show that almost half of the output (48 per cent) of firms employing 115 or more employees was subcontracted in 1980. The data in Table 7.4 give a more detailed firm-size breakdown, and it can be seen that the larger the firm the greater is the amount of work subcontracted.

It should be remembered that subcontracting is being calculated as a proportion of the value of output, not of the value added by the industry. Given the likely economies of scale in bulk purchasing of materials, plant, etc., the proportion of value added done by subcontracting could easily be higher. The DoE data from 1975–80 show only a slight increase in the proportion of work subcontracted. Leopold (1982), however, when looking at the growth of self-employment, suggests that it grew significantly from the late 1960s onwards, which indicates that subcontracting has increased substantially over time.

Table 7.4 *Size of construction firms and the amount of work subcontracted, 1982*[1]

Size of firm	No. of firms	Employment[2] (%)	Gross output[3] (%)	Value of work done (%)	Average value of work subcontracted[4] (%)
1–7	125,619	28	18	20	15
8–24	13,624	18	14	16	17
25–114	4,324	20	21	22	23
115–599	714	16	22	20	33
600–1,199	76	6	8	7	34
1,200+	38	11	18	14	40
Totals	144,395	100 (998,000)	100 (£6,712m)	100 (£4,900m)	37 (£1,814m)

1 Data are for October 1982, or third quarter 1982 where relevant.
2 Employment includes working proprietors as well as employees.
3 Gross output is value of work done plus value of work subcontracted.
4 Expressed as a percentage of the gross output of the size category.
Source: Housing and Construction Statistics 1972–1982

The ownership characteristics of construction firms

One noticeable characteristic of construction firms is the prevalence of family ownership, even amongst the largest concerns. It is not surprising that the smaller enterprises are frequently run by a proprietor-owner, particularly in an industry where the life of a small firm can be short. However, given the size of the largest concerns, family ownership there is more remarkable.

The divorce between management and ownership characteristic of so many advanced capitalist enterprises is less pronounced in the British construction industry. Many of the largest firms are still predominantly owned by one individual, family or family trust (e.g. Laing, Wates, the McAlpine groups, and Bernard Sunley, to name but a few of the largest contractors). Others have family names still on their boards of directors or as managing directors: L. Barratt of Barratt the housebuilders; J. P. and D. J. Gleeson of Gleeson; B. J. and A. D. D. Hill of Higgs and Hill; etc. Even the few firms from outside the industry that have taken over large construction firms in the last fifteen years often have close links between management and ownership (e.g. Nigel Broackes of Trafalgar House).

Giant companies exist in construction, therefore, with nineteenth-century-style ownerships. This has been possible as the marked increase in the size of major construction firms since the inter-war period has not been associated with a commensurate increase in the scale of capital tied up in production. A need for wider access to sources of capital and credit deriving from greatly increased investment in production consequently has not forced a dilution of personal ownership to the same extent as in other industries. Similarly, the forced centralisation of firms caught during economic downturns with large amounts of idle productive capital has not squeezed out family ownership. Coercive pressures of concentration and centralisation are weak in construction. Firms have got big, but for reasons other than investment in costly methods of production.

A hierarchical industry

What the patterns of firm size, ownership and subcontracting indicate is that construction is an industry in which firms are highly interlinked through subcontracting relationships, and where personal contact and trust are of considerable importance. Sectors of the industry vary in the scale of the dominant enterprises, but even among small firms subcontracting of specialisms and of the simplest of labouring tasks is commonplace, as anyone is aware who has dealt with the industry in its repair and maintenance roles.

It is impossible to deduce what the effect of widespread subcontracting is on the market power of particular enterprises. Firms that subcontract a lot obviously control a greater proportion of total construction output than the official statistics indicate. This helps to explain the paradox of company accounts showing many large firms increasing their workloads during the 1970s and 1980s, as the next chapter will show, whereas the official statistics described in this chapter seem to indicate a dramatic loss of market share for the largest producers. Because the largest firms subcontract so much of their work, which is then not counted as being done within that size category by the official data, the influence of the largest firms is considerably underestimated by the data.

If this line of reasoning is correct, smaller firms must to a degree have changed their role within the industry, from being independent medium and small 'main' contractors to being subcontractors on projects run by larger firms. It is unlikely that such trends have occurred in the R&M sector because of large firms' generally weak competitive position there – a sector which, as the last chapter noted, now accounts for almost half of all construction work. This means that the change to subcontracting in new work would have had to have been substantial, given its proportionate decline and the work-done-by-size category figures. Such reasoning is, of course, conjectural and cannot be verified by the available data, but it does fit in with commonly-held views about how the industry has changed and it is difficult to see how else the different pieces of data can be reconciled. Personal contact and trust are central to the market relations associated with hierarchical relations of subcontracting. Although subcontracting is a market phenomenon, with rates of remuneration being broadly determined by market forces, the market cannot work on an entirely atomistic, independent basis. Prior networks of information are needed to bring the various elements of the market process together, and to give firms and their local managers some idea that subcontractors can actually do the work they claim to be able to, and that they are reasonably reliable and punctual. Such informational requirements create the possibility of intermediaries arising who control access to particular types of work, particularly in such fragmented activities as labour-only subcontracting, and especially in a large but diverse market such as London. The role of labour agents is well known in arranging work for British construction workers in Europe, but their role in the UK itself is less well documented.

The information networks and personal contacts required within construction in order to make some of its key markets operate are open to abuse. Adam Smith's warnings about merchants' and producers' propensities to collude and fix prices (Smith, 1776) would seem to be apposite for construction. A series of price-fixing arrangements have been discovered over the years, and builders, architects and public employees are periodically jailed or fined when a scandal comes to light (Direct Labour Collective, 1978). Common views about the building industry – ones frequently portrayed in the media – play on corruption. However, while they undoubtedly exist to a degree, corrupt and monopolistic practices should not be seen as the driving forces in the industry. Theories based on the operation of market forces on the social agents in the industry seem to have far more explanatory power, as the following chapter shows.

CHAPTER 8

Keeping up profits

The dramatic slump in workloads since the early 1970s has induced substantial restructuring in the construction industry. However, for the largest firms at least, it has not caused a commensurate slump in profits. For many firms, profits in fact increased. This chapter will document this 'profits paradox' and provide explanations of why it occurred.

The inapplicability of standard models of industrial restructuring

Looking at profitability within the construction industry during the 1970s and early 1980s shows once again how the industry cannot be subsumed under a simple, general theory of corporate behaviour. The 'profits paradox' would confound any conventional analysis.

It is useful to contrast the consequences of the collapse of demand on construction capital with a standard model of the impact on an industry of such a decline. While ascribing no particular proponent to the model, it would fit happily within a number of varieties of Marxist and neo-classical economic analysis because it generalises from the empirical consequences of large amounts of fixed capital characteristic of most large-scale modern industry.

Conventional wisdom suggests that falls in output of the magnitude experienced in construction lead to forced rationalisation of the industry through a massive devalorisation of capital, and the centralisation of ownership of what remains. The centralisation could take place gradually through cartels and 'gentlemen's agreements' on pricing policy, plant closure and amalgamation, as were common in Britain in the inter-war years (Alford, 1981), and in industries like cement today. Alternatively, fierce price wars could break out as firms with large overheads and economies-of-scale-inducing fixed-capital strive to maintain or expand market shares. Gradually the weakest high-cost producers go to the wall, leaving a more centralised and technically efficient industry.

Whichever path is taken, the theory would suggest that there are reduced profits during the restructuring phase of the downswing, plus extensive company amalgamations or collapses and widespread closures. This model may apply in varying degrees to manufact industries, although the story is frequently not so simple (Massey and Meegan, 1982), but it certainly does not apply to construction. There have neither been falling profits nor widespread collapses and amalgamations between the major firms (except, for special reasons, in speculative housebuilding). There has been a 'restructuring' of construction, but of a very different sort. To illustrate the reasons, this chapter will look at what has happened to construction firms' financial performance, concentrating on the years of decline and depression from the mid-1970s to the early 1980s.

A restructuring of social relations

Faced with dramatic declines in workloads, construction firms have had only three options, or a mix of them:

1 accept real declines in output;
2 fight for a bigger share of a declining market;
3 diversify into new activities.

The last, of course, could include getting out of construction altogether, either voluntarily or forcibly through company failure. Yet no large building firm has substantially withdrawn from the industry. All, instead, have experienced various mixes of the three options, whilst remaining firmly tied to the fortunes of UK construction activity.

Change for construction firms does not simply lead to higher or lower accounting profits, or even just to bankruptcies, mergers and restructurings of capital. A sharp industrial slump alters the contemporary state of class relations. Workers get laid off, for example, weakening or removing the ability of the workforce as a whole to resist changes in work practices demanded by capital. Construction is no exception. Company performance reflects the transformation of power relations in the industry. When looking at the dry statistics of published indicators since the mid-1970s, this point should be kept in mind, as it crucially affects data interpretations.

Whose profits?

It should be noted that only the profits performance of large firms is being examined here. The difficulty of obtaining adequate data for smaller companies makes it impossible to consider them. For some of the smaller firms, the market power of the bigger concerns might lead to a squeezing of their profits. On the other hand, smaller firms might have been able to operate in similar ways to the large concerns. There is no way of knowing what actually happened.

Detailed investigation of firms operating predominantly in speculative building (notably housebuilding) will not be undertaken in this chapter. As has already been explained, the economics of speculative building and contracting are very different; speculative builders profit from land development, contractors do not. So speculative builders have to invest capital in land purchase and assembly for success, necessitating proportionately much larger advances of capital than contractors. The profitability of speculative housebuilders, for instance, depends, amongst other things, on cyclical variations in the level of housing-market activity. And that market's fluctuations differ considerably from other construction markets. Most speculative housebuilders have done well in the mid-1980s, following the revival of the owner-occupied housing market in 1983.

Because a number of the largest contractors have substantial speculative housebuilding divisions, and they also deal in a smaller way in industrial and commercial schemes, it is impossible to segment off speculative building neatly from the rest of the construction industry. The two largest building firms, Wimpey and Tarmac, have particularly large speculative housebuilding subsidiaries. However, this chapter concentrates on the large contractors, so a number of independent speculative housebuilders are omitted, notably one of the largest, Barratt.

The profits performance of larger building firms, 1961–81

Estimating comparative rates of profit is fraught with theoretical and empirical difficulties. Three problems of particular relevance here are that companies may not report their 'true' profits or assets; that inflation plays havoc with traditional historic cost-accounting procedures; and that consistent time series data are difficult to obtain. The Bank of England in the early 1980s developed a consistent (if not necessarily unambiguously accurate) method of calculating the real rate of return for British industry (see *Bank of England Quarterly Bulletin*, June 1982). Williams (1981), using this method on *Business Monitor MA3 Company Finance* data, has estimated real rates of return for twenty-two industrial sectors. His calculations enable comparison of profitability in construction with the rest of British industry from 1961–77. The time period is particularly useful as it includes both part of the post-war upswing in building and part of

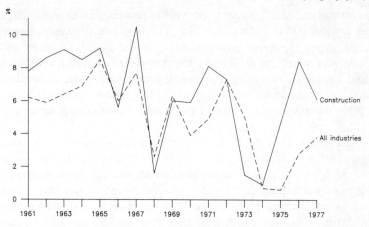

Figure 8.1 Construction and manufacturing industry: post-tax real profitability, 1961–77. Note: post-tax real rate of return on the equity stake in trading assets. For data and method of calculation see Williams (1981).

the subsequent downswing. Figure 8.1 plots Williams' estimate of the real post-tax rate of profit for construction and for manufacturing industry as a whole from 1961–77.

A number of interesting points emerge from the data. The first, and perhaps most surprising given the 'hard-up' image presented by employer's organisations in the industry, is that with the exception of one year, 1973, rates of return in construction are consistently higher than in manufacturing. Moreover, 1973 was a crisis year for construction, as many firms, with the collapse of the early 1970s property boom, were reeling under the impact of over-hasty property and land speculation.

The second point to note is that construction profitability has a cyclical variation which is similar to that of manufacturing. During downturns the differential between the rates of profit narrows, whilst in the profits-upturns it widens again. The similarity of the cycle of construction profitability with the rest of the economy suggests that it is the general state of the economy rather than the volume of aggregate demand for construction work that determines variations in profitability. The influence of the economy as a whole presumably operates through the effect on input costs, through the interest rates charged on loan finance, and possibly on building firms' tender-pricing strategies.

A third point to note is the break in the level of profitability between the 1960s and 1970s. The downturn of 1968 marks a long-term downward shift in the average level of profitability. For construction this might indicate a squeeze on profits resulting from the collapse of workloads that started in 1968. The evidence, however, is very inconclusive. The general rate of profit in the British economy as a whole was in secular decline, so the downward shift in construction could simply be reflecting the general trend. Moreover, to attribute the fall in profitability to a collapse in construction workloads cannot explain the dramatic increase in construction profitability again after 1974.

Another sector of the British economy that did considerably better than average in Williams' data is retail distribution. Retailers are the epitome of merchant capital in their buying and selling operations. It is generally accepted that the big retailers have considerable muscle over manufacturers because they buy in bulk, can dictate quality standards, influence product design and packaging, and squeeze purchase prices through the threat of withdrawal of their business from suppliers (Morris, 1979). The relative profitability of construction firms could also be indicating the importance of their merchanting functions, a point that is taken up in detail later.

One final point to note is that the consistently higher rate of profit for construction in comparison with much of the rest of the economy implies that there are significant barriers to entry to the most profitable activities in the industry. If capital could move freely in and out of construction, the rate of profit should be no greater than the average for the economy as a whole, as competitive pressures would quickly reduce any additional profit. While it might be easy to set up a small construction enterprise, to join the ranks of the largest firms is exceedingly difficult. Entry can probably only be achieved quickly through takeover of an established concern, which might be hard to do. Large firms appear to have significant advantages of scale over smaller concerns (for reasons outlined in Chapter 5). Even though large construction firms have relatively little fixed capital, they have market presences and organisational structures which cannot be replicated quickly – either by themselves when they want to expand or by potential new competitors.

Unfortunately, comparable data are not available for later years. The *Bank of England Quarterly Bulletin* periodically publishes historic-cost profitability data, and a comparison of construction and all industries on this basis is given in Table 8.1. The data base and calculation are not the same as those of the Williams study, so not surprisingly the numbers are different. The cycle of profitability does not stand out in these data but even so there is no secular decline of construction profitability; instead it is similar to that for all industries, except for a marked fall in the mid-1980s. The mid-1980s decline is odd, as it occurs at a time when the construction industry was coming out of the worst of the earlier 1980s slump and when some companies were reporting record profits. The decline could reflect the problems of some large individual companies, like Barratt, or alternatively could indicate that construction firms' restructuring strategies had not been as successful as they might have been.

Table 8.1 *Rates of return on capital employed, valued at historic cost, 1970–85*

	1970	1971	1972	1973	1974	1975	1976	1977
Construction	15	17	18	18	17	17	18	18
All industries	14	15	16	18	17	16	18	18

	1978	1979	1980	1981	1982	1983	1984	1985
Construction	18	16	15	14	13	12	13	14
All industries	17	16	14	14	14	16	17	17

Source: Bank of England Quarterly Bulletin, passim

The largest independent contractors

This section considers what has happened to the turnover and profits of the ten largest independent contractors during the years of decline, from the early 1970s to the early 1980s (Figures 8.2–8.5).[1] Turnover and profits are taken direct from company accounts for the period 1970–81; for comparability over time the figures are deflated to 1975 prices. The analysis is not as sophisticated as the Bank of England treatment of profits. Even so some interesting features emerge.

THE UNIVERSAL BUILDERS
Looking first at the hierarchy of firms, there is a clear divide between the turnovers of the top five and the rest (although the merger of Press and Fairclough in December 1982 put the new AMEC holding company into the super-league as well). The top five in the table can all be described as 'universal builders'. They operate in most fields of construction activity in the UK and to varying degrees also have strong international presences. Most of the five have significant non-construction interests as well, especially in the related fields of property and building materials. The second five, on the other hand, specialise mainly in the engineering spheres of construction, particu-

131

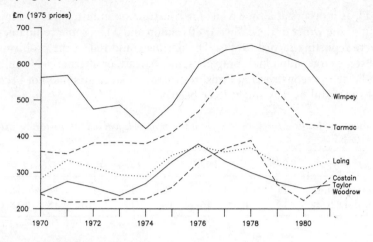

£m (1975 prices)

Figure 8.2 Deflated turnovers of major contractors: universal builders, 1970–81. *Source: company accounts.*

larly large-scale civil engineering, although again they have subsidiary interests but on a much smaller scale. The second group, because of specialisation, have been severely hit by the decline in non-housing public sector work.

Changes in turnover for the five universal builders are given in Figure 8.2.[2] The size order of the top five is remarkably constant throughout the eleven-year period. The closeness in size of the smallest three of the five, Laing, Costain and Taylor Woodrow, means that their pecking order varies in the tumultuous years after 1975. However the general trend of output is similar for all five; significant real increases in turnover until 1978 for four of them (up to 1976 for Taylor Woodrow), then fairly steep declines for all bar Laing, who, as we shall see, tried to buck the downward trend by taking some very large, but ill-advised, overseas contracts in the late 1970s.

The common trend of turnovers of the top five to an extent illustrates the effectiveness of diversification in this risky industry once over a critical size level. Detailed investigation of each firm would show that they have all adopted distinct market strategies since the early 1970s. Yet they all managed to achieve similar aggregate turnover patterns. The pattern of the two largest firms' turnovers is virtually the same from 1974 onwards, after one of them, Tarmac, had expanded rapidly in construction through takeovers (see Chapter 10). The next three firms exhibit a greater variability around similar trends, possibly indicating that even at their substantial size they cannot diversify to the same extent as the top two. Even so, for all five of

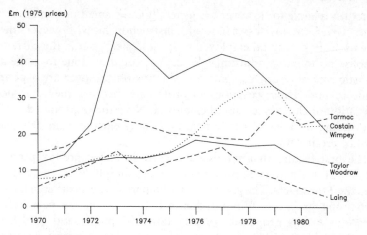

£m (1975 prices)

Figure 8.3 Deflated pre-tax profits of major contractors: universal builders, 1970–81. *Source: company accounts.*

the top firms, differences in the patterns of turnover can be explained to a great extent by their distinct market strategies. For instance, Taylor Woodrow felt the bite of increased world competition more rapidly than Costain. Tarmac and Wimpey, on the other hand, put far more emphasis on speculative housebuilding. Wimpey's output decline in the earlier 1980s owes much to its disastrous performance in speculative housebuilding. Overall, Wimpey failed to implement substantial restructuring strategies until 1984, years after its competitors.[3]

The general experience of these five firms would seem to indicate that extensive diversification has not enabled any of them to buck the turnover trend for their size of enterprise. Extensive diversification means less risk of failure, but also less chance of outstanding success in increasing market share relative to competitors of a similar size.

What is most remarkable about the real turnovers of the largest five contractors is that until the late 1970s they all managed to increase their turnovers significantly, despite the precipitous drop in the overall UK construction industry workload. Some of this increase is the result of diversification out of construction and overseas, but they are not the only factors; the biggest contractors managed to increase their share of UK building output as well. Costain, for instance, in the depressed year of 1981, managed to increase its UK building and civil engineering turnover by 47 per cent above the 1980 level (*Construction News* 13 June 1982).

Turning to the profits of the big five, a different picture emerges. Only the absolute size of deflated profits are given in Figure 8.3. Rates of return relative to turnover are generally quite small (around 5 per cent). Given the low asset-base of construction firms, however, the rate of profit on capital employed is much higher – but in the current exercise no inflation adjustment of capital could be done to make a realistic rate-of-return comparison. Margins on turnover are a poor guide to underlying variations in profit rate, because they give no indication of changes in capital employed. Nevertheless, some idea of the varying fortunes of the sample firms does emerge from deflated pre-tax profit data.

The first feature that stands out clearly from the pre-tax profits data is that the pattern of profits varies more sharply between the five than their turnovers. The greater variation partly reflects differences in accounting practices. Wimpey, for example, has in the past been notorious for its propensity to play down its profits and to delay recording them within the limits of accounting conventions and company law in an attempt to reduce its tax bill (Hird, 1975). A more important factor over the long term is the speculative nature of a contractor's operations. It is far easier to adopt market strategies to sustain turnover than profits. This is illustrated most clearly by Laing, especially after the hiving off of its substantial property port-folio into a new company in 1978. Moreover, what is a successful strategy for a few years might easily turn sour. Costain's profits in 1978 and 1979, for instance, benefited from high overseas earnings in the Middle East, whereas the 1980 and 1981 figures were depressed by the lack of new work there. The Middle East accounted for 40 per cent of Costain's turnover in the later 1970s, dropping to 20 per cent in the early 1980s (*Financial Times*, 9 September 1981). Wimpey's problems in the private housing market in the early 1980s have already been mentioned; earlier that division was a mainstay of profitability.

Despite the variability of the profits performance, a cycle similar to that of the early Bank of England data can be discerned in the defated profits of the big five. The peaks and troughs vary, but within a four-to-five-year cycle. Profits generally rose in the early 1970s, fell in the mid-1970s, rose again in the late 1970s, and fell again in the early 1980s (and picked up in 1982). Once again, the cycle seems to corre-late more strongly with the general level of profitability in the economy as a whole rather than with variations in construction turnover.

The profits data do indicate that the mid-1970s were a make-or-break period for the biggest contractors; the slump in orders in the UK had been under way for a number of years and some strategic restructuring decisions had to be made. The ways in which the paths of the companies' respective pre-tax profits diverge after 1975–6 shows that not all firms met with success in their restructuring. Wimpey's profits, for example, slid each year for five years after 1977 to only half their earlier magnitude, whereas Tarmac's dramatic restructuring in the mid-1970s, after some initial false starts (see Chapter 10), paid off. The most remarkable change in fortunes can be seen in the second tier of firm size, that of Laing, Costain and Taylor Woodrow. From 1970 to 1976 the profits pattern is virtually identical for the three, but after that date they diverge sharply: Costain is buoyed up by work in the Middle East; Taylor Woodrow struggles to maintain profits in the face of rapidly-declining output (echoes of a not-buying-work-at-suicidal-prices strategy); while poor John Laing makes a series of disastrous mistakes after hiving off its property interests in 1979.

THE ENGINEERS
The second tier of construction companies, the six 'civil engineers' shown in Figures 8.4 and 8.5, have far more varied fortunes than the big 'universal builders'. Of the six companies listed, three distinct pairs can be isolated on the basis of the respective changes in their turnovers; namely, Newarthill and French Kier, Marchwiel and Fairclough, and William Press and Mowlem.

Newarthill and French Kier Both these companies traditionally have specialised in roadbuilding. During the late 1970s, as Figure 8.4(c) shows their turnovers both declined by about a third – classic instances of stricken public-sector builders during a period of state expenditure cuts. Newarthill is the holding company, formed in 1973, of Sir Robert McAlpine, one of Britain's leading motorway builders. French Kier also was a new company formed in the early 1970s from the merger of two previously independent civil engineering firms, and taken over in 1985 by C. H. Beazer (see Chapter 10).

Profits show a very different pattern from turnover (Figure 8.5(c)). French Kier got off to a very bad start because of disastrous losses on fixed-price motorway contracts (a similar problem led to the demise of Cubitt as an independent contractor at roughly the same time). French Kier, however, managed to avoid Cubitt's fate through the generosity of the then Labour government. Yet, if those particular years are discounted, because their outcome for the company was so dependent on the failings of one major project (the M25/M23 interchange in Surrey), a creditable profits record can be seen. Both firms' strong profits performance belie the collapse in their respective workloads. Real pre-tax profits were kept steady despite falling tender prices.

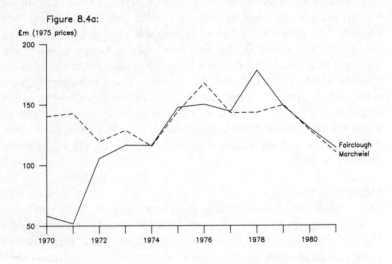

Figure 8.4a:

£m (1975 prices)

Fairclough
Marchwiel

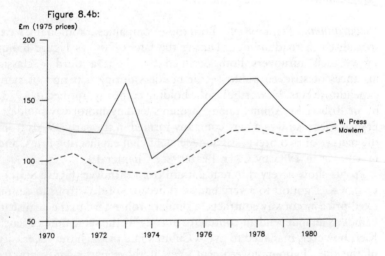

Figure 8.4b:

£m (1975 prices)

W. Press
Mowlem

Figure 8.4 Deflated turnovers of major contractors: the engineers, 1973–81.
Source: company accounts.

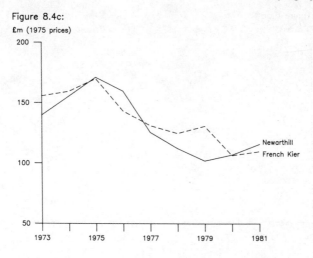

Figure 8.4c:

£m (1975 prices)

In the 1980s, French Kier became one of the most profitable UK construction firms, partially as a consequence of a successful policy of overseas diversification, although that strategy finally ran out of steam, leaving it vulnerable to takeover.

Marchwiel and Fairclough   Both of these firms are heavily involved in public-sector work; yet until the 1980s their turnovers did not slump like the previous two's (Figure 8.4(a)). It is not surprising that Marchwiel and Fairclough should be paired together as they have been closely involved in motorway consortia (see Chapter 10). Fairclough managed a spectacular growth up to 1978, after which turnover started to decline quite rapidly (highlighting the logic of the merger with William Press in 1982). Marchwiel's performance, on the other hand, is one of more mixed fluctuations. Both firms, none the less, managed to go against the trend of declining workloads for most of the period, even if the bottom of the construction output trough in 1980 did finally bite into their workloads. (Marchwiel has subsequently changed its name back to Alfred McAlpine.)

Pre-tax profits for the two firms (Figure 8.5(a)), unlike the previous cases, closely follow changes in turnover – with Marchwiel's fluctuating and Fairclough's steadily rising until the end of the 1970s, although its subsequent profits decline is not so pronounced as the drop in turnover. Marchwiel had a bad year in 1980 because of problems with overseas work.

Figure 8.5 Deflated pre-tax profits of major contractors: the engineers. Source: company accounts.

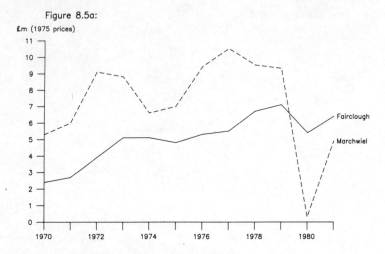

Figure 8.5 Deflated pre-tax profits of major contractors: the engineers. *Source: company accounts.*

William Press and Mowlem   The final pair of firms, whilst having some similar characteristics to the other constructional engineers, also have tended to specialise in particular fields. Mowlem, for instance, is well-known for its tunnelling activities and Press for its dealings with the British gas industry over projects like the conversion from coal-based to natural gas in the early 1970s. Although turnover fluctuations (Figure 8.4(b)) for each bear some resemblance to Marchwiel's, both have managed to maintain long-term output levels. Mowlem did so with only minor variations, whereas Press's is more erratic.

Mowlem's profits record closely follows its turnover (Figure 8.5(b)). Press, on the other hand, had its worse profits year at the time of its highest turnover, 1973 (perhaps because of fixed-price contracts). Profits then boomed until 1978, but from 1979 onwards a sharp decline set in.

The overall picture   The example of these six firms shows again how difficult it is to generalise about the performance of construction firms. However, some common features emerge which tend to set limits on the extent of the variation between the firms. The most important conclusion is that declines in overall construction output do not necessarily lead to declines for the larger firms in profits, *even for the firms whose turnovers actually fall.* The next section explores the reasons for this profits paradox.

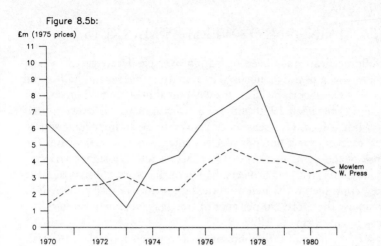

Figure 8.5b:

£m (1975 prices)
11
10
9
8
7
6
5
4
3
2
1
0
1970
1972
1974
1976
1978
1980
Mowlem
W. Press

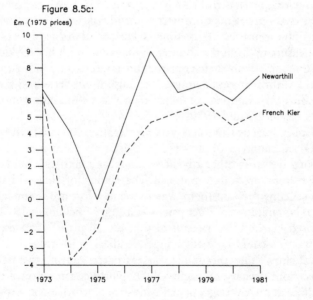

Figure 8.5c:

£m (1975 prices)
10
9
8
7
6
5
4
3
2
1
0
−1
−2
−3
−4
1973
1975
1977
1979
1981
Newarthill
French Kier

Figure 8.5 Deflated pre-tax profits of major contractors: the engineers. *Source: company accounts.*

Factors sustaining construction profitability in the downswing

DIVERSIFYING INTO OVERSEAS MARKETS

UK building firms have been operating overseas for over 150 years, but there was a dramatic upsurge in activity in the second half of the 1970s. Overseas work by UK firms went up almost six-fold (in current price terms) between 1970 and 1978, with much of it concentrated in the Middle East. Overseas work proved to be an important source of new markets for a number of UK contractors, especially after the collapse of the home market in 1974. Size is an important barrier to entry for many overseas projects. Much of the work consists of large turnkey contracts, for which only the largest firms can compete. Not surprisingly, therefore, 90 per cent of overseas work was undertaken by only twenty firms in 1978–9.[4]

Most of the diversification into overseas markets took place through firms shifting their marketing focus from the UK to other countries. Costain, for example, increased the proportion of its turnover attributable to overseas projects from 39 per cent in 1970 to 67 per cent by 1977. Sometimes problems of project size and risk were overcome by instituting joint ventures. They took a variety of forms and often involved a company from the country in question. Both Bryant Holdings and Tarmac set up their construction interests in Saudi Arabia in this way. All-British joint ventures were also used; French Kier and F. J. C. Lilley, for example, combined to win a £60-million contract in Hong Kong in the mid-1970s.

The boom in overseas markets was principally associated with the effect on OPEC countries of the 1973 oil-price rises. Contractors from Britain, like those from other advanced capitalist countries, won large contracts at very profitable margins. The timing of this oil-based international construction boom was extremely fortuitous for large UK firms. The building-contract price explosion in Britain in 1972–3 had collapsed, partially as a result of OPEC's oil price increases, so some contractors could take advantage of others' misfortune.

Table 8.2 shows the volume of overseas output during the 1970s and 1980s, both actual and 'deflated'. A world-construction price-index is difficult to envisage, so UK construction prices have been used as a proxy to try and take account of price inflation. Output obviously lags a few years behind the initial winning of orders, especially on large turnkey projects. The boom in output started in 1974–5 and lasted for about four years, dropping sharply in 1979–80. The 1979 oil price rise added a new, though for construc-

Table 8.2 Value of British construction work overseas, 1974–85, in £ million

	1974–5	1975–6	1976–7	1977–8	1978–9	1979–80	1980–1	1981–2	1982–3	1983–4	1984–5
Actual	1,086	1,284	1,596	1,676	1,385	1,385	1,366	1,870	2,780	2,252	2,391
Deflated*	2,585	2,568	2,956	2,890	2,130	1,731	1,366	1,781	2,699	2,165	2,214

Work of British companies and their overseas branches and subsidiaries.
*Deflator used is British all-construction work index, 1980 prices.
Source: Housing and Construction Statistics

tion, slight impetus. But by 1982–3 both OPEC and non-OPEC Third-World markets were severely depressed by falling oil revenues and debt-rescheduling crises. Sharply growing involvement in the Americas (particularly the USA) partially offset the decline, but workloads in real terms still did not match those of the 1970s. The regional shifts in overseas work have been substantial, as Table 8.3 shows, with the major shift of focus from OPEC to N. American markets. The latter have been primarily achieved through takeovers of indigenous firms, whereas the former were very much 'foreign' and, as it turned out, temporary markets.

Table 8.3 *Overseas work by region*

	1975–6 (%)	1979–80 (%)	1984–5 (%)
Europe	5	8	4
Middle East	40	47	32
Rest of Asia and Africa	40	21	24
Americas and Oceania	15	24	40

Source: Housing and Construction Statistics

The despondency should, however, be qualified, as overseas work is still important for contractors. In 1984, for example, total work overseas was equivalent to 17 per cent of all new orders won in Britain – a useful supplement to domestic activity.

British contractors have a number of intrinsic advantages over competitors in Third-World markets. They include the network of informal links derived from Britain's imperial past (neocolonial links are very important in determining which firms win contracts); the financial skills of the City in drawing up attractive international finance packages[5]; and, finally, the unprecedented success of British designers and consultants in formulating the projects to be built. Yet the relative performance of British contractors has been poor, not simply in the face of the meteoric rise of cheap-labour-based South Korean enterprises, but also relative to other Western European and North American companies. In 1981, for example, West Germany, France, Italy and the Netherlands all had significantly higher overseas construction earnings than the UK.[6] In 1981, only one UK contractor featured in the world's top thirty international construction contractors; it was Davy Corporation, the second largest international contractor (and subject in 1982 to an unwelcome and unsuccessful bid from the Bechtel Group of the US, the largest international contractor).[7]

Overseas work has also proved to be risky, reflectin
local knowledge, political turbulence and financial crises
Tarmac, for instance, made substantial losses on contracts
in the mid-1970s; the Bath and Portland group was almos
into liquidation as a result of the Iranian revolution; while
wrote off £18 million in its 1982 accounts because of 'unreliable
information' leading to spectacular losses on contracts in Venezuela
and the Middle East. As the *Financial Times* noted: 'Most of Laing's
UK competitors, while extracting themselves less painfully, have
shared the same retreat from markets which offered jam for all
through the mid-70s (*Financial Times*, 29 April 1983). Not everybody
shared in the jam; some were forced to retreat to safer havens with
little or no return on their investment. The overseas market brings
out strongly the speculative nature of the contracting world.

A number of the largest contractors did take advantage of the mid-
1970s overseas boom to offset the declining UK market, and some as
a result seem to have remained more internationally inclined, though
only one or two can be regarded as truly international-orientated
firms. For most, the UK market is still the centre of activity. Company
accounts show similar patterns of change during the 1970s in the
share of overseas work in total turnover for the five 'universal builders' described above. All show sharp rises in the mid-1970s and
subsequent declines, but all have noticeably higher overseas turnovers
at the end of the period. Only one, however, has a majority of its
work overseas, Costain, and that firm has traditionally been overseas
orientated – a legacy of Britain's imperial past. And even Costain
switched dramatically back to the UK in the mid-1980s as the international contracting market collapsed. High overseas turnovers, as
was noted above, are not necessarily equated with high profits. In
1981, Wimpey, for example, had 34 per cent of turnover outside the
UK but only 27 per cent of its already poor profits came from that
source.

Overseas work in Third World markets in retrospect constituted a
few golden years for a handful of contractors, and developments in
North America are too recent to evaluate. Even at its peak in 1978,
however, overseas construction work represented only 17 per cent of
new construction work in the UK. Going overseas, therefore, hardly
constitutes the saviour of UK construction capital.

CASH AND PROPERTY INVESTMENTS
Building contracting has a big advantage over continuous production
industries with large amounts of fixed capital – cash in hand. The
income and profits from contracts flow into a firm over a period of

ars and they are not swallowed up by funding and maintaining a stock of fixed capital. If workloads begin to fall for construction contractors they begin to accumulate cash from current projects which cannot be reinvested directly into more contracts. Profitable contracts have this beneficial effect for a number of subsequent years. Firms in other industries can also build up cash mountains, especially from their own contracting activities; the engineering firm, GEC, had a well-publicised cash mountain in the early 1980s. However such firms can only do so by running down existing plant and curtailing new investment; building firms do not face similar dilemmas. Their favourable liquidity position gives building contractors a financial breathing space during which to restructure: by running down building operations and administrative overheads; by reducing outstanding debt; and by using the funds to diversify into new areas of activity.

The mid-1970s illustrate the phenomenon clearly. Table 8.4 shows *Business Monitor* data on construction firms' cash and investments. Investments can be seen to be heavily associated with unlisted securities rather than government stock or equities. Both investments and cash rise sharply after the end of the tender-price boom in 1973. The rise in cash holdings is especially noticeable. Between 1971 and 1973 the increase in cash holdings did not keep pace with inflation, but then in the next three years they rose steeply, almost doubling in one year, 1976. Individual company accounts show a similar story: in 1973 Taylor Woodrow had cash holdings of £8.8 million, yet by 1976 they had risen to £38.2 million; Marchwiel had £6.7 million in 1973 and £23.4 million in 1977; whilst Costain had amassed £36.7 million by 1976, compared to £6.6 million in 1973.[8]

Table 8.4 *Construction firms' cash and investments as a proportion of their total use of funds, 1971–6*

	(1) Total use of funds (£ thousand)	(2) Increase in cash holdings (£ thousand)	(3) Increase in cash and investments (£ thousand)	(2) as a % of (1)	(3) as a % of (1)
1971	239,297	23,303	29,263	9.7	12.2
1972	458,436	602	−16,898	0.1	−3.7
1973	658,600	9,527	23,490	1.4	3.6
1974	431,477	33,875	40,799	8.3	9.9
1975	410,342	93,582	108,162	22.8	26.4
1976	626,467	69,761	101,877	11.1	16.3

Source: Business Monitor MA3

The cash, of course, does not lie idle but is invested in the money markets. The cash holdings of Gleeson, a medium-sized civil engineering and building contractor, illustrate the dramatic short-run impact these investments can have on a firm's profitability. In the year to June 1977, Gleeson made virtually the same pre-tax profit (£1.4 million) as it had done in the previous year on virtually the same turnover (£54 million). Yet its ability to sustain profits resulted from the interest (£1 million) earned on money investments because trading margins had fallen by over half (to £400,000). As the Chairman, J. P. Gleeson, noted in the annual report:

> In my statement last year I mentioned the Group's improved liquidity position and the related prospect of having substantial moneys on deposit with our bankers on short call from time to time; it is gratifying that the interest earned on these short-term deposits (at the higher rates then attainable) has made such an important contribution during the year under review. (Gleeson Annual Report, 1977, p. 7)

Firms, of course, do not sit on cash holdings. They have other short-term options as well. The cash income from completed contracts could be distributed to shareholders, for example, and the business run down to a lower level of activity commensurate with the reduced likelihood of profitable building work. Few firms have taken that path, however. Managerial theories of the firm, based on the twentieth-century divorce between legal ownership (by shareholders) and effective control (by salaried managers), may help to explain this characteristic. But the 'family' nature of many construction firms suggests that the divorce is not so great for construction firms. And for tax reasons 'family' shareholders do not want large irregular dividend incomes. Such ownerships, plus the generally higher rate of profit, may explain the traditionally low dividend-to-profit-payment ratio of construction firms compared to manufacturing enterprises. The average payout ratio, for example, between 1973 and 1977 for manufacturing industry was 25 per cent, whereas for construction firms it was only 19 per cent, according to *Business Monitor* data.[9]

Contracting income has been used instead, amongst other things, to run down borrowings. Figure 8.6 shows trends in capital gearing, that is the ratio of borrowed funds to funds provided by ordinary shareholders, for the period 1961–77. (The trading assets used in this calculation are inflation adjusted by valuing them at replacement cost.) It can be seen that the gearing ratio rose from 14 per cent in 1964 to a peak of 36 per cent in 1973, only to fall rapidly back to 13 per cent in 1977. The extent of borrowings by the construction

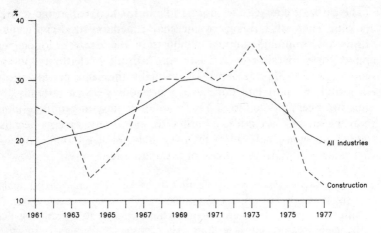

Figure 8.6 Capital gearing of trading assets, 1961–77. Note: trading assets valued at replacement cost. *Source: Williams (1981).*

industry in the early 1970s was enormous, as construction firms were very active in the land and property speculative booms of 1972–3. Between 1971 and 1973 the real value of outstanding loans by banks to construction companies more than trebled. Most of this debt was used in land and property deals. The collapse of the boom at the end of 1973 sent some firms into liquidation and left others highly geared. Much of the debt, however, was paid off quickly (or written off by banks when firms went into liquidation). Between 1974 and 1976 actual outstanding loans fell by over a quarter (*Financial Statistics*). In real terms, the effect was even more dramatic as inflation eroded the real value of the outstanding debt. Since then construction firms have been more careful with their borrowings, which in real terms have never again reached their 1974 level.

A number of firms in the years following 1973 wrote off large sums in their company accounts because of the depreciation in the land and property assets purchased earlier in the speculative boom. Higgs and Hill, for example, wrote down their property assets by £1 million in 1974, and Tarmac in a similar exercise wrote off £4.8 million between 1974 and 1976. Land revaluations reduced Laing's asset values by £7.8 million between 1974 and 1976, Bryant's by £2.7 million between 1974 and 1975, and the Royco Group's by £4.3 million between 1974 and 1976. Many other firms similarly wrote down assets. Others in the same predicament did not revalue, out of fear of the effect on creditors and share prices, and waited for inflation to make the book values realistic again.

The early-1970s property boom and its effects on the construction

industry are indicative of a general characteristic of construction fir.
Income from contracting is frequently invested in property to provide
future revenue to compensate for the decline in construction activity.
All the large building contractors have significant property divisions.
They operate either as developers, selling off completed schemes, or
as investors, holding on to developments once completed. Some firms
build up property portfolios as long-term investments in a similar
way to pension funds (Massey and Catalano, 1978). Others vary their
involvement in line with fluctuations in the property cycle. Wimpey,
for example, astutely sold most of their property holdings at the
peak of the 1972–3 office boom, thereby avoiding the later debt and
depreciating-asset problems of many of its competitors. Similarly,
in 1982, when the next office boom turned sour, Trafalgar House
announced its intention to rundown its property portfolio.

Although there has been increased involvement in property, the
extent should not be over-emphasised. Rental income from property
investments for most companies represents a supplement to
contracting profits rather than a replacement of them. The reason is
obvious. Property requires large investments of capital and the
resultant rents make a substantial impact on most firms' income only
after a lapse of time. Large scale short-term borrowing to provide the
property-investment capital reproduces the problems of the mid-
1970s as the property sector itself is subject to profitability cycles.
Moreover, yields on property investments historically are comparatively low because of the nature of competing investors, particularly
pension funds and insurance companies (Massey and Catalano, 1978).
The return on capital invested in property holdings, therefore, is
likely to be far less than in mainstream construction and development
activities. Property investment is not a simple substitute for construction work. Rental income, rather, is a useful, predictable alternative
source of revenue. Only when tax considerations are important is a
strong involvement in property likely to provide an adequate substitute for construction activities. Firms with significant 'family' ownerships, therefore, might switch towards property holdings as a means
of minimising personal tax incidence.[10]

Evidence of the overall impact of rental income from property
investments on construction firms' profits can be derived from
published company accounts. An analysis of thirty-eight publicly-
quoted building contractors' accounts from 1971 to 1978 showed
little change in the proportion of gross profits derived from rental
income. The proportion varied between 12 per cent and 16 per cent
of aggregate profits, the variation reflecting as much changes in
trading profits as variations in rental income. An analysis of the

nty-two speculative housebuilders shows the same
income rose slightly as a percentage of aggregate
6 per cent to 8 per cent between 1971 and 1978, and
ror cyclical variations in the housebuilding profitability

INVESTMENT IN NON-CONSTRUCTION ASSETS

Investment in property is only one diversification construction firms can make. The most obvious alternative is to invest in other industries, especially through acquisition of existing firms. Since the early 1970s most construction firms have pursued this strategy. Frequently the move is into industries with complementary links to construction, as they represent less daunting prospects for effective management control. Construction firms, for example, have been active in North-Sea-oil-related industries, in particular oil-rig fabrication and the service industries associated with the oil field. They have also moved into mechanical service industries, whose clientele extends way beyond the construction industry, and have acquired firms overseas, especially in the USA. Details of these acquisitions of new assets are given in Chapter 10.

Again, diversification activity has not changed the overall nature of most construction firms. They remain overwhelmingly dominated by construction. One consequence of the decline in construction workloads, however, in combination with the diversification into property and elsewhere, has been a lowering of the ratio of turnover to net assets (as defined in the *Business Monitor* analysis). This means construction capital is not as flexible as it used to be; a progressively greater proportion is being tied down in less liquid assets.

Business Monitor Company Finance data indicate the significance of this trend in the late 1970s, one which has continued through into the 1980s. In 1969 the classic image of construction capital, having a high turnover relative to net assets, is clearly shown. Construction firms' aggregate turnover was over four times its asset base, whereas that of manufacturing was less than two. Over the next nine years, however, the two sectors exhibited a marked convergence in their turnover ratios as manufacturing's rose and construction's fell. In 1969, construction's turnover ratio was 2.3 times higher than that of manufacturing; by 1977, it was only 1.5 times higher.

As the data are historic-cost based, the rise in the turnover ratio for manufacturing could be the consequence of inflation alone; turn-over grows in line with rising prices, whereas valuing assets at historic cost increasingly under-represents their true value. Such inflationary characteristics, however, make the fall in the turnover ratio for construction all the more remarkable. It occurred against the inflationary trend and in replacement cost terms would be even more marked.

MARKET POWER WITHIN THE CONSTRUCTION INDUSTRY

Given the continuing predominance of construction in Britain in their turnovers, the financial strength of construction firms in the face of collapsed workloads can be explained only by their structural position in the UK building industry. The key concept needed to understand what has happened is the notion of construction firms as merchant-producers, elaborated earlier in Chapter 2. Construction firms have been able to use their position of market power to pass most of the costs of the slump on to others. Many of the means by which they have done this were described earlier, and so will not be gone over in detail again.

The low overheads of construction firms have enabled the prudent firms to avoid 'buying work at suicidal prices', to use the industry's well-known cliché. Companies can let real turnover fall if sufficient new profitable orders cannot be won, using their current income to reduce even further the burden of fixed costs as they do so (cf. the section on gearing ratios above). The marketing strength of the larger, established firms has enabled them to take a greater share of their traditional markets. The annual statement by the board of Turiff Corporation in 1980 illustrates the principle clearly:

> The group has stayed away from road and housebuilding where profits are volatile, to concentrate on the heavy engineering construction it knows best.
>
> While contract labour has been cut back, the board says all key staff have been kept on to await the upturn. Most significantly Turriff is unborrowed and remains a net interest earner. (quoted in *Guardian*, 18 October 1980)

The degree of flexibility over workloads places main contractors in a strong position relative to subcontractors, materials suppliers and building workers. Contractor R. M. Douglas, for example, has experienced both sides of the pressure. In 1981 they were commenting that 'Douglas has found that the margin-pressure lets up only when a major contract is landed; that brings a temporary increase in the contractor's power to bargain with local subcontractors' (quoted in *Financial Times*, 26 August 1981). Eighteen months later, when the company made its first ever six-month loss, the Chairman, John Douglas, was complaining of the squeeze on the firm's own specialist subcontracting divisions: 'In the specialist subcontracting and supply industries, the general shortage of work and pressure from main contractors has resulted in a very severe squeeze on margins' (quoted in *Construction News*, 17 February 1983).

Another contractor, Croudace Holdings, reported a similar story of increased market power:

> work taken on by the contract building division at what seemed scarcely economic rates, turned out more profitable as the year 1980–81 progressed.
>
> This was because materials, and particularly labour, became more easily available at lower rates than provided for at the time of tender. Labour becoming more easily available enabled Croudace and others to organise jobs so that more work was done in less time. (quoted in *Construction News*, 15 April 1982)

In other words, what happened was that although real tender prices fell from the mid-1970s through into the 1980s, contractors in general have been able to sustain or increase profits as input costs fell even further. Published data on input costs, moreover, do not reflect the severity of the squeeze on input prices as many firms were able during the period to negotiate substantial discounts on quoted prices. As one commentator noted:

> The solution to the profits paradox is that, as middlemen, the contractors have been able to place more pressure downstream – labour, materials, specialist subcontractors – than the clients have exerted on them; fortuitously . . . the very severity of the recession has come to the contractors' rescue.[12]

Two final pieces of data highlight the consequences for two different social groups of the financial performance of construction firms over the years of long decline in workloads. During 1982 the *Financial Times* contracting and construction share price index rose by 40 per cent – a 'buoyant performance', largely due to the profits of medium-size companies sheltered from the increased competition of international construction markets (according to the Lex column, *Financial Times*, 8 January 1983). Meanwhile, in May 1982, construction unemployment rose to a record 366,000, double the level of four years previously and a staggering 25 per cent of total construction employment (*Monthly Digest of Statistics*, April 1983). No wonder input costs could be pushed so low.

Implications for management strategies

This chapter has looked at why the profits of the major building contractors have not collapsed with the decline in construction workloads. The arguments used have considerable implications for understanding the options open to the managements of construction firms in expanding accumulation in the face of varying market opportunities. Construction managements to an extent have a flexibility denied to firms operating in many traditional manufacturing activities. The flexibility arises only partially from the famous lack of fixed capital of construction firms; as important are some economic consequences for firms of the social structure associated with the contracting system.

When traditional markets start to collapse, profits within those activities need not be detrimentally affected. The sharp depression of input costs, however, is likely to be gradually counteracted as structural adjustments take place in those input markets – the number of subcontractors begins to decline, and unemployed workers move to other types of work, for instance. So big construction firms have to start thinking of new opportunities for accumulation. The profits paradox and the cash inflows from reduced contracting give them considerable breathing space in which to make those decisions. They also cushion firms from the consequences of making bad decisions in those restructuring strategies. As Chapter 10 will show, some construction firms have made absolutely disastrous mistakes in their diversification strategies, but continued profits from their traditional activities and limited borrowings have enabled them to survive and try something else.

Continued profits also mean that contractors do not immediately have to run down their overhead costs, even if reduced workloads make many of those costs unnecessary. Firms can wait for a while, in the hope that the downturn is only temporary. In this way, all the organisational features (core staff, etc.) that give the large firms 'muscle' within a market sector can be retained. However, after a time, if orders do not revive, a substantial restructuring must be implemented to avoid a rapid slide in profits.

Chapter 5 introduced the notion of a portfolio of contracts to understand contractors' tendering strategies. It was also suggested that the concept could be extended beyond contracts to all situations when a building contractors' capital becomes liquid. They have to decide whether to reinvest in the same activity or to diversify elsewhere. The rationale of profit-making for construction firms rests on such speculative decisions. If they move in the right direction, profits rise; a mistaken investment, however, can spell disaster. Again, construction firms in this respect are in principle no different from other capitalist enterprises. However the proportionate importance of such decisions for the senior management of construction firms is significantly greater than in many other productive enterprises, because of the limited scope open to builders of gaining advances over competitors through changing methods of production in their dominant activities.

Of course, construction firms are interested in making more profits from their traditional activities as well as diversifying. Firms try both in order to improve their competitive marketing position, in order to be able to win a greater share of the available contracts at favourable prices, and to increase the cost effectiveness of production itself.

One of the major effects of the slump in construction work since the early 1970s is that firms have tried to find new areas of activity: searching out new markets in construction; playing the property, money and securities markets; and investing in non-construction industries are options on which management strategies have been focused. Due to the barriers to entry in different construction markets and in other industries, takeovers of existing firms have been one of the main means by which construction managements have tried to change the direction of accumulation. Mergers and acquisitions play a particularly central role for construction firms. So, by looking at the pattern of takeovers, a good impression can be obtained of the transformation of construction capital over the past twenty years; this is done in the next chapter.

CHAPTER 9

Takeovers for growth

Industrial restructuring is a rather vague term commonly used to denote processes of structural change within an industry. The changes referred to could be associated with: new technologies and the destruction of outmoded plant; a relocation of the points of production; a change in the relations between capital and labour; or, finally, a reconstitution of individual capitals through failure, concentration or centralisation. Obviously, for most industries these processes are interlinked. Yet, for construction the situation is somewhat different. Earlier, certain distinctive features of the construction industry were highlighted which suggest that restructuring over the past twenty years is more closely linked to changes in the ownership of capital than to new methods of production. The extent to which they are associated with a redrawing of social relations in the industry is still an open question, which Chapter 11 will consider.

This chapter explores the changing ownership of construction capital by examining the pattern of, and reasons for, mergers and takeovers in the British construction industry since the early 1960s. Mergers, of course are only one means of creating changes in the ownership structure of an industry. Some firms may disappear through bankruptcy and voluntary withdrawal, whereas others may expand rapidly through internal expansion alone. The importance of takeovers, however, is clearly linked to specific phases of economic change in the construction industry and to economic pressures on the individual sectors that form its components. For this reason, takeover activity is a particularly useful means of examining the process of firm change.[1]

Takeovers are important for individual firms at specific points in time. For an acquiring firm the takeover is undertaken to speed up growth, stabilise a market position or avert a threatened decline in turnover and/or profitability. For an acquired firm, it is specific historic circumstances that make them objects of takeover. The company, for instance, could be in temporary financial difficulty or have size constraints to further growth; both may be overcome by merger with a larger organisation. The existence of such economic pressures results from the position of the firm within an industry, the overall state of that industry, and the general level of economic activity. The direction of causality, however, is not one way. The possibility of takeover itself affects the accumulation process for individual firms. Mergers should be seen as only one possible response to specific problems or constraints. An examination of merger activity therefore increases the understanding of the nature of capital accumulation in construction.

The following argument and empirical evidence is divided into two main sections. The first considers why construction firms are involved in takeover activity; the second then looks at the actual incidence of takeover activity by examining the aggregate pattern of acquisitions from 1960 onwards.

Why do construction firms take-over and merge?

The nature of the construction industry limits the range of potential advantages to be achieved from acquisitions. For this reason diversification plays a dominant role, and the level of takeover activity is closely linked to the state of aggregate and sectoral demand for construction work.

Economies of scale in production are a much vaunted advantage of mergers, yet they are of little relevance in construction. Continuous production runs are necessary for many scale economies, yet difficult to achieve in construction, simply because a production process comes to an end when a project is complete; furthermore the social relations of production make any potential continuity within and across projects difficult to achieve. Mergers that increase firm size only affect the possibility of continuity indirectly by increasing the size and range of contracts for which a firm may tender. But they could equally have the opposite effect on continuity; labour turnover (a proxy for continuity of work) is, after all, highest in the largest firms. The impact of mergers on production is far less than in manufacturing, a fact which might explain the lack of vertical integration in the industry.

There is another situation in which mergers can have an indirect impact on production, which is when there is current or potential excess capacity. This could occur when competitive investment by two or more firms threatens to expand capacity faster than demand, or where a declining market necessitates plant closure. Mergers can avoid duplication of investment, speed up closure of plant, and have the added advantage of increasing market power (cf. George and Silbertson, 1975; Massey and Meegan, 1982).

The secular decline in new construction work since the early 1970s might appear to make firms in the industry ideal candidates for defensive mergers in order to reduce capacity, particularly in those sectors where workloads have declined very rapidly (e.g. public-sector work). There is, however, little evidence of this occurring. This is not surprising given the nature of building contracting. In many sectors of the industry, technical barriers to entry are small. Technical expertise in many building processes is highly substitutable, especially in traditional building work. Specialist plant can be hired (and where it is not, it is often written-off over a very short period by charging the cost to one contract). And specialist work can be subcontracted. A corollary of limited technical barriers to entry is a low cost of exit from a sector.

Mergers to reduce the costs of cutting capacity are therefore of little importance. Excess capacity for most types of work means potential capacity for the firms concerned. It does not imply high overhead costs to finance that potential, as so much of the plant, equipment and labour-force is hired temporarily. Potential capacity simply means that the firm has an organisational structure capable of gearing up to higher levels of work rather than actual idle capacity owned (and financed) by the firm. This does mean, however, that when there are upturns in workloads there are many firms trying to bid for the available resources to undertake that work, leading to a strong upward pressure on costs. However, these costs of flexibility are born by clients in higher tender-prices rather than by the firms submitting tender bids, who all face the same input costs; thus, even in a competitive situation, each firm can pass on those higher costs in their tender bids.

Having stated that, though, for certain types of work, barriers to entry for new firms are substantial, especially in large-scale civil engineering projects. Given such barriers to entry, mergers might be advantageous to stop the erosion of profit margins with reduced workloads through competitive undercutting of each others' tender bids. The merger option, if used to maintain margins however, is likely to induce client response to the potential abuse of monopoly power, or to encourage established civil engineers from other regions or countries to tender as new local entrants. Clients themselves can encourage new entrants by inviting newcomers to select-tender lists or by encouraging foreign contractors to submit bids. A strategy that is likely to have more success in such situations is for contractors to try to maintain the existing market and administrative barriers to entry through operating covert restrictive practices, sharing out the available work at agreed tender prices. This type of market response occurred amongst blacktop (i.e. asphalt, tar, bitumen, etc.) contractors, who were discovered in the mid-1970s to be operating price rings throughout the UK.

Mergers can bring substantial economies in marketing and finance (e.g. bargaining power in relation to suppliers and clients, and access to and the cost of credit). Construction firms can benefit from such advantages. The firm size required to gain these advantages depends on the type of work undertaken (it is, for example, much greater for motorway building than small-scale house improvements). Some mergers in construction have been partially to gain such size advantages, and often they can be combined with an attempt to diversify into other markets. But many companies actively involved in acquisitions are well above the size where such economies are substantial. Most contracting work, moreover, does not require large amounts of loan capital for long periods of time, so financing constraints are rarely substantial for all bar the smaller contractors.

One marketing factor which has a strong bearing on company size concerns entrance to select-tender lists, which is often dependent on the company attaining a minimum turnover requirement. The larger the project, the higher the turnover that must be achieved. Clients use turnover as a proxy for competence and financial strength. Once again, many of the medium and large contractors are well above most potential turnover limits. There might still be occasions where mergers are induced by the need to reach a given turnover to tender for work. This is particularly the case with large turnkey projects overseas, although consortia can help solve the problem. The relatively small asset base of many British firms has been cited as one of the reasons for the comparative lack of success of British contractors overseas (*Construction News Magazine*, November, 1979).

There is one other financial advantage of size which does explain why construction firms are interested in takeovers. Contractors try to maintain a portfolio of building contracts and, frequently, non-construction assets which maximise expected profits (see Chapter 5). A broad portfolio minimises the risk of financial disaster arising from one loss-making contract, enables greater bargaining power with clients (as there is other work to fall back on) and advantage can be taken of differential rates of profit between construction markets. The larger the firm size, the broader can be the portfolio. In this way, size is an advantage almost without limit. This advantage, however, has no positive effect on productive efficiency and costs. If anything, the effect is likely to be adverse as the large firm can temporarily withdraw from a market rather than attempt to cut costs if competition pushes profit margins below an acceptable level.

Mergers can both increase overall firm size and, through diversification, stretch the range of work for which a firm can tender. Takeovers in this context have two simultaneous benefits on a firm's portfolio of contracts. And it is in terms of the attainment of an improved portfolio of contracts and non-construction assets that takeover activity must be understood. It is one means, out of a whole series, of changing the structure of a company's portfolio of work. A new market can be entered with minimum likelihood of retaliation, as the acquired company will already have a standing there. The acquired firm will have the management expertise, a portfolio of contracts and contacts, and membership of select-tender lists where necessary. Takeovers enable rapid access to new markets and, consequently, make sense for firms with no previous presence.

Whether a strategy of diversification through acquisition is adopted by a firm depends on its structural position within construction and on the overall state of the industry and economy as a whole. In some areas of work, specialisation may produce the most profitable portfolio (e.g. certain types of civil engineering, specialist sub-contracting, and speculative housebuilding). On the other hand, long-term decline of markets will encourage diversification. If takeover activity is closely linked to attempts to diversify into new markets, it is to be expected that the aggregate level of takeover and type undertaken will depend on the overall state of demand for construction work and on the relative variations in workloads between sectors of the industry.

Acquisition is only one option open to a firm. It is to be expected, therefore, that different firms have wide variations in their takeover activity (or in whether they become potential takeover candidates). Much depends on a firm's position in the industry, especially the sectors in which they operate, their size and the style of management. Acquisition as a strategy (like anything else done to adjust a portfolio of contracts) might also be unsuccessful, either because the intended acquisition does not succeed or because the acquisition turns out to be a financial disaster.

Takeover activity and the building cycle

As Chapter 6 showed, over the course of the past thirty years there have been considerable changes in the level and type of construction work in Britain. This section considers the aggregate level of construction mergers in the context of those changes.

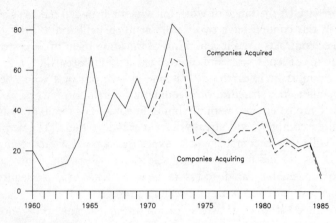

Figure 9.1 Acquisitions in the construction industry, 1960–85. *Source: Business Monitor MQ7.*

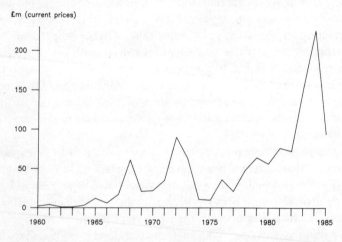

Figure 9.2 Value of construction acquisitions, 1960–85. *Source: Business Monitor MQ7.*

Figures 9.1 and 9.2 give data on the number and value of acquisitions in construction from 1960–85, taken from *Business Monitor MQ7* data. Some definitions and qualifications need to be clarified before the data are described. The most important definitional point is the classification of a construction takeover, and the most important qualification is the potential inaccuracy of the data.

Business Monitor acquisitions and mergers data are based on reports in the financial press, supplemented by special inquiries to companies to determine the form, value and timing of particular acquisitions. A construction acquisition is defined by classifying takeovers to SIC industry groups on the basis of the predominant activity of the acquiring firm. Where no activity predominates the company is classified under a general category of mixed activities. This means that diversification into and out of construction by firms who are not predominantly construction companies is not included in the construction data, yet such moves are obviously of interest when considering diversification. Similarly, takeovers of non-construction companies by construction companies are classified as a construction takeover, although there has been no change of ownership of capital within construction. Overseas acquisitions are particularly poorly represented as only direct acquisitions are counted, whereas acquisitions by existing foreign subsidiaries or associates of UK companies are ignored; yet many acquisitions of foreign companies are effected through existing affiliates.

Potential inaccuracies in the data must also be born in mind. First, not all acquisitions and mergers can be traced via daily searches of the financial pages of newspapers. Smaller takeovers, especially those between non-quoted companies, may not be recorded in the press; added to which is the inevitable possibility that some reported takeovers may not have been noticed in the search process. The problem of omission necessitates the second qualification that the data are likely to be biased towards public companies and towards larger firms. It is to be expected that they are likely to be the ones most accurately reported by the press. This bias is particularly likely in construction, where many firms are small and/or are private companies, including some of the larger ones. One possible consequence of this bias is that the purchase of smaller builders caught in financial difficulties during a downturn is likely to be understated by the *Business Monitor* data. The sharp rise in the value of construction takeovers in the mid-1980s is not reflected in the numbers of takeovers, which declined considerably after the late 1970s. The value data instead result from a limited number of large mergers at a time of general share price boom.

Data qualifications apart, the information provided by *Business Monitor* simply states the number of acquisitions and firms acquiring (Figure 9.1) and the total value of acquisitions (Figure 9.2). Whilst useful, this information may give a poor guide to the extent of changes in firm ownership taking place at a particular point in time. If only the number of firms acquired data is looked at, a false impression of the scale of changing ownership may be drawn. One large takeover, for instance, obviously has a much greater impact than a number of smaller ones (cf. 1965 and 1968 in Figures 9.1 and 9.2). Alternatively, the value data alone might be heavily influenced by a takeover whose timing is due more to chance or individual company circumstances (like the death of an individual majority-shareholder) than to contemporary economic pressures in the industry. The scale of intervention might also be understated, as in the situation where a relatively small firm is acquired to gain a market presence and then a substantial amount of additional capital pumped into it, so that the acquiring firm becomes a major new entrant through acquisition into the sector.

Additional problems arise with the valuation of the size of acquisitions. *Business Monitor* data take the purchase price of the acquired company (shares and cash) where possible, and estimated net asset value otherwise. The two are obviously not the same. The purchase price of a company depends on the overall state of the stock market and of construction shares in particular. Companies can be acquired cheaply (judged by net asset value) when share prices are depressed. Fluctuations in the total value of acquisitions consequently depend on the number of firms acquired, their size, their share prices relative to other companies, and on the general level of share prices (apart from net asset value/share price measurement discrepancies). This may explain the difference between the number of acquisitions and their total value. It is likely that the greater volatility of the value series reflects the wide variation in share prices over the period. Construction firms shared in the property boom of the early 1970s and the price of their shares rose substantially, so the value series would exaggerate the importance of takeovers for the peak of that boom. Construction firms also felt the effects of overgearing when the speculative boom came to an end; their share prices were consequently very low at the end of 1973 through to 1974. Most contractors' profits, however, were extremely buoyant during the slump of 1975–6 and again later, which was reflected in share prices. General price inflation also played its part in pushing up the value of acquisitions throughout the 1970s.

Turning to the data itself in Figures 9.1 and 9.2, it can be seen that the numbers of acquisitions was much greater from 1965 to 1973 than at any other time period, although there was a resurgence of acquisitions in 1979 and 1980. The value data show a slightly different picture, with much shorter takeover waves in 1967–8, 1971–3 and 1979–82. The 1965 and 1969 peaks in the number of acquisitions looks particularly perverse in terms of the value data, which show no corresponding change. A combination of the numbers and value data, however, does give a rough indication that there have been three periods of relatively intense merger activity; the late 1960s up to 1969, 1971–3 and the late 1970s/early 1980s. Even so, the intervening periods were important for some sectors of the industry, as will be shown later.

Interestingly, the first two merger peaks are closely associated with years when new orders for some types of work also reached peaks. In 1967, public-sector work and private housing showed simultaneous upturns, and in 1972–3 it was public non-housing, private and commercial, and private housing that boomed (see Chapter 6). During this period of the late 1960s and early 1970s the extent of fluctuations of orders for specific types of work and the variations between them were large. Takeovers, therefore, may have been closely correlated with these sectoral demand upturns to enable previously excluded firms to bid for new types of work.

The value-of-acquisitions data indicate a difference between the late 1960s' and early 1970s' merger booms. The merger boom in construction in the early 1970s corresponded almost exactly with the timing of the boom in orders itself (1971 to 1973), whereas the peak of the previous merger boom in the late 1960s occurred a year after the sharp drop in new orders in 1967. The difference may be explained by the earlier peak being a response to a drop in traditional workloads, whereas the later one was a reaction to the rise in new orders for certain types of work. In the boom of the early 1970s mergers helped in the winning of contracts and the higher profits of the peak demand types of work. Speed is necessary to enter a market before the boom conditions end and tender prices and profit margins weaken. A lagged response to the latter would simply have meant that the orders boom had been missed.

The situation in the late 1970s and early 1980s is different. Variability in sectoral demand had significantly increased by the 1980s, while long-term decline of some sectors had become obvious, especially those related to government and local authority non-defence work. The upturn in merger activity at this time could be reflecting firms' attempts to find any new markets in the context of a fairly desperate overall shortage of demand. This may have involved looking for niches at a more specialised level than the five broad work categories as a whole, or it may have involved acquisitions overseas or in other industries.

The two periods of relatively low merger activity in the early to mid-1960s and in the mid-1970s need to be explained. Again the most probable reasons related to the state of the construction market at the times in question. During the first period, most construction markets were rapidly expanding, whereas in the mid-1970s construction firms generally were facing flat or even catastrophically bad markets, depending on the sector in question. Both situations led to the low level of merger activity, as the following brief histories show.

TAKEOVERS IN THE 1960S UPSWING

Notwithstanding the increase in merger activity in the late 1960s, the 1960s as a whole were characterised by the construction industry having one of the lowest levels of takeover activity of any British industry. Aaronovitch and Sawyer (1975) ranked the construction industry lowest in merger activity in the distribution sector for the years 1955 to 1968. Kuehn (1970) in a survey of 3,566 publicly-quoted UK firms found that in his sample of 178 builders and contractors, forty were lost in takeovers from 1957 to 1967, a reduction of 22 per cent. This was, however, the second smallest loss of any of his sixty-seven industry classifications. Civil and construction engineers experienced a similar loss, fifty out of 187, a reduction of 27 per cent (ranking them sixty-second in the takeover league).

A survey of mergers between 1958 and 1968 by the Monopolies Commission (1970) found an even smaller effect than Kuehn, using a slightly different sampling procedure. Only two takeovers within construction were noted for the whole of the eleven-year period. There were also nine mergers, each of which involved a construction company and a firm from outside the industry. The grand total, however, is hardly large, and does not indicate any major restructuring of the ownership of construction capital through acquisition in this period. During the period, however, total construction output more than doubled, and the Commission found that the net assets of its sample of construction firms grew by 115 per cent, the third fastest rate of all industries. (A related industry, construction materials, was ranked second.) Much of this growth was also concentrated in the largest contractors; the Commission found that only five companies held 50 per cent (or more) of the net assets of the industry by 1967.

The findings of the Monopolies Commission report correspond to the view that most of the growth in the construction industry during the long post-war upswing occurred through the internal expansion of firms rather than through extensive mergers and acquisitions. Faced with buoyant demand in all sectors, firms could plan steady expansion and place new investment in the areas which promised greatest profit. Some companies opted for expansion across all sectors (e.g. Wimpey and Laing) whilst others concentrated on sectors where specialisation, given their size, generated a market advantage, for example, in civil engineering (e.g. the McAlpine family's companies), public housebuilding (e.g. Bryant) and private housebuilding (e.g. Leech and Comben).

Fairclough is a good example of a company which grew rapidly through the 1960s by concentrating on one specialist activity, bridge building. A long-established Lancashire-based company, which built its first bridge in 1905, it expanded rapidly with the motorway building programme by forming consortia, firstly with Sir Alfred McAlpine and later with others (e.g. Amey and Cementation). From its involvement in the Preston bypass, the first British motorway, in 1959 through to the 1970s it was in consortia which built more miles of motorway in the UK than any other contractor (according to its *Annual Report and Accounts*, 1973). Turnover, and especially profits, rose rapidly throughout the period. To sustain expansion by the end of the 1960s, however, it had to undertake an active policy of acquisition as its traditional market started to decline. Finally, in late 1982 it merged with William Press in one of the biggest construction mergers of all time. This final merger came after four years of rapidly declining real turnover (see Chapter 8).

TAKEOVERS AND THE MID-1970S SLUMP IN DEMAND
In 1974 demand collapsed in every sector bar public housing. Total new orders fell by 30 per cent in one year (1973–4). Merger activity collapsed and remained low until 1978. Diversification has been argued to be the main reason for construction takeovers, so it might seem paradoxical that takeovers fell so dramatically at a time when diversification into new markets seemed of paramount importance.

The sharp drop in merger activity at the end of 1973 can be explained by the crisis that hit the industry at the time. The crisis was not only one of a sharp drop in new orders but also a financial crisis, as many firms had become overgeared by borrowing too much to finance speculation in land and property – assets whose value dropped sharply and which could not be sold, even at the new depressed prices. The crisis, nevertheless, was very uneven in its impact. Many firms continued to make record profits, but these profits were not usually based on the magnitude of new orders won (see Chapter 8). So acquisition of even a profitable company did not necessarily mean that a firm in a strong position in a new market (for the acquiring firm) was being acquired. Taking over a heavily-overgeared company, alternatively, could spell disaster unless the price was very cheap and arrangements had been made with the firm's creditors.

In the face of such uncertainty, many firms adopted a wait-and-see attitude to diversification (though some did diversify overseas or out of construction). Many could also afford to adopt such a strategy as they could live on profits from past contracts and on the returns from investing cash in the money markets. Those that could not hold off in this way were, on the other hand, in no financial position to diversify through acquisition but were more likely to become either objects of takeover bids themselves or forced into liquidation.

This broad survey of linkages between merger activity in the construction industry and the state of demand for construction work in the 1960s and 1970s shows that there is not a simple relationship between a particular phase of the building cycle and the level of merger activity. In the early 1960s mergers were low because construction was booming, whereas in the mid-1970s they were low because the industry was in slump, for instance. This does not mean, however, that a whole series of reasons for merger activity have to be searched for to explain the apparent lack of correspondence. Instead the link between the state of construction demand and the level of construction activity has to be mediated by considering whether or not takeovers were necessary or feasible for firms in order for them to enter new markets at the time in question. The difference between the role played by merger activity after the 1967 slump in new orders and in the post-1973 slump does not, for example, have to be explained in terms of different reasons for take-over but in terms of the distinct historical (especially financial) contexts in which the slumps occurred.

The other main reason for take-over in the immediate post-1973 period was cheap acquisition. This is most clearly seen in the private-housebuilding sector, where very cheap land banks could be built up via acquisition. The process also occurred amongst general contractors. Often, however, such cheap acquisitions were, at the same time, a diversification for the acquiring firm. It could be geographical, such as Barratt's acquisition of H. C. Janes in 1975 in order to move into speculative housebuilding in southern England. Otherwise, it was product diversification, as in the case of Tarmac's acquisition of Maclean in 1973 (to enter private housebuilding), and Fairclough's takeover of Sir Lindsay Parkinson in 1974 (partly to aid overseas expansion).

Reasons for takeovers, 1970–9

So far, the level of takeover activity has been linked to changes in construction workloads over time. Reasons for the role of takeovers were advanced but, because of the aggregate nature of the data, they could only constitute suggestive hypotheses. In order to try to substantiate more clearly why construction firms acquire others, a search of the financial and trade press was undertaken for the 1970s. The purpose was somewhat different from the *Business Monitor* inquiries; interest was principally in the reasons given for individual takeovers associated with construction, rather than the numbers-and-value approach for rigidly-defined SIC classifications of the *Business Monitor* inquiry, useful though they are.

The main body of data used is derived from a search of the financial pages of the quality press (especially the *Financial Times*) and of the trade press (especially *Construction News* and *Building*). Each takeover or merger was listed by its date of reporting, the size of the firm acquiring, the price paid (where available) and by the reasons given for acquisition. The reasons were derived from statements made by the acquiring company, press commentary or, failing all else, our own judgment. The reasons were then classified into one of sixteen categories listed in the appendix to this chapter. Where more than one reason was given, they were graded into the dominant reason and others.

To get an overall picture of the changes in ownership of construction firms, takeovers were listed when either the acquiring *or* the acquired company was a construction firm. The definition of a construction company also differs from the *Business Monitor* approach. What is of interest to us is firms that have a significant presence in construction, as the object is to examine the relationship between capital accumulation in construction and takeovers by the firms that constitute that capital. 'Significant presence', however, is difficult to define; firms with over one-third of their total turnover in construction are treated as being construction firms. It is also useful to consider the extent to which firms are diversifying out of construction, in the sense that construction represents a smaller proportion of total turnover. This adds a further potential category of firms to the lists of relevant takeovers, because some firms have fairly large construction divisions yet do not have a third of their total turnover in construction. The major non-construction acquisitions of such companies were also collected and are reported separately in Table 9.1 under the 'others' category.

Data presented in the lower half of Table 9.1 compare the differences in the results between this method of data collection and that of *Business Monitor*. Our approach should give a higher figure, and this is generally the case, except for 1971–3, when there is a substantial shortfall compared to *Business Monitor*. The companies 'missed' by us are likely to have been very small and therefore poorly reported in the press. This conclusion is born out by the value-of-acquisitions data, where the discrepancy is reversed for two of the years in question. It does not seem, therefore, that the major trends being picked up in Table 9.1 are at variance with the *Business Monitor* information. The conclusion was reinforced by comparison with disaggregated takeover data kindly made available to us by the Department of Trade and Industry, which showed that generally we had a similar identification rate in our search to that of the official statistics.

Results

Tables 9.1 and 9.2 present reasons for takeover by year. Table 9.1 gives the dominant reason only, whereas Table 9.2 also includes other reasons where important (e.g. a takeover could be both cheap (dominant) and enable diversification). Table 9.1, in effect, reports the number of cases and Table 9.2 the number of reasons quoted in those cases.

There are notable differences between the reasons given in each year, and broadly those differences correspond to the contemporary economic state of the industry. The most striking feature of Table 9.1 is the differential importance of takeovers in each sector of the industry and their timing. Plant hire, for example, experienced a large number of takeovers in the early 1970s as a number of the fairly small independent companies grew rapidly through acquisition. In later years takeover activity dropped sharply, but the size of the mergers increased substantially as the enlarged firms merged together with companies outside plant hire.

Takeover is also important within speculative housebuilding, particularly during rising market conditions (1971–3 and 1978–9). Such takeovers are predominantly to acquire land, often in a new area. Takeovers associated with speculative housebuilding constitute almost a quarter of the total takeovers within construction (excluding plant hire). Acquiring a land bank through takeover seems often to be a way of purchasing land cheaply, and it is most important during the slump period after the land-price boom of the early 1970s (and significant again in the mid-1980s).

In two areas where Chapter 8 indicated that construction firms have been active, rental income and overseas markets, takeovers do not feature strongly. Property portfolios were built up via development or purchase of individual properties rather than through the acquisition of property companies. Similarly, much of the move overseas has been undertaken by an internal shift of resources rather than through acquisition. There was, in fact, a significant falling off in takeovers associated with overseas markets after 1974, even though this was the main period when firms were diversifying overseas. Overseas, however, is more important in the multiple-reason table. A comparison of the last two categories with the previous two indicates that the importance of takeover depends on the sector, the timing and on which firms are trying to increase their presence there.

Cheap acquisitions, not surprisingly, are most important after the 1972–3 boom. They are also more significant in the multi-reason table, as are the catch-all explanations of potential or current profits.

Table 9.1 Dominant reason for takeovers involving construction firms 1970–9

Reason	1970	1971	1972	1973	1974	1975	1976	1977	1978	1979	Total
Sectoral diversification into or within construction	7	3	9	12	6	1	3	6	1	2	50
Product diversification within construction	6	5	7	7	1	2	4	2	5	3	42
Product expansion by specialist housebuilders	2	10	15	9	0	3	2	1	5	6	53
Product expansion by specialist contractors	2	3	3	4	5	3	3	6	3	2	34
Product expansion by other contractors	8	4	3	9	3	4	13	6	6	5	61
Land bank	0	0	0	2	4	2	3	2	4	6	23
Potential or current profits	0	0	0	0	0	1	0	0	0	1	2
Ability to win contracts	0	0	0	0	0	1	0	2	0	1	4
Available investment cash	0	0	0	1	0	0	0	0	0	0	1
Complementary activities	0	1	0	2	2	0	0	0	0	2	7
Cheap acquisition	0	0	0	3	3	0	4	6	1	5	22
Rental income	0	0	0	0	0	1	0	1	0	0	2
Product expansion or diversification outside construction	4	4	13	4	13	11	9	11	8	13	90
Geographic diversification, national	3	2	1	0	0	0	0	2	1	0	9
Geographic diversification, international	1	3	1	4	1	0	0	3	0	3	16
Plant hire, expansion of or diversification into	9	5	14	9	6	6	2	6	3	2	62
Not known	0	0	0	0	3	1	0	2	0	0	6
Total	42	40	66	66	47	36	43	56	37	51	484

Table 9.1 cont–

Business Monitor total	41	59	83	77	40	35	28	29	39	na	na
No. of acquisitions reporting value of acquisition	25	24	40	42	33	19	26	37	21	28	296
Value of reported acquisitions (£m)	38.5	48.5	58.4	70.4	54.5	23.1	47.3	74.8	47.4	68.6	531.5
Value of acquisitions Business Monitor (£m)	21.7	35.8	90.3	62.8	11.1	10.3	37.0	21.1	48.0	na	na
Product expansion or diversification outside construction (others)*	5	2	5	3	5	7	5	4	15	9	60
No. of acquisitions reporting value of acquisition	1	0	2	0	3	5	2	2	12	5	32
Value of acquisitions (£m)	0.9	0	4.3	0	4.0	22.1	1.6	16.5	18.0	19.9	87.3

*Others refers to firms with less than one-third of turnover in construction.
A detailed explanation of the reasons for takeover categories is given in the Appendix to this chapter.

Table 9.2 *Multiple reasons given for takeovers involving construction firms, 1970–9*

Reason	1970	1971	1972	1973	1974	1975	1976	1977	1978	1979	Total
Sectoral diversification into or within construction	7	4	9	12	7	1	3	6	1	2	52
Product diversification within construction	8	8	7	7	3	2	5	7	8	6	61
Product expansion by specialist housebuilders	2	10	16	11	0	3	2	1	5	7	57
Product expansion by specialist contractors	2	3	3	4	5	3	4	6	4	3	37
Product expansion by other contractors	11	6	4	12	5	6	14	8	7	8	81
Land bank	2	8	9	13	4	3	6	4	8	11	68
Potential or current profits	6	2	4	7	1	2	3	3	3	4	35
Ability to win contracts	1	2	1	2	1	2	0	5	1	2	17
Available investment cash	0	0	0	2	0	0	0	0	0	0	2
Complementary activities	1	2	0	4	3	1	1	2	3	4	21
Cheap acquisition	2	2	2	5	5	4	4	9	2	8	43
Rental income	0	0	0	0	0	1	0	2	0	1	4
Product expansion or diversification outside construction	4	5	13	6	16	11	10	11	10	17	103
Geographic diversification, national	10	7	7	5	6	4	4	6	4	4	57
Geographic diversification, international	1	4	4	5	2	3	2	7	4	6	38
Plant hire, expansion of or diversification into	9	5	15	14	7	6	2	6	3	2	69
Not known	0	0	0	0	3	1	0	2	0	0	6
Total	66	68	94	109	68	53	60	85	63	85	751

It is difficult, however, to decipher the extent to which such statements are *ex-post* self-justifications by management.

Overall the two tables indicate the importance of diversification as a reason for the takeover. The takeovers recorded in Table 9.1 within construction numbered 303 in total. Broadly they can be subdivided into a hundred cases of product or geographic diversification, ninety-four cases of contractors acquiring other contractors, seventy-six cases of speculative housebuilders and land, and a miscellany of thirty-four. This subdivision grossly understates the importance of diversification. Many of the purchases by speculative housebuilders of land, for example, imply moves into new regional housing markets (i.e. geographic diversification). Similarly many of the acquisitions of contractors are of firms specialising in different areas of building work/specialist trades.

With regard to the takeovers of contractors, a detailed examination of the cases for 1976 showed that the majority of acquisitions were diversifications into different spheres of contracting. The importance of speculative housebuilding and contracting categories indicate the limits to the types of diversification that are feasible for many firms, rather than a total absence of diversification.

The rest of the takeovers given in Table 9.1 fall into four main categories. There are ninety cases of building firms diversifying out of construction, with a marked upward shift after 1974; sixty-two cases of acquisitions in plant hire; and twenty-three cases of sectoral diversifications into/within construction which consisted of non-construction firms buying into the industry in the hope of high profits during the 1972-3 boom, or cheap acquisitions in the immediately-following years. The final group is non-construction firms with construction interests (i.e. the others) category who increased their acquisition of non-construction firms in later years, reducing further their relative dependence on construction.

Takeovers by firm size

Our survey of takeovers in the 1970s enabled us to examine the size of acquiring construction firms. They were grouped into three categories based on their annual turnovers; large (£100 million and over), medium (£25 million to £100 million) and small (less than £25 million). Obviously, by the standards of an industry with tens of thousands of firms in it, all of the firms acquiring others are big. It is size differences within the largest enterprises consequently that are being considered.

There were marked changes in the sizes of construction firms involved in takeover during the 1970s. It is the change in relative importance that is particularly interesting, as there are obviously far less medium and large firms than small ones. *The Times 1000* (1978) shows that in 1976 there were only seventeen construction-related firms with a turnover of £100 million or more (our large category) and only thirty-five between £25 million and £100 million (our medium category). So, *a priori*, it might be expected that small firms would always dominate in the numbers acquiring. They did not, however.

As Table 9.3 shows, in the early 1970s takeovers were dominated overwhelmingly by smaller firms acquiring other companies. This position changed with the slump in 1974, after which smaller firms became far less active in the takeover market. Medium-sized firms became the main acquirers, although large firms also increased their activity, particularly in the exceptional year of 1976 when just four large companies (Wimpey, Tarmac, Trafalgar House and Matthew Hall) undertook fourteen out of the nineteen acquisitions by large firms.

Table 9.3 *Construction takeovers by size of acquiring firm, 1970–9*

	1970	1971	1972	1973	1974	1975	1976	1977	1978	1979	Total
Large	9	6	15	8	9	6	19	12	15	17	116
Medium	10	8	13	20	27	17	13	28	27	21	174
Small	22	25	32	21	13	11	12	10	10	11	167
Not known	3	1	6	7	0	4	0	5	3	4	33
Total	44	40	66	56	49	38	44	55	45	53	490

Size defined by turnover:
    Large ⩾£100m (£75m prior to 1975)
    Medium £25m–100m (£15m–75m)
    Small <£25m (<£15m)

The size of acquiring firms indicates the relative importance of takeover for firms of different size when moving into a new activity. The largest firms already have many divisions and subsidiaries operating across a wide range of activities. A change of product or geographic emphasis is consequently less likely to necessitate an acquisition, as it can be achieved through an internal switching of resources. Only when a completely new field is entered is takeover likely to be necessary, or encouraged when a financially attractive acquisition can be made.

Medium-sized firms, on the other hand, frequently have a smaller spread of activities, particularly if they are involved in specialist activities like civil engineering. In rising markets they have a relatively low incentive to diversify into new sectors where the rate of profit is apparently higher, because what they gain in higher tender prices could easily be lost in reduced economies of specialisation. Diversification tends to take place only when it is forced upon them, through rapid growth or because traditional markets contract permanently.

The small firms are the most difficult to explain. To an extent the change in their position is the converse of the increased merger activity by medium-sized firms. However this is only part of the explanation, as there was a significant drop in the absolute number of takeovers by small firms after the boom year of 1973. There appear to be three factors. First, some small firms that were very active in takeovers in the early 1970s became medium-sized firms as a result (e.g. some plant-hire firms, the HAT Group of specialist subcontractors and builders merchants, and Barratt the housebuilders). There were, furthermore, more acquisitions of speculative housebuilders by other speculative builders during the boom years of the early 1970s, and during the early 1970s speculative housebuilding was dominated by firms in our small category (Ball, 1983). Finally it is to be expected that small firms tend to be the most highly specialised, so that growth implies diversification and possibly, therefore, a takeover. Growth was more likely to be achieved by such firms in the early 1970s than in the period of rapid long-term decline of the late 1970s.

Conclusion

Takeovers and mergers have played important parts in the restructuring of the British construction industry. This chapter has tried to explain the reasons for construction takeovers, and has analysed the 1970s in detail in the light of these explanations. Market diversification has been highlighted as the dominant reason for acquisition in construction and it has been shown that periods of substantial takeover activity are related to rapid changes in the level and types of demand for construction work. The overriding importance of diversification as the reason for takeover distinguishes construction from many other industries.

What has been the impact of takeovers on the centralisation of capital in construction? Have takeovers and mergers led to the industry becoming increasingly dominated by a few large producers? Chapter 7 has already considered the available evidence on the market shares of different sizes of producer. It was shown that the data are too poor to draw any definite conclusions about relative market shares. However, it does seem plausible, given the evidence available, to suggest that the UK market share in new construction work of the largest firms has increased over the past decade or so. The extent of takeovers during this period supports this view. Certainly in speculative housebuilding and other key sectors, the largest producers have increased their market shares dramatically. The following chapter gives further elaboration of some of the changes. However, as earlier chapters have argued, what is particularly important is the new hierarchical structure of the industry, and takeovers have aided its formation. Construction may not be in danger of becoming dominated by a giant monopoly, but relations of market power between different types of firm are now on new footings.

One thing that has come out strongly from the evidence has been the differential importance of takeover for certain sectors of the industry, and for specific types of enterprise. The next chapter takes up this theme and looks at the changes in particular sectors of the industry.

Appendix: Definitions of categories used in Table 9.1

Sectoral diversification within/into construction Acquisition in construction sector by company not previously engaged in that sector or, possibly, construction.

Product diversification within construction Acquisition in a construction sector, in which the acquiring company is already established, in order to enter a new product market.

Product expansion by housebuilders Purchase of a housebuilding company by another housebuilder.

Product expansion by specialist contractors Purchase of a contractor engaged in specialist work by another specialist. Here, specialist means mechanical, electrical and hydraulic engineers and heating, plumbing, ventilating, roofing, glazing, etc.

Product expansion by other contractors 'Other' refers to all construction sectors not previously categorised, i.e. excludes speculative housebuilding, specialist contracting (as defined above) and hirers of contractors' plant. This category refers principally to general building contractors and civil engineering.

Land bank Purchase of a company to acquire its land bank for private housing development.

Potential or current profitability Purchase of any type of company by a construction company where the dominant reason given was potential or current profitability.

Increase ability to win contracts Self-explanatory.

Available investment cash The dominant reason was that the acquiring company had cash available for takeovers.

Complementary activities Acquisition in which at least one party is a construction company where the dominant reason was the benefits accruing from combining complementary activities in production, marketing and purchasing.

Cheap acquisition The dominant reason for the acquisition was the exceptionally low share price of the acquired company.

Rental income The dominant reason for the acquisition was that it would generate a significant stream of rental income.

Product expansion outside, or diversification outside, construction Self-explanatory.

Geographic expansion: the national market Purchase of a company, regardless of from which SIC it originates, by a construction company where the dominant reason for the acquisition was an improvement in the geographical coverage of its products within any region(s) of the British Isles.

Geographic expansion: the international market As above, where the coverage relates to world markets excluding the UK.

Plant hire, expansion of or diversification into Purchase of a plant hire company either by another plant hire company or by any other company. In the former case the acquisition represents product expansion, in the latter diversification.

CHAPTER 10

Sectoral restructuring

The last chapter showed how large construction firms use takeovers as a means of reacting to changes in their economic environments. This chapter shifts the focus to particular sectors of the industry, looking at how each has changed over recent decades and the reasons for the changes. Takeovers are a key part of the changes, so emphasis will be placed on them. Four sectors are taken as illustrative of the changes taking place within the industry as a whole; speculative housebuilding, civil engineering, overseas markets, and plant hire. Each has had a distinct history over recent decades.

Speculative housebuilding

Owner-occupied housing is built by speculative housebuilders. In many ways this sector is distinctive because of the large amount of capital that has to be invested, prior to production, in land purchase and development. In addition, the profitability of investment in speculative housebuilding is exceptionally risky (Ball, 1983). It is not surprising, therefore, that many acquisitions are attempts to minimise risk or are results of the unfavourable outcomes of the speculative decisions. Four major reasons for takeover can be identified; three relate to land (its cheapness, and the speed and the scale of development), and the other to attempts to diversify out of housebuilding. Their relative importance depends on the state of the housebuilding cycle; speed is hardly of paramount importance in a downturn and cheap land is more difficult to come by in an upswing.

The slump period after 1973 illustrates a number of the reasons for takeover. After the intense speculative boom of the previous two years, the sharp downturn in 1973 created liquidity problems for many housebuilders. Creditors were calling in loans, whilst falling demand left many firms with borrowed capital tied up in unsold houses and overvalued and unsaleable land. Such firms were either forced into liquidation or their net worth (and Stock Market valuation when publicly quoted) fell dramatically. In both cases, their assets became attractive for acquisition. Many land banks were purchased direct from receivers or creditors; in other cases the enterprise was taken over as a whole. Although it is takeover which strictly is of concern here, the distinction between takeover and land-bank purchase can often be merely a formality concerning the precise timing of the acquisition (relating to the contemporary corporate status of the firm). In many cases, where all work is subcontracted, the only assets acquired by taking over a speculative housebuilder are its land bank plus part-completed dwellings and a small office.

A number of firms outside speculative housebuilding took advantage of the situation to enter the industry during the mid-1970s with a view to cheap acquisition and longer-term profitability. Between 1973 and 1975 for example, John Maclean, Galliford Estates and Bovis (48 per cent of whose profits came from private housebuilding in 1973) were respectively taken over by Tarmac, Sears Holdings and P & O Steam Navigation. Here the firms were presumably interested in management expertise and goodwill as well as land, whereas takeovers within the industry were primarily simply to acquire land. Examples of the latter are Barratt's acquisition of H. C. Janes in 1975 giving it entry to markets in Southern England and substantially increasing its turnover, Wm Leech's purchase of Hugh Owen & Son (Cheshire) and Trafalgar House's purchase (via its subsidiary Trolloppe and Colls) of Midland builder, W. J. Simms, Sons and Cooke. New regional housing markets were entered cheaply and quickly through such acquisitions.

A similar spate of acquisitions of housebuilders with poor profits in a slump occurred during the housing market downturn in 1980–1. Milbury Estates (then a subsidiary of St Piran) acquired Dares Estates in 1981 and Comben bought the land bank and work-in-progress of Wiggins Construction in the same year. Two other firms decided to sell off their poorly-performing housebuilding divisions in 1981; Federated Land disposed of its housebuilding interests in a management buyout, whilst Rush and Tompkins (once just a civil engineer) began to sell off its housing land-bank.

During 1977–8 the private housing market picked up and land prices rose rapidly. In a rising market, acquisitions can also be a good way of acquiring land. Housebuilders in early 1978 were claiming that acute shortages of building land existed in many localities. In that sort of situation, acquisition of another housebuilder may be one of the few ways of obtaining reasonably priced land. But there are also more general reasons why takeover can be a good means of acquiring land. The assets of the acquired company (i.e. its land bank) could have been undervalued; hence land is being acquired at below its current market price. Alternatively, acquisition can bring beneficial tax advantages for both the acquired (especially when the owner is a private individual) and the acquiring firm. Housebuilders' land banks are classified as stock and work-in-progress and, therefore, were eligible for tax relief under the deferred tax for stock appreciation scheme introduced in the 1974 Finance Act, until its abolition in the mid-1980s. The tax relief was transferrable to an acquiring firm and, once taken into account, could make the effective purchase price of the land through acquisition much less than its current market price.

Another advantage acquisition brings is speed. Buoyant market demand rarely lasts for more than a few years in owner-occupied housing, yet the overall construction process can take many years from conception to completion (National Economic Development Office, 1978). As a result takeover can be an attractive option, for the acquired firm will have sites with planning permission or already under development. The speed advantage is particularly important if the acquiring firm is moving into a new locality, because it will have no previously-purchased land in the development pipeline and no contact with local market conditions, landowners and planners. Like any land purchase, however, acquisition is a speculative calculation. Takeover may involve the purchase of a land bank which contains a number of unattractive plots of land and of other business activities which are of little interest to the acquiring firm.

A few speculative housebuilders have used takeover as a means of diversifying out of housebuilding. A prime example is Crest Securities, which diversified out of construction to become a conglomerate. Originally only a housebuilder, Crest merged with Camper Nicholson, a firm specialising in the production of yachts and other leisure products, to form Crest Nicholson in 1972. The enlarged group's interest in housebuilding was reduced to around 50 per cent of turnover. This initial diversification marked the beginning of a policy of sectoral and product diversification through acquisition over the next seven years, which included moves into engineering (Lamson Engineering in 1976) and the export market for optical equipment (the Crofton Group of companies in 1979). The process is uncommon, however, as considerable management economies are generally felt to be derived from specialising within housebuilding. When speculative housebuilders do diversify out of housebuilding they usually concentrate on commercial and industrial developments, that is alternative activities involving land development.

The final reason for takeover in the sector is scale economies. It is difficult for a speculative housebuilder to grow on a gradual, incremental basis. Particular organisational structures are geared to producing a specific number of houses each year; above or below that figure substantial management diseconomies result. Moreover, local markets can become saturated so that growth requires expansion elsewhere, possibly in another region. The additional distance necessitates setting up a new regional office, once again with an optimal output for the organisational structure. There is consequently a stepped-size optimal-output function. Its precise shape depends on the types of house being built, the markets served, and individual company and management competence (Ball, 1983). Firms which want to grow have a considerable incentive to look for a favourable acquisition. Takeover combines the advantages of scale economies and speed of development.

A good example of this type of merger is Comben Group's takeover of Orme Developments in 1978. Comben's output was doubled and its geographic spread increased substantially, so this acquisition enabled scale economies to be achieved. The actual picture is complicated as Comben had already been involved in a series of takeovers (principally as victim) during the 1970s, primarily by conglomerates from outside construction looking for land-development investment opportunities. In 1970, the then Comben and Wakeling was taken over by Carlton Industries, via a merger with its subsidiary Carlton Homes. The Comben Group thereby became a subsidiary of London Merchant Securities, a property company and parent of Carlton. Carlton already had interests in batteries and whisky distilling. Hawker Siddeley, an engineering company, took a majority interest in Carlton Industries in 1978, enabling Comben to have the financial backing to bid successfully for Orme Developments (*Building*, 16 December 1970 and *Sunday Times*, 30 April 1978). Later, in 1984, Hawker Siddeley in turn sold Comben to Trafalgar House, partly because Comben had managed to misjudge trends in the housing market for a number of years.

SPECULATIVE HOUSEBUILDING TRANSFORMED
Centralisation in the speculative housebuilding industry has continued throughout the 1980s. Through the process of firm entry, particularly through acquisition, the industry was transformed from its small-firm characterisation of the 1960s. The consequences for the ways in which land is purchased, and houses are built and sold, have been enormous (Ball, 1986).

By the mid-1980s, private housebuilding was experiencing another major boom. The sector was becoming an increasingly important proportion of total new building work, and an area in which good profits could be made. Table 10.1 lists some of the major private housebuilders, shows their rapidly-expanding outputs during the period, and gives the estimated percentage of the firm's total profits derived from speculative housebuilding. Some noticeable trends can be observed in speculative housebuilding in the 1980s, relating to the mid-1980s housing boom and the previous shift in the 1970s to large-scale producers.

Table 10.1 *Contractors' profits from housebuilding*

	House sales (thousands)		% group profits from housing
	1983	*1986 (est.)*	
Wimpey	9.5	11.0	40
Tarmac	7.0	10.1	25
Barratt Dev.	11.0	8.1	100
C. H. Beazer	0.8	5.5	56
Trafalgar House	4.0	3.8	25
Y. J. Lovell	1.4	2.7	70
John Laing	1.3	2.7	40
W. Connolly	1.8	2.3	90
Bryant Holdings	2.0	2.1	80
Costain	0.9	2.1	10
Bellway	1.4	1.7	100
Westbury	1.5	1.7	100
A. McAlpine	0.9	1.5	12
English China Clays	0.5	1.5	10

Source: Financial Times, 10 December 1986

In the first place, all building firms have taken a growing interest in private housebuilding. The prime reason is obvious; the sector is not undergoing secular decline and is one of the most profitable. Housebuilding has been the mainstay of many large contractors' profits during the mid-1980s, as Table 10.1 shows. Virtually all the major contractors now have housebuilding divisions, whereas in the late 1970s only a handful were seriously active in the sector. For some the shift has been through internal organic growth, especially when there was already some activity in the sector. This occurred with firms like Costain and Laing, who built only around 400 and 700 houses in 1980, yet 2,100 and 2,700 in 1986 respectively (CNFR, 1986). The biggest builder, Tarmac, even announced a large target market-share – planning to build 10 per cent of all new dwellings by 1990 (it built none prior to 1973). Others took the takeover trail. Beazer became one of the major housebuilders through takeover (Monsell Youell, Second City Homes and Wm Leech, amongst others). Civil engineers Mowlem bought housebuilder Alfred Booth in 1985. Higgs and Hill had earlier virtually renounced its traditional contracting activities to concentrate on property and housebuilding, picking up a series of small housebuilders on the way (such as Southend Properties in 1986).

Another reason cited for the shift into housebuilding, for instance when Beazer acquired French Kier in 1986, is that contracting generates cash that can be invested in ever-more-expensive land banks (see *Financial Times*, 28 December 1986). If this is true, it indicates a shift in construction firms' management philosophies. In the 1970s, speculative housebuilding and contracting tended to be two relatively independent spheres of the construction industry, precisely because both required distinct management skills (Ball, 1983). Housebuilding required marketing and land-assembly skills and contracting tender-pricing and large-site management skills. The greater merging of the two spheres could partly have become easier because of the drift in contracting away from its traditional focus of production management towards that of project management (see Chapter 11).

Associated with the greater merging of ownership of contracting and housebuilding firms has been a concomitant relative decline in the large independent family producer. Barratt's mid-1980s troubles have been well-aired. Other large independents have been swallowed up (e.g. Leech by Beazer in 1985, and English China Clays' purchase of E. Bradley in 1984), or subject to hostile bids (English China Clays' bid for Bryant in late 1986). With the growing interest of construction firms in housebuilding, some conglomerates found it a good time to sell off their speculative housebuilding subsidiaries, a move doubtless encouraged by the changed British corporate tax regime in the mid-1980s. Insurance company Guardian Royal Exchange sold its Broseley housebuilding subsidiary to Trafalgar House late in 1986; Christian Salvesen disposed of all its housebuilding subsidiaries during the second half of 1986; and Hawker Siddeley sold its Comben subsidiary in 1984. Previously all three had been among the country's top ten major housebuilders. In all cases, the prime reason given by the purchasing firms for buying them was acquisition of substantial land-banks.

Civil engineering: motorways and other public works

Civil engineering grew rapidly during the 1950s and 1960s. Motorways were particularly important. However the motorway programme and other public work as a whole slowed down considerably at the end of the 1960s. This led to attempts by virtually all the firms concerned to diversify. Acquisitions by firms who had major interests in the sector were greater than for the rest of construction, and there were important differences in the response of large and medium-sized firms.

For a number of companies, the problem was compounded by a regional shift in new motorway contracts towards the South of England. The amount of motorway and trunk roadwork in Scotland and N. England fell sharply from 1970. The two largest Scottish civil engineering firms – Carmichael and Duncan Logan – both went into liquidation in 1970. Others, like Fairclough, attempted to win more work in the South. Fairclough did this by forming consortia (with Amey on the M40 and Cementation on the M5), and by the acquisition of C. V. Buchan in 1970, the Fram Group in 1972, Lindsay Parkinson in 1974 and Robert Watson (Constructional Engineers) in 1978. Norwest Holst, another civil engineer in a similar predicament, also diversified through acquisition, particularly by moving south (e.g. Marshall-Andrew of London in 1979) and into open-cast coal mining (e.g. via MacGregor, bought in 1978). By this approach, Norwest Holst managed almost to treble its turnover in six years (1973–9).

Some of the bigger civil engineers are divisions of the very largest contractors (e.g. Wimpey, Costain and Laing). Consequently they were not forced to diversify through acquisition, resources instead being switched out of those divisions into other areas. Laing, for example, was involved only marginally in takeover activity during the 1970s. It nevertheless was reported at the beginning of the decade to be 'determined to become one of the most diversified companies in the construction industry' (*Construction News*, 7 October 1971). New regional operations were set up and expanding markets, like property development and North Sea oil platforms, were entered. Expansion into platform fabrication proved short-lived, whilst the property division was hived off as an independent company in 1979. A poor profits' record in the early 1980s led to further disposals, including the ending of a twenty-five-year link with the blockmaking industry in 1983 with the sale of its Thermalite subsidiary in, at the time, the second-largest ever UK management buyout. So, from having pursued a strategy of diversification in the early 1970s, by 1983 Laing was again principally a building contractor and speculative housebuilder. A change in management strategy was announced in 1985, however, and Laing was back on the diversification trail (*Financial Times*, 21 August 1985).

Virtually all of the rest of the major roadbuilders were involved in acquisition activity during the 1970s: French and Kier merged in 1973 (subsequent financial problems led to the new firm withdrawing from UK road work); Dowsett was acquired by Concrete (1976), Parkinson by Fairclough (1974), Fitzpatrick by Tarmac (1971) and

Cementation by Trafalgar House (1970); South African mining company Charter Consolidated purchased Shand, whilst Davy International bought a substantial (approximately 30 per cent) shareholding in Monk in 1978 and purchased the firm outright in 1986; the largest change occurred when Fairclough merged with William Press in 1982. Another civil engineer, Balfour Beatty, had been taken over by cable-makers BICC earlier in 1969.

Of the largest independent civil engineers, only the McAlpine family firms and Mowlem have remained intact. Mowlem's response was almost a casebook example of the reaction by building contractors to workload declines in traditional activities. Buoyant profits (despite lower real turnover) in the early 1970s were used to expand in the UK and overseas. The civil engineering interests of Ernest Ireland were bought from that firm's receivers in 1975. Mowlem actively purchased companies overseas whose activities were progressively more remote from construction: in 1980, for example, US-based Soiltest was acquired to enhance Mowlem's position as a major supplier of test equipment to world construction markets; later in 1983 Buehler, a specialist instrument-maker, was added to its technology division whose links with construction were increasingly tenuous. The result of the diversifications was that the company did not have to 'buy' construction work in the UK at loss-making margins. Its position of market-power in relation to UK work consequently was not threatened, so the growing margins-differential for work undertaken in the UK, described in Chapter 8, could be taken advantage of. In 1982 profits were at an all-time high. Mowlem since then has consistently kept up its diversification strategies – becoming, for instance, involved in constructing and managing a new airport in East London, and acquiring scaffolding-specialists SGB and housebuilders Alfred Booth.

Medium-sized civil engineering firms have been particularly active in the takeover field, as each sought new outlets as a means of recovering from the long-term decline in their staple workloads. Takeover offered the only rapid solution since they often had no internal base from which to diversify. Failure to diversify could mean bankruptcy, so that the incentive to acquire is great. A variety of acquisition strategies were adopted. Some acquired the assets of others that went into liquidation (e.g. Mears Brothers was bought by Edmund Nuttall in March 1979 and Bacal Civil Engineering was purchased by Galliford Brindley in 1975). Others acquired going concerns between 1975 and 1979 (e.g. W. and J. Glossop, F. J. C. Lilley and Rush and Tompkins). Some firms used takeovers to diversify outside construction. Two of the most striking examples of this last strategy are the acquisitions by the small firms J. B. Holdings and Brown and Jackson. The former, a small civil engineers based at Redhill, Surrey, acquired a US firm in 1978 which manufactured and assembled road-cleaning equipment. Brown and Jackson, a rapidly-growing company from Fleetwood in Lancashire, were solely civil engineers originally. However, acquisitions transformed them into a conglomerate. Knitwear products were entered via an acquisition in 1975, and takeovers in 1979 took them into systems building, footwear and car retailing. In a similar move out of civil engineering, Charles Hill of Bristol, late in 1982 sold its construction and civil engineering subsidiaries, B. B. Kirk and Kirk Developments, in a management buyout for only half the price it had paid for them in 1973.

An indication of the outcome of these changes in civil engineering is given by comparing the top road contractors in the late 1960s with those in the early 1980s. The Department of Transport periodically publishes data on major road contracts let, Table 10.2 shows that for 1968–70. More recent data for the 1980s indicate reinforcement of the role of the major firms although a number of earlier ones have disappeared through merger or bankruptcy. Laing and Tarmac between them had over 30 per cent of the work listed for 1980–2. Fairclough and McAlpine had another 26 per cent between them. Regional breakdowns show big shares for other firms. Balfour Beatty, for example, won 30 per cent of the work listed for Scotland. The large market shares of so few firms might surprise those used to the image of a fragmented perfectly-competitive construction industry, yet they help to explain why main contractors can exert such power over their input costs.

Table 10.2 *Top 12 firms in all trunk road and motorway contracts let in 3 years to 31.12.70 (Ministry of Transport Data)*

1. W. and C. French	£47.3m		7. Lindsay Parkinson	£21.6m
2. Sir A. McAlpine/Leonard			8. Wimpey/J. L. Kier	£21.2m
Fairclough	£43.1m		9. Christiani-Shand	£17.2m
3. A. Monk	£30.3m		10. A. E. Farr (Bovis)	£13.8m
4. R. Costain	£29.7m		11. Tarmac	£13.1m
5. J. Laing	£24.9m		12. Fitzpatrick	
6. Dowsett	£22.2m		(Limmer Holdings)	£10.8m

Also, individually: Sir Alfred McAlpine £21.3m,
Leonard Fairclough £2.3m

consortia: Fairclough/Amey Construction £2.0m;
Fairclough/Cementation £10.0m;
Costain/Sydney Green £5.5m (English China Clays).

Source: Construction News, 8 February 1971

Diversifying into overseas markets

Mergers have played only a small part in the move into overseas construction markets for most firms. The ability to form joint ventures with other UK or local firms is the most likely explanation for their relatively minor role. Firms could, in effect, temporarily merge their resources for a few well-defined projects by the use of consortia, instead of the permanent merging of all their interests implied by a takeover. This indicates, once again, that acquisition is only one of a series of options open when considering diversification, even into markets where entry presents difficulties.

There were none the less some notable acquisitions whose purpose was to move into overseas markets. Fairclough's purchase of Sir Lindsay Parkinson in 1974 was undertaken partly to effect entry into overseas markets. Similarly, the group's purchase of Robert Watson in 1978, a firm of constructional engineers specialising in structural steelwork, was undertaken to expand workloads in Africa and the Middle East. Richard Costain paid £8 million for Kwikform (September 1977), a firm of scaffolding manufacturers, to take advantage of the fact that nearly 50 per cent of the latter's business was overseas and could be rapidly expanded to coincide with those markets in which Costain already had substantial contracts. Not all such acquisitions have proved successful, however. Tarmac, for example, had to make provisions totalling £16 million in their 1978 accounts to cover losses incurred by their Nigerian subsidiary acquired in 1976 when Holland, Hallen and Cubitts was purchased from Drake and Scull.

The downturn in overseas markets, at least for UK firms, in 1978–9 led to the reverse effect, of mergers being used to move out of overseas markets. Bath and Portland, who had a road contract in Iran contributing over 30 per cent of their total revenue, were severely affected by the struggles following the Shah's overthrow. To avoid subsequent financial collapse they were forced to find a partner. Arrangements were made in 1979 with Anglo-American Corporation, a multinational with South African mining interests, whereby the latter could by 1981 purchase 21 per cent of their equity as well as guaranteeing financial help in the form of a £3 million bank loan through a South African construction subsidiary. It was intended that Bath and Portland should embark upon a policy of joint ventures with this subsidiary and also diversify and expand its non-construction activities. Later, the firm was to end up in the Beazer fold. Another medium-sized contractor, Streeters of Godalming, also suffered substantial losses in the Middle East. Their response was to become an associate of Costain. Again, the aim here was for the two companies to tender jointly for work in excess of £5 million (for example in London's Docklands).

The larger firms heavily involved overseas have similarly been active in looking for new outlets through sectoral and geographical diversification. Costain used part of their huge cash resources to negotiate the deal with Streeters. In July 1979 they also acquired an Oklahoma-based company, costing over £2 million, with a view to diversifying into gas process engineering in the USA. Then, in October 1979, they bid for Whessoe, a process engineering firm based in North-East England. This bid backfired (and lost Costain £3 million in share dealing) when Whessoe were sued for over £10 million for damages arising from a contract undertaken, ironically, in the Middle East in 1975 – precisely the area from which Costain was trying to diversify.

Other large firms, such as George Wimpey and Taylor Woodrow, by the late 1970s adopted joint ventures or acquired foreign companies to try to break out of stagnant overseas sales – particularly by making acquisitions in North America. Wimpey announced expansion of their North American activities and Taylor Woodrow reported a move into US open-cast mining (*Construction News*, 5 October 1978 and 13 April 1978). Later, Costain joined in the moves towards US mining, and by 1986 its total mining interests provided 44 per cent of all its activities' profits (*Financial Times*, 18 December 1986). British materials producers joined other European manufacturers in purchasing large numbers of US companies in aggregates, cement and brick- and block-making. Bovis in 1986 bought a 50 per cent interest in the sixth-largest US construction-management company, Lehrer McGovern, in order to increase its US presence and to win more work worldwide from US multinationals (*Financial Times*, 18 December 1986).

There has almost been a stampede by UK building firms into the USA. Barratt is now one of the largest housebuilders in California following the purchase of two West-Coast housebuilders, American National Housing Corp. and McKeon Construction, in 1980 and 1981 respectively. Initially Barratt experienced severe trading difficulties but did not suffer the misfortune of Comben, who had to withdraw quickly from an ill-fated move into the Texas housebuilding market.

Materials and aggregates in the USA have been a favourite area for acquisition. All the major UK ready-mixed-concrete firms moved into the USA in the late 1970s and early 1980s, including Ready Mixed Concrete, Amey Roadstone and Tilcon. The expanding sun-belt states have been the focus of activity. Tarmac embarked on a series of acquisitions in the south west states in 1980. 'Since they arrived and took us over, they have gone on to buy out companies which I wanted to acquire for a long time' stated one admiring new Tarmac employee in Florida (*Financial Times*, 8 March 1982). As with all construction-related activities, management with local knowledge and experience is essential; so Tarmac retained key local staff, learning from the bitter experience of acquisitions earlier in the 1970s in W. Germany, where it was blackballed by the local blacktop cartel and had to withdraw after substantial losses.

Specialist subcontractors have also been actively trying to increase their geographical spread within the same activity. Both the HAT Group, a major British building maintenance-and-repair group, and SGB, scaffolding, formwork and access equipment specialists, expanded rapidly in the UK through acquisition in the 1960s and early 1970s. The decline of the UK market led to overseas expansion by both of them.

> David Telling (chief executive of the HAT Group) is convinced he can build a national painting network in the US, using Slince (a recent acquisition) as a foundation stone. The American painting industry is highly fragmented. What the US seems to lack, as far as David Telling can see, is a group like HAT interested in buying a selection of medium sized building services companies. (*Financial Times*, 22 March 1983)

Both specialists have themselves since been taken over, as large construction-related firms move into areas of specialist subcontracting. Specialist work has become increasingly attractive to some large firms as a result of current trends in the industry, particularly the increased sophistication of some construction work, the strength of some sectors where specialists traditionally have had a comparative advantage, like office building and R&M, and because of the general growth of subcontracting in the industry.

Plant hire

As the plant-hire industry is a major repository of the fixed plant and equipment of the construction industry, a discussion of restructuring in construction must include it. Although plant-hire firms managed to survive most of the years of construction decline during the 1970s with considerable success, the early 1980s saw substantial over-capacity and tumbling hire-rates in real terms. One major firm, Richards and Wallington, collapsed in 1981, whilst the chairman of British Electric Traction, parent of three major plant-hirers (Eddison Plant,

Grayston and J. D. White) dramatically stated in 1982 that it looks 'as though a black hole had opened up and sucked away their profits'.

The industry is large, with an estimated turnover of £250 million to £300 million in 1978 (National Economic Development Office, 1978); three-quarters of its business is with the construction industry; and it accounts for more than half the total construction-plant investment in Britain.[1] The industry started after the Second World War with small proprietor-managed firms. It expanded rapidly during the 1960s and became centralised into a few large firms, often operating in specialist areas of the industry (e.g. cranes, earth-moving equipment, fork-lift trucks, scaffolding, etc.). In 1975 over half the turnover was handled by 5 per cent of the firms (i.e. 126 companies). There has been significant structural change in the industry since the mid-1960s and there is likely to be further centralisation in future years. The economics of the plant-hire industry obviously are different from those of general contracting.

The economic rationale for a large plant-hire industry rests with the problems of general contractors holding large stocks of plant and equipment. A better way for contractors to manage their plant-and-equipment needs is to purchase only equipment that is used virtually all the time or to buy specialist equipment only when it gives them a competitive edge. The rest of their equipment, given the existence of such a sophisticated hire industry as the British one, can be hired. As plant is rarely fully utilised, and specialist equipment is difficult to monopolise, the scope for plant hirers is great, especially as they can take advantage of taxation laws and financial packages in ways not open to individual contractors. By taking advantage of economies of scale and balancing off the temporal requirements of individual contractors for plant, plant hirers can thrive in an environment of sharply fluctuating individual-contractor plant needs. Major construction output downturns, however, create problems. Because hirers satisfy contractors' marginal plant needs, they are disproportionately hit by the reduced use of plant.

One implication is that construction-equipment investment cycles are more pronounced with a large hire industry than when contractors buy equipment for their own use, as contractors' replacement investments have to be more directly related to the physical life of the equipment and their own plant needs. When a re-equipment phase by hirers comes just prior to a dramatic slump in plant use, the plant-hire industry is left in severe difficulty. This is what happened in the early 1980s.

This brief description shows that the plant-hire industry is strongly affected by variations in construction output, but that the economic

187

effects of those variations are different from the effects on general contractors. Plant requires heavy investment in fixed assets, contracting does not. Plant hire firms, consequently, do not have the same flexibility of capital. Downturns in workloads may lead to crisis, lower margins, bankruptcy and a restructuring of financial ownership in an industry in which takeover plays an important part. Quite what happens depends on the specific historical circumstances, as a brief examination of the plant-hire industry since the 1960s shows.

During the 1960s most large construction companies had their own plant subsidiaries, mainly providing plant for companies within the group. Other plant-hire firms tended to be small and serviced the requirements of the smaller building firms. By the late-1960s, however, the situation was changing, with some independent plant-hire-only firms adopting an aggressive expansionist policy. The independents grew rapidly. Into this category fell what became in the 1970s the two largest plant-hire firms, Richards and Wallington, and Hewden-Stuart Plant. The latter resulted from the merger of two Scottish firms; the former, through its subsidiary British Crane Hire Corporation, grew rapidly to its leading position by means of a number of purchases of smaller companies during 1968 and 1969.

The 1960s were boom years for plant-hirers. H. Cox and Sons (Plant Hire), for example, operating in the South London area, expanded consistently from 1964 to 1968, achieved the highest return on net capital employed within the industry and went public in 1968. Yet, when construction slumped at the end of the 1960s, they had to report a fall in profits of 28 per cent in one year, 1970.

In such conditions of faltering demand at the end of the 1960s, acquisitions were adopted as a means of achieving two objectives. First, some companies sought to specialise in one particular section of the market. This policy was especially attractive to those hire firms dealing with heavy equipment, notably cranes, where the capital outlay required is high. Second, others sought to expand their share of a declining market by extending their geographical sphere of activities.

To illustrate the two trends, it is worthwhile considering further the activities of Richards and Wallington and Hewden-Stuart Plant (HSP). Based in central Scotland, HSP sought to extend its geographical range. In early 1970 they bought a Castleford-based firm, Stanley Davies Plant. This was followed by the acquisition of two more firms in 1971 – one of which had a Manchester depot whilst the other was intended to extend HSP's servicing of the motorway-building programme. Richards and Wallington had already made a series of important acquisitions in 1968–9 to extend its crane-hire activities. In 1971 it acquired the crane hire subsidiary of Thos

W. Ward and in 1972 bought a controlling interest in Cardiff Plant, a firm which had experienced rapid growth through acquisitions itself and operated in the South Wales area.

Poor market conditions during 1969–71 meant that some of the fastest expanding firms were caught in a liquidity crisis. Falling demand for plant hit worst those companies who had recently heavily invested in new plant. As a result they were, in some instances, cheap acquisitions for their competitors. Such was the case of Harvey Plant's takeover of Vanguard Plant in the latter part of 1971. Vanguard had recently acquired a public quotation, valuing the company at £1.2 million. When Harvey Plant stepped in to buy it, however, it was faced by an acute crisis of liquidity and was acquired for only £300,000.

Another effect of the problems of the early 1970s led to further pressures towards centralisation of the plant-hire industry by encouraging contractors to sell off hire subsidiaries and to hire more of their plant and equipment from outside agencies. Many contracting firms still continued to operate with poorly-organised plant-hire subsidiaries which, in declining trade conditions, became an increasing burden that could be overcome by selling plant and hiring it instead. Greene and Company's 1970 *Investment Report on Plant Hire* discussing these subsidiaries noted that, 'turnover rarely exceeds 2/3rds of gross book value of plant and is often lower. This is due to the reasons that business is geared too much to one customer, the customer is allowed to fix the price, high maintenance costs . . . etc.' In other words, large contractors had grossly under-utilised plant capacity and were usually the only client making use of it, and at a non-commercial price. In 1972, Greene and Company reiterated the view that many companies were still buying plant when it would be more economical to hire the plant as and when it was required. It argued that medium-sized contracting firms in particular seemed to have small, probably unprofitable, plant assets and plant-hire subsidiaries.

Certainly for Shellabear Price, at least, the old style of plant subsidiary was still the dominant practice. Reporting the group's results to shareholders during 1972, the Chairman was questioned and criticised for this policy (*Construction News*, 17 July 1971). On a more disastrous note, the failure of Mitchell Construction, a large Midland-based civil engineering contractor, was in part ascribed to its inability to use its plant adequately (*Construction News*, 22 February 1973).

The mid-1970s saw the large hire firms continuing to expand geographically and to specialise in particular markets. The process of centralisation, with fewer companies dominating the industry, was further encouraged by the economic problems of small and medium-sized hirers. For a number of years competition from very small hire operators had kept plant-hire rates at low levels. Such firms (often consisting of the proprietor only) have virtually no overheads and can, therefore, undercut larger firms, but they are very vulnerable to recessions, so many went bankrupt from the mid-1970s onwards.

Other effects of the long-term decline in new building work throughout the 1970s was that new plant was purchased less often, while much was sold off, especially overseas. Contractors, as well as plant-hire firms, sold idle plant so that capacity was reduced quite rapidly and shortages of some equipment subsequently arose.[2] The shake-out of plant consequently bolstered the margins of those firms remaining.

The process of rationalisation was further accelerated by the increasing technical sophistication of some types of plant. Only the large firms have the expertise, markets and finance to purchase such equipment. The importance of financial resources was also enhanced by the impact of inflation. Hirers' plant costs rose by an average of 180 per cent from 1973–9; new investment in plant was consequently beyond the internal resources of many companies. The result was that a trend developed of plant-hire firms being taken over by large holding companies who had the financial resources for re-equipment and who wanted the tax benefits to be derived from equipment leasing (e.g. SGB purchased Contractors Services in November 1974, and Lex Services acquired Harvey Plant in 1973 and L. Lipton in 1977). Another holding company, BET (British Electric Traction), itself a victim of the mid-1980s merger boom, owns three of the largest hire firms.

The restructuring of firms in earlier years described above, into larger individual units, frequently under the control of financially-strong tax-sensitive parent firms, paradoxically led to an upsurge in investment in the plant-hire industry throughout the 1970s. From 1971 to 1978 the volume of plant held by the plant-hire industry increased by 103 per cent, yet in the same period the volume of plant-hire output rose by only 12 per cent.

High interest rates and an acceleration of the slump in construction demand in 1980–1 forced the pace of rationalisation. A gross over-supply of plant for hire led to bankruptcies, amalgamations and the destruction of substantial amounts of equipment.

The two largest independents, Richards and Wallington and Hewden-Stuart, were badly hit. After a failed rescue attempt by its bankers, Richards and Wallington went into receivership in 1981, whereas Hewden-Stuart reported in 1981 that 'capacity utilisation is running at between 50–60%, rates have weakened materially . . .

cannibalisation of parts is now said to be rife and Hewden maintains that a rising element of the national hire fleet will never be operable again'.

Takeovers played their part in capacity reduction. The trend of general contractors divesting themselves of their plant-hire interests was continued in 1981 when Taylor Woodrow sold its Greenham Plant Hire subsidiary to Scotts Cranes in one of the largest-ever plant-hire acquisitions. One reason given for this merger was Scott's desire to expand without increasing the amount of equipment in the industry, which would have intensified competition.

Faced with over-capacity, firms tried to find new specialist markets, to set up permanent depots overseas (most of Western Europe has poorly developed plant-hire industries), or to diversify into new activities. Vibroplant, for example, acquired a video leisure firm in 1981. Its venture into video jukeboxes involved substantial investment with little payoff. The main tendency however has been for firms to try to gain a competitive advantage by having the most up-to-date and extensive equipment range. This was Scott's justification for the purchase of Greenham. The managing director of Grayston in 1981 predicted the demise of the medium-sized enterprise: 'the giants of the industry are likely to continue their domination, with possibly fewer but larger fleet holding depots' (*Construction News* Plant Hire Supplement, 22 October 1981). By the mid-1980s this prediction seemed accurate; the heavy end of the crane-hire market, for example, was reduced to only three firms with the acquisition of Sparrow by BET.

In the mid-1980s the prospects for plant hirers looked good. The earlier shake-outs had reduced capacity; the abolition of capital allowances discouraged contractors from buying their own plant; the growth of subcontracting encouraged more plant hire; and some major projects, particularly in the South East, made strong demand a good prospect.

Conclusion

The plant-hire industry exhibits some of the features of industrial restructuring generally attributable to manufacturing industry, especially centralisation and accumulation through investment in plant and equipment. But for construction as a whole, one of the principal areas where the coercive effect of economic crisis induces changes in methods of production – investment in new plant and equipment – has been effectively hived off into a separate industry. Firms in the main sectors of construction have been left with one

191

major worry; how to find new markets to replace those in decline. Diversification has been an important interest of management throughout the 1970s and 1980s. Takeovers, as has been seen, have been used as a major method of gaining access to new markets (including land markets with speculative housebuilders).

One feature that has come out strongly from this chapter is linked to the theme of earlier ones. The strong profits record of the major firms has weakened the coercive effect of crisis forcing them to change. Diversification has been a relatively casual affair; some financial disasters that have resulted have generally only dented firms' profits records temporarily rather than encouraged an industry-wide shake-out.

Another possible consequence of the takeovers and mergers of the past twenty years is an increased centralisation of construction capital and the increasing domination of specific markets by a shrinking number of firms. It is possible only to get hints of this process from the information presented in this chapter. A small number of firms, constituting long-term development capital, undoubtedly came to dominate speculative housebuilding during the 1970s, while the importance of a few large road builders also seems to have grown.

Finally, whilst it is difficult to argue that the changing pattern of ownership of construction capital has been a major determinant of broader social relations in the industry, it has played a part. Changes in the position of social agents in the construction industry was argued in Chapter 4 to be the product of a long-term historical dynamic. However the influential position of the building contractor in that development must have been aided by the changing pattern of firm ownership. Weaker enterprises or those that have tried to go against trends in contracting have either gone to the wall or been taken over during the long workload decline. Crisis in the construction industry does not blast firms into innovative restructuring; it leads instead to even greater attempts to take advantage of the imbalance of the social relations existing in the industry.

CHAPTER 11

A *new social balance in the construction industry?*

One of the principal themes of this book is that the British construction industry contains a variety of social relations associated with the process of building. The most important are those embodied in the Contracting System – the specific but ambiguous roles for architects and other design professionals, surveyors, building contractors, and for organised labour. This chapter will try to assess whether the Contracting System has survived the past decade of traumatic change in the construction industry unscathed. Although by its nature the discussion must be tentative, there is good evidence that the larger building firms have been able to take advantage of their superior economic position and their ability to ride the crisis to improve their position in relation to building workers and professionals. In part, the Contracting System has actually crumbled, though there is still a lot of life in the industry's traditional social relations, and future developments are unclear. What is certain, however, is that in a number of key respects building firms face severe problems.

To focus the argument, this chapter will look at the position of the large building firm in relation to the other social agents in construction to see what advantages they have gained from the changes. Before examining those relations in detail, however, it is useful to recap and expand upon previous comments made about the development of the construction industry since 1945.

The three post-war phases

Post-war developments in the construction industry can be divided into three periods. The first is the early post-war years of reconstruction and consolidation of the dominant relationships between agents in the construction process, lasting from 1945 up to 1953–4; second are the 'golden years' of rapid eexpansion and full employment, from the mid-1950s through to the early 1970s; and, finally, come the years of retrenchment and restructuring up to the present day.

RECONSTRUCTION AND CONSOLIDATION

During the late 1940s and early 1950s, contracting in the form that was to dominate the subsequent years of boom was reconstructed out of the pre-war forms of industrial organisation, but with some key changes, some of them created out of war-time conditions.

These years were ones of almost total dominance of contracting, as all forms of speculative building were severely curtailed by state building controls. The state's role as a client for the industry had grown rapidly during rearmament in the late 1930s, and most construction work during the war was undertaken for it. Although the share of the public sector in total demand inevitably fell after the war, it was still predominant – especially because of reconstruction and the public housing drive (Smyth, 1985; Merrett, 1979). Contracting under the direction of the state helped to consolidate the post-war social relations of the industry, with architects (often as public-sector employees) playing a major management, as well as a design, role (Bowley, 1966; Saint, 1983).

Much of the post-war contracting system was a carry-over from the pre-war years, but two other crucial aspects, apart from the increased role of the state, had changed – the size and scope of the major contractors and the role of the unions. The major contracting firms had reached unprecedented sizes during the war, had introduced new working practices, and had been forced by labour shortages to develop a new relationship to their workforces based on retaining and rewarding a core skilled labour-force. Contractors' abilities to deploy rapidly a competent workforce had been crucial to their success during the war years, and was to remain so during the post-war years of acute labour shortage (Smyth, 1985). The large contractors could work in all spheres of construction, and so could develop a strategic attitude to different markets in ways which were to grow in importance over the next forty years. Big building firms were also used to dealing with, and taking maximum advantage of, their relations with the state, both in terms of work directly undertaken for the state and political lobbying. Lobbying took the form of pressures over contract forms, criticisms of the constraints of building controls, encouraging an ideological environment that ensured minimal state interference in the actual process of production, and demands to limit the power of organised labour.

For the trades unions the post-war years had greatly enhanced their position because of the chronic shortage of labour. Political support for the post-war Labour government, however, forced them to conform to the new pressures and rewards of contracting by abandoning their opposition to piece rates, as Chapter 4 noted. Corporatism, at least in a limited way, had come to the British construction industry.

THE GOLDEN YEARS

Rapid expansion of construction output during the years from the early 1950s to the early 1970s consolidated the position of the large building contractors in the industry. It also kept to a minimum any potential conflict between contractors and design professionals over their contradictory management tasks and responsibilities within the construction process. Clients could be forced to endure the consequences in the form of high costs, delay and poor quality, in a frequently overstretched construction market. It was during this period that Marion Bowley wrote her famous indictment of the negative effect of the design 'Establishment' on the construction industry (Bowley, 1966). Both builders and designers, in fact, could profit from the inefficient working of the construction process: contractors through contract claims procedures; and designers through their fixed percentage fees. They were, in effect, both rewarded for creating higher costs!

The major problem for contractors centred on their relations with their workforces. Along with many other industries, they managed to politicise their difficulties to their own advantage, gaining easy acceptance of the notion that workers' demands for higher wages and better conditions were the bane of the industry, particularly when those demands led to unofficial trade union action.

To combat attempts to raise wages, and worker resistance to reorganisations and speed-ups of the construction process, construction firms could use a variety of methods, many of which contained inherent contradictions for them. Pay could be tied to work rates through bonuses and overtime, with the construction process divided up into a series of separate tasks not requiring the full range of traditional craft skills. Such Taylorist strategies, however, met general trade union resistance, so that only a relatively small proportion of workers were on genuine bonus schemes by the end of the 1960s; while the strategy also exacerbated site-level disputes centring on disagreement over what constituted a reasonable speed for each task and the appropriate rate for it (see Chapter 4, especially the well-documented case of the Barbican dispute discussed there).

One method of trying to circumvent such difficulties was, of course, greater use of subcontracting. Subcontracting either pushed the labour relations problem on to another firm or removed the role of trades unions altogether, for example by employing workers on labour-only self-employment. Such a strategy was increasingly used during these years, as Chapter 4 noted; however in the context of acute labour shortage, frequently prevalent at the time, the strategy had clear limits and problems.

First, firms could gain a competitive edge by being able to mobilise a 'core' workforce, as they had in the first post-war reconstruction phase. And the core had to be quite large when a firm straddled a wide variety of sectors and order books were variable but generally full. Greater use of subcontracting weakened the ability to maintain a sufficient core workforce. Semi-permanent relationships with subcontractors may have been possible, but were unlikely to be so extensive or secure.

The other major problem was that subcontracting transformed rather than removed the labour difficulties faced by contractors. Subcontractors, rather than the main contractor, would negotiate with shop stewards and other union officials. Main contractors, therefore, lost control over site labour relations. The behaviour of just one maverick subcontractor could endanger a whole carefully-constructed edifice of procedures and attitudes built up on a site. The difficulties on large construction sites, for instance, arising from such a fragmentation of industrial relations seems to have grown over these years and increased further in the mid-1970s, according to evidence presented by NEDO's Building and Civil Engineering Economic Development Committees (National Economic Development Office, 1970 and 1976a).

RETRENCHMENT AND RESTRUCTURING

The long fall in workloads from the early 1970s heralded significant changes in the relative position of the social agents in the construction process. Yet it would be wrong to suggest that it has simply been the workload-decline that has induced change. A wide variety of other factors are important, many of which have been alluded to in early chapters. Changes in techniques and types of work are two examples. It is unlikely that the situation in the early 1970s could have been sustained, whatever the level of demand. The relations between the different social agents were already in a state of flux. The inability of anyone to exert sustainable forms of control over the production process was creating escalating building costs, declining productivity and extensive project delays. Fragmentation, self-interest and minimal liability for the costs of inefficiency were producing increasingly adverse consequences. What the collapse in workloads did, in conjunction with a right-wing political climate, was to shift the balance of power firmly in the direction of the contractor. As Chapter 8 showed, large building firms survived the slump in workloads relatively unscathed, which cannot be said for either design professionals or building workers. Given their economic and political advantages during the years of crisis, any change that did occur was likely to favour the interests of the major building firms. What the following sections will do is to run through key aspects of the shifting social terrain facing the large builders and contractors.

The state

The contours of political debate over the building industry have changed considerably since the early 1970s. Then emphasis was on the relations of building firms to the state as client, and on labour problems. However, since the mid-1970s, falling public-sector demand has reduced the importance of the ways in which public-sector work is allocated, and debates over forms of public-sector contract and steady allocations of work have slowly evaporated. Reduced trade-union militancy, widespread acceptance of self-employment, and general Tory labour legislation resolved, as far as employers were concerned, many of the industry's labour problems. Active public-sector building was also curtailed. In particular, competitive threats from local-authority Direct Labour Organisations (DLOs) were weakened by the rundown of council housing, Tory legislation which forced DLOs to operate financially more like private contractors, and by a continued drift of DLOs towards adopting the organisational and employment practices of the private sector. Some local authorities still opposed contemporary trends in employment practices through stipulations written into contracts, but even this irritant was to be legislated against at the time of writing. Many political issues of the 1970s, in other words, had been resolved by the mid-1980s in the construction-employers' favour.

Nationally, building firms in the 1980s have had three successive Conservative governments whose broad political stance they support, either through their employers' organisations or directly through political donations and active participation. Building companies are substantial financial supporters of the Conservative Party, and prominent Conservative political figures have past or current ownership links with construction firms (e.g. ministers and ex-ministers such as Keith Joseph and Cecil Parkinson, and McAlpine, the Party Treasurer for much of the 1980s). It cannot be said that builders have had the perfect political climate, however, as construction has suffered from public expenditure cuts, from a reluctance of government to fund major new training programmes, and from restrictions on housebuilding land in attractive Tory-voter heartlands especially in the South East.

Construction firms' political image in recent years has been greatly enhanced by the demand made by many non-Thatcherite politicians to lower Britain's high levels of unemployment through rapid expansion of construction demand. Although some commentators are aware of capacity constraints within the industry, limiting its ability to expand, none are critical of the current organisational structure of the industry. By implication, construction firms are in an enviable political position. Members of all the major political parties are pushing their case, not because they support construction capital in particular, but because they either want more jobs or more products from the industry. In the late 1970s, building firms were particularly hostile to the Labour Party because of (exaggerated) fears of building nationalisation (Economist Intelligence Unit, 1978), and because of Labour's traditional support for local-authority direct labour. By the mid-1980s, Labour's leading politicians in a variety of ways were offering building firms considerable encouragement. Labour's housing spokesperson late in 1986 even publicly argued the housebuilders' case for large-scale green-field-site land release (*Guardian*, 13 December 1986).

Construction workers

An important shift of power within the construction industry over the past decade and a half must undoubtedly be the greatly weakened position of the labour force. Unemployment and the growing drift towards subcontracting have severely restricted the ability of construction workers to improve their wages and conditions, to resist management encroachments on traditional working practices, or to influence the restructuring of the labour process.

Mapping out the detailed contours of workers' loss of power is virtually impossible, given the variety of ways in which individual workers can impose their will within the production process, either through collective action with others or through their own attitudes and work practices.

It is also mistaken to see industrial relations simply in the stark terms of immediate confrontation. A decline of strike activity, for example, could arise from a change of tactics as well as from less ability to effect change in the industry. To an extent, a redrawing of the ways in which workers influence industrial development is precisely what has happened in construction. Industrial conflict and worker resistance to management direction have become more fragmented and individualised than before, and far less based on strike action – though by no means less disruptive as a result.

It would be wrong anyway to see workers as necessarily adopting a confrontational attitude to management. Such a stance requires an ideology to sustain it and a particular understanding of the nature of the employer/employee relation, neither of which many workers have. Workers also have a strong material incentive to support the success of the firms they work for, because they might end up with higher bonuses, more regular employment and greater job satisfaction – though none of them are, of course, guaranteed. Construction is an industry, however, where such basic homilies of the industrial-relations literature frequently do not operate. There is little evidence that construction firms in general have tried to mobilise their work-forces by winning their support for company objectives. Firms, in attempts to increase the flexibility of their capital, have created a greater distance between management and workforce. Subcontracting, for example, at best gives workers an incentive to improve the performance of the actual enterprise for which they work, not that of the firm that hires a subcontractor. And the enterprises for whom they work might only consist of themselves. Because of its social structure, construction has always been an industry in which there is an ever-present threat of conflict (Higgin and Jessop, 1973), and the changes of the last decade have in no sense reduced that threat, only transformed the ways in which conflict becomes manifest.

During years of mass unemployment, construction firms have had little incentive to adopt innovations in industrial-relations techniques. Years of labour shortage have been replaced by excess supply, though tight labour markets in Southern England were reappearing for some trades in the mid-1980s. Retaining a core labour force was no longer essential once unemployment in construction became endemic. Gener-ally, labour was readily available, and once subcontracting was wide-spread it could always be acquired at short notice, though sometimes only at a premium price. Divesting themselves of a directly-employed core of workers also fitted in with contractors' desires to increase the flexibility of their capital.

Changes in construction firms' employment practices have had consequences for the ways in which firms can arrange their industrial-relations strategies. A reduced role for direct employment and, there-fore, direct management supervision, combined with the industry's industrial relations has meant that firms now have to rely more on trade unions to discipline their members to stick to agreements or on the rigours of a legally-enforceable subcontract.

In Chapter 4 three levels of action open to construction workers were highlighted: at national and regional level, through 'official' trade union activity; local site-level responses, of an official or generally unofficial kind; and, finally, within the confines of a worker's direct work group. Each level has a different space for action and distinct methods that can be put into practice – reactions that themselves depend on the type of employment contract in operation.

One sphere of action that has declined dramatically in the 1980s is the strike. The last national strike in the construction industry was in 1972, though there have since been calls for 'days of action', particularly in support of the coal miners in 1984. Most strikes in the 1960s and early 1970s, as Chapter 4 showed, were site-based and only made official if success was not immediate and if the conflict conformed to the national or regional policies of the union in question.

Table 11.1 shows the fall in construction disputes since the mid-1970s. The data include public-sector building workers, who were involved along with other public-sector workers in major wages struggles in the late 1970s. Similarly, the upsurge in strikes in 1984 arises from action in support of the miners. Once these two factors are taken into account, there is precious little strike activity left in the 1980s. The 1985 figure, for instance, represents only three short-lived local actions (*Department of Employment Gazette*, August, 1986).

Table 11.1 *Industrial disputes in construction, 1976–85 (days lost)*

	Index number (1976=100)	
	Construction	All industries and services
1976	100	100
1977	52	309
1978	73	286
1979	146	898
1980	49	364
1981	15	130
1982	9	162
1983	12	114
1984	59	826
1985	9	195

Actual days lost in 1976: construction, 570; all industries and services, 3,284.
Index calculated from *Department of Employment Gazette*, August, 1986 data.

Trade unions, and particularly their shop stewards, have lost considerable power since the mid-1970s. Memberships have fallen substantially because of unemployment, subcontracting and the decline of the unions' stronghold, local-authority direct labour. The weakness of the unions is highlighted by the continual rumours of another round of mergers of construction unions, especially the long-awaited drawing of UCATT into the TGWU fold. Many private-sector sites are now unlikely to have any direct trade-union represen-tation on them at all, though there are no data available to verify this belief. The extent of subcontracting, however, is now enormous, and its widespread use is often synonymous with no unions. A Building Employers Confederation-sponsored survey of construction sites in Britain and the USA found that 'specialist trade contractors' did about 90 per cent of the site work in Britain (a similar percentage was reported for the USA) (Building Employers Confederation, 1986a).

Although trades unions have been considerably weakened, they have in no sense disappeared from the industrial relations scene. Their current position, to an extent, reflects losses inflicted on workers during a downturn in the construction cycle which might be regained during another phase of labour shortage, a pattern repeated many times in the past.

In certain sectors of the industry, the position of the official trades union machinery has actually been enhanced. A classic 'corporatist' model can be seen, for example, in engineering construction – an area of considerable industrial strife during the 1970s. In 1981 a National Agreement for the Engineering Construction Industry was reached between the construction unions and employers, leading to a fall in local disputes and less project delays. Committees consisting of management and union officials now adjudicate over any area of conflict, utilising the contents of the National Agreement. Within its framework, national and area union officials have gained power, while the independent authority of local shop stewards has been undermined. As one manager stated, 'Increasingly, they [union officials] think of it as their agreement as much as ours. Whereas under the old systems they thought it their duty to try to get round agreements they now police it more stringently than we do' (quoted in the *Financial Times*, Engineering Construction Survey, 7 May 1985). Here the ambiguous role of trades unions is once again high-lighted, though it is unlikely that workers were chafing against such union-imposed constraints, as Price (1980) suggested their earlier brethren did. By 1986, however, there were signs of growing resent-ment at the lack of benefit received by the workforce from the Engin-eering Construction Agreement. In their submission for the 1987 pay claim, the unions suggested that 'all full-time officials of trades unions have experienced increased militancy and increased demands from shop stewards and from branches. . . . Without a balanced settlement

. . . they may no longer be able effectively to impose the disciplines which are necessary to the agreement' (quoted in *Contract Journal*, 23 October 1986). Though flavoured by the exigencies of negotiating rhetoric, the fear does indicate the difficulties of maintaining agreements imposed at times of mass unemployment.

One major revolution in union policies in the mid-1980s could have significant repercussions for contractors in the future – unions have started to recruit members from the ranks of the self-employed and to negotiate on their behalf. Given their long-standing opposition to labour-only subcontracting such moves are extremely difficult for unions to make, but in the long run they are inevitable unless unions are prepared to see their industrial role further whittled away.

A position of representing self-employed members, moreover, is not necessarily in contradiction with opposition to its existence. To accept that there is an inevitable contradiction between, say, the Lump and union membership is to argue that opposition to any situation not liked by a union is impossible when that union agrees to work within its confines. Such a position would mean that opposition to casual employment in the industry, or to particular aspects of contemporary employment legislation, or even to the private sector itself when unions demand nationalisation, would all be equally impossible. Surely, the manner in which union opposition is implemented – through boycotts, reluctant acceptance with attempts to ameliorate the worst aspects of the situation, or whatever – must be a tactical question. For the trades unions in the mid-1980s, total boycott of workers on the Lump must be bad tactics; limiting the use of Lump labour, on the other hand, may not be.

Obvious things that unions can do for self-employed workers are to improve their rates of pay, working conditions, health and safety, and to protect them from the worst of the (illegal) abuses to which they may be subjected. Earlier it was argued that employers like self-employment because it enables them to offer differential rates of pay, depending on how urgently they require the task to be done. At times of high demand, unions may be able to reduce that benefit by negotiating the higher rates for all their self-employed members in the locality. Through such means, unions could even undermine the overall attractiveness of self-employment to employers.

Unions in other countries, such as Australia where construction union membership is much higher, have adopted such tactics with regard to self-employment – limit it, but unionise it. In Britain, at the time of writing, similar developments seem to be underway. Both the two major construction unions, TGWU and UCATT, were negotiating with labour-only bricklaying subcontractors. The catalyst was an initiative to set up a Federation of Brickwork Contractors by a group of labour-only subcontractors in the South East (*Contract Journal*, 23 October 1986).

One of the reasons for union initiatives over self-employed brick-layers was the high demand at the time for skilled workers in certain parts of the country, especially the South East. Building Employers Confederation state-of-trade enquiries showed a tightening of skilled labour markets after 1982, particularly for bricklayers and carpenters. Only 60 per cent of respondents said these trades were readily avail-able by June 1986, although this figure was far higher than the last severe shortage in June 1979, when less than 10 per cent of respon-dents said such labour was readily available (*National Builder*, September, 1986).

A similar shortage of labourers was not reported in the 1980s, although in previous cycles the availability of labourers had closely followed that of the skilled trades. Such a disparity indicates that construction labouring is still a haven for the young and the unskilled in general, but that mass unemployment does not necessarily affect skills shortages. By the mid-1980s the industry's training crisis was beginning to hit firms' abilities to hire the workers they want, whether directly or from the self-employed.

One factor ameliorating employers' shortages of skilled labour – and unions' abilities to take advantage of them – was the growing disparity between the demand for labour in the North and South of Britain. Building Employers Confederation surveys showed that labour shortages were particularly marked in the South. The June 1986 state-of-trade survey, for example, showed that less than 40 per cent of respondents in the South found bricklayers 'readily available', whereas in the North almost 70 per cent did (*National Builder*, September, 1986). Construction workers from the North have trav-elled South, either temporarily or permanently, to find work. In doing so they have lowered pressure in Southern markets for key trades. In this way the growing North/South divide has benefited building employers. For the construction industry, Marx's reserve army of labour now lives north of the Watford Gap.

Labour shortages or not, directly-employed, supply-and-fix or labour-only workers still have power at the level of the work group. Even without recourse to strikes, workers can still respond to manage-ment instructions they do not like. In particular, they can be bloody-minded and not do quite what is expected of them. Such tacit oppo-sition can take many forms; poor-quality work, a slower pace which means that tasks are not completed exactly on schedule, or incorrect execution of a task so that it has to be redone or the fault covered up are just a few options open to a disillusioned worker. The possibility of using one of them is greatly enhanced, with less chance of recrimination, if the whole of a work group does it. Subcontractors and the self-employed have other sanctions as well. They can turn up late or walk off the site before completing a task, causing massive disruption with little probability of legal redress being sought.

The power of the work group, in fact, may have been enhanced with widespread subcontracting in situations of excess demand. There are no unions or shop stewards to put the case of the wider interests of the whole workforce above the immediate grievances of the work group, or to question the disruptiveness of the group's tactics. Building firms then have truly lost control of industrial relations, a point which a number of them implicitly admit in their interviews in the construction press. Widespread subcontracting in no sense removes the possibility of conflict between ultimate employer and workers, even if the terms of the conflicts and the ways in which they are played out have changed.

Architects

Of the design professionals, architects have had the most influential role in the building process. Examining their changed position, particularly in relation to building contractors, is therefore likely to be indicative of the current roles of other design professionals as well. Here the key question is not so much whether architects still design and give technical advice within their remit. The answer to that is simple: they do. The most important issue is the extent to which architects' design capabilities enable them to influence the sequence and direction of the construction process. Do they, in other words, still play the central, if ambivalent, management role they did in the heyday of the traditional contracting system? The answer to that question appears tentatively to be that their management role has been considerably weakened, because construction firms have been able to draw more of that function under their control. The rest of this section will bring together the evidence pointing to this conclusion.

The extent to which architects managed to bring construction work under their management control in the years of the long post-war building boom is almost without precedent. The type of organisational structure of the construction process described under 'main contracting' in Figure 5.1 was almost universal by the mid-1960s in projects requiring any significant architectual input. Within this structure the architect represented the client, as an overseer of the construction process, as well as being the designer (see Chapters

4 and 5, and Bowley (1966)). Civil engineering work and modern speculative housebuilding require little or no architectural input; even so, between 1964 and 1969 private architects managed on average to supervise 40 per cent of all new construction work (Monopolies and Mergers Commission, 1977). Added to this figure must be the work supervised by public-sector architects, especially the mega-public-housing projects of the era. Thus precious little contract building at the time could have fallen outside the architect's managerial remit.

Saint (1983) describes the British architectual profession in those years. One of its prime, and worrying, characteristics was the inefficiency of the average architectual practice. Despite architects' managerial roles within the construction process as a whole, their ability to run their own profession left much to be desired. A RIBA survey of 1962 found that most architectual firms were too small, and their management incompetent and unrealistic, faults it put down to the nature of architectural education and the failure to coordinate design and construction (Royal Institute of British Architects, 1962). Such findings did not augur well for the recipe of successful construction management under the direction of the professional architect. Criticisms of the failings of architectural practices and education are still being voiced in the 1980s. To see how far architecture has actually changed since RIBA's 1962 report, the *Architectural Journal* intended to undertake a similar survey of the profession during 1987, and the tone of the editorial announcing the survey was not an optimistic one (*Architectural Journal*, 7 January 1987).

The average architectural practice, however, was not necessarily the most significant within the construction process. In the post-war years a number of private-sector practices grew to pre-eminence, while the large local authorities built up extensive architectural departments with considerable autonomy from client departments such as housing. The scale of such architectural empires is indicated from RIBA membership-data for the 1960s. Roughly half its members worked in the public sector, and at least another quarter were employees in private offices; almost 80 per cent of RIBA members, therefore, were salaried, and clear management-hierarchies within architecture existed (Saint, 1983).

Marriott (1967) estimated that up to three-quarters of speculative office-building in London in the twenty years since the war had been designed by a mere ten architectural firms, who had achieved such success partially through their ability to manipulate restrictive planning regulations. The role of architects for the developer was clear. According to Marriot:

> What the developers wanted from their architects was a commercial service. They needed functional buildings designed to a certain price, usually the lowest possible, that the estimate should not be exceeded at the end of the day, and that the architect should organise the builders so that the development was finished at a specific date. (Marriott, 1967, p. 41)

Although many architects regarded such commercial work as sordid, Marriott's description shows that for those that undertook it, the management and advisory tasks of the architect went way beyond the sphere of design (aesthetic quality, in fact, was usually of minimal concern). Public-sector architects had similar architectural briefs, even if with more concern for contemporary design fashions. They had to organise builders to ensure that buildings were built properly, to estimate and on time. On all counts, both private- and public-sector architects failed miserably, and the situation seems to have deteriorated into the 1970s, if the catalogue of building disasters and cost- and time-overruns is any indicator (see Direct Labour Collective, 1978).

Some of the leading lights of the profession in the 1960s were concerned that the architects should retain and extend their control over the building process, albeit with greater cooperation amongst the participants in building. Two of the contributors to the debate were concerned that architects should develop genuine skills of comprehensive building management, adding, prophetically, 'that if they do not achieve this capability they will find themselves sooner than they expected on the fringes of decision-making rather than at the centre, acting as stylists for other people's products' (Esher and Davies, *RIBA Journal*, 75, October, 1968, p. 450, quoted in Saint (1983)). By the mid-1980s that prophesy had gained considerable credibility.

It would be unfair to suggest that architects were simply misguided or grandiose amateurs incapable of managing the complexities of the building process. The building world was changing, and architects' place within it made their status as 'coordinating supremos' increasingly tenuous. The growing complexity of building work and the expansion of subcontracting were both greatly increasing the fragmentation of the construction process. Architects had neither the means nor the will to impose the necessary organisational discipline on such trends. Building firms' whole rationale is based on organising, within a disciplined framework, the construction process. The rationale for the role of the architect is far more ambivalent, and virtually all architects would regard tasks associated with the organisation and disciplining of a workforce as unsavoury. Arts-and-crafts-style harmony in the construction process was far more to their liking, which, it was claimed, could be achieved with a little more under-standing on the part of all agents, under, of course, the guiding hand of the architect. The whole ideology of architecture made architects singularly unsuitable as tamers of the building jungle of late-twentieth-century Britain.

That ideology, however, enabled building contractors to take advantage of the ambivalent role of the (managing) architect. Lack of concern with discipline within the construction process on the part of architects made it easy for contractors to achieve architectural approval for short-cuts and cost- and time-overruns. Contractors, in fact, had a considerable incentive to take advantage of the ambiguities of architects' design and management roles.

Such a situation could not last. Alternative models already existed in Britain in the 'fee system' of management-contracting and from overseas, particularly new practices emerging in the USA. As late as 1985 a BEC-sponsored survey found that 'US sites are dealing with fewer drawings, fewer variation orders and less managerial involve-ment by the architect. This means that US sites are not so swamped with paperwork' (Building Employers Confederation, 1986a, quoted in the *Building Trades Journal*, 9 October 1986, p. 17).

The new forms of management contracting and fast-tracking that have become prevalent over the past decade in Britain have already been described in Chapter 5. What is of interest here is their impli-cations for the respective management roles of architect and contractor. All these new forms of contract topple the architect from the central management coordinating role of the traditional main contract. Construction firms now claim (and, it would seem, far more successfully implement) the brief Marriott's developers assigned to their architects in the 1960s – build to cost and on time. In addition, by being drawn into the construction process at the time of its concep-tion as is generally the case with the new forms of contract, contrac-tors have been able to circumscribe architects' room for manoeuvre in influencing the sequence of the construction process through imposing on it the imperatives of design. 'Buildability' – a contem-porary buzz-word in the industry – means in reality 'management power' to the contractor. In fast-tracking techniques, where the contractor starts construction before the architects have finished completing the drawings for subsequent stages, Esher and Davies' prophesy has come home to roost.

ARCHITECTS FIGHT BACK

Architects have been under strong pressure in the 1980s. Unemploy-ment in the profession has been high; architectural education has been severely criticised and several schools closed; RIBA's mandatory-fees system was abolished in 1982, following strong pressure from the Monopolies and Mergers Commission; RIBA itself has been in turmoil, with an unprecedented series of hotly-contested elections for its presidency; the government failed to appoint an architectual representative on a key committee to deal with 'cowboy' builders in 1986, a sign of how low the political status of architects had fallen; and public distaste for modern building design reached new heights, with a member of the Royal family giving vent to criticism of the aloof architect and renewing mass publicity. To cap it all, architects in Britain for the first time felt the threat of sustained competition from foreign architects, particularly from large American firms induced to set up offices in London to win some of the lucrative contracts generated by the financial-services revolution (*Architects Journal*, 7 July 1987). Style, on the other hand, had become very fashionable, so there was greater interest in architecture as 'art'.

Some architects were acutely aware that the profession would be in a much weaker economic position if it was forced back into the uncertain world of aesthetic design alone. One attempt to redress the situation was a proposal for an Alternative Method of Management (AMM). Under AMM, the main contractor was cut out of the building process altogether; the architect is the central design and management figure, delegating the details of construction management to a building manager who is his/her employee. AMM recognises the dominance of subcontracting in construction, as all work is undertaken by subcontractors, with architects rather than building firms getting the advantages of the minimal capital required to superintend building work through total use of subcontractors. The advantages of this form of building organisation are claimed to lie in the direct contact made possible between the designer and the producer, so that problems can be quickly sorted out as they arise without incurring additional claims and variation orders. An unnecessary layer of management and 'bureaucracy' is said to be cut out – this time the offending layer being the building contractor. One well-publicised scheme in central London was undertaken under the approach; it was generally successful but did not achieve any cost economies over the use of a contractor, as hoped for (*Building*, 2 November 1984).

As a method of building management, AMM has failed to catch on. In part, its lack of success can be put down to the weak position of the profession in relation to building contractors in the 1980s. But there is also a fundamental problem about design and production within the capitalist organisation of the building process, which all proposals to put the architect at the top of the building-management pyramid fail to address. There is a permanent tension between the relative freedoms available within the sphere of design and the imperatives of the construction process itself, which the independent architect with his/her bias towards design cannot satisfactorily resolve. Of course, there are many solutions to the contradiction, but to be successful the solution either has to take on board the current social relations in the industry, or be prepared and able to change them. On both counts, architecturally-inspired solutions fail.

Buildings can take many structural forms, be dressed in a variety of 'skins', consist of widely different materials, and within limits all of these elements can be changed as work progresses. Designers' technical skills and their ability to conceive of completed structures from a handful of drawings inevitably place them in a key role in the construction process. Being able to communicate those ideas to building workers directly, and in turn learn about the practicabilities of construction from workers, as embodied in the AMM and in most influential architectural ideologies from the mid-nineteenth century onwards, are obviously aids towards efficient and economical building. To implement such schemes, however, requires that all relations in the construction process are harmonious – and it has to be a harmony which fits in with architectural dominance. Even in currently-fashionable community architecture, where architects claim only to help ordinary folk realise their housing dreams, the architect is still treated as the expert on building and takes management responsibility for the whole building process. But, as previous chapters have shown, conflict rather than harmony characterises modern building, and no-one – apart from architects – unquestioningly accepts the role architects assign themselves.

One example of the practical consequences of architects' inability to outdo building contractors can be seen in the Alternative Method of Management. Emphasis for architects is on cooperation and communication, not on controlling a workforce and continually transforming the labour process, so the ability to keep costs at a level compatible with those achieved by management contractors is slight. Whether architects are the top dogs or not, the cold building world of the 1980s offers no space for those who dream of an organically-generated harmony shorn of the state power needed to bring it into effect.

One final postscript can be added to developments in the architectural profession in the mid-1980s. It concerns the changing role of the architect, as illustrated by the fortunes of two of its most fêted British practitioners. Norman Foster and Richard Rogers in 1986, along with another architect, were given the accolade of having a well-publicised exhibition of drawings at the Royal Academy in London. Treated as masters of style, their other roles in the construction process were forgotten. Foster was managing architect of reputedly the world's most expensive office block, the Hong Kong and Shanghai Bank building in Hong Kong. He was relieved of his management functions in 1985 as costs escalated, and a management contractor was appointed with the brief to 'cut all possible corners' to save money. Rogers, on the other hand, purchased in 1986 a site in central London with two colleagues with the aim of undertaking speculative development, a role made possible under RIBA's revised rules (*Building*, 19 December 1986). Loss of management prerogative might not necessarily lead wealthy British architects to have nothing left but style.

New clients, new aims

One development that has helped building firms consolidate their new-found strength in relation to workers and design professionals has been not only the shift away from public-sector work but also the type of private-sector client now involved. Public-sector work relied on criteria of fairness in selecting contractors and supported the managerial role of the design professionals, although the revolution in contract-management procedures, in turn, had begun to penetrate the public sector by the mid-1980s. In addition, much public-sector work actively encourages unionisation and discourages use of labour-only self-employment. Private-sector clients do not feel inhibited by such criteria of social fairness; they just want building work done in the most expeditious way. They consequently are hardly likely to hamper contractors in their attempts to reorganise construction.

Much new private-sector work is now also speculative. Speed is important, as are clearly-defined time-schedules and costs. Delays mean extra interest charges and loss of revenue. Most jobs are not prestige headquarters office-projects for fickle clients. Instead they involve fairly standardised, if still complex, office and other commercial projects. Each of these elements give contractors a competitive advantage over alternative forms of construction management, put architects at a disadvantage, and enable the benefits of specialist subcontracting to come to the fore.

Consequences of the new forms of building contract

The new forms of building contract, associated with the various types of management contracting, have facilitated and reflected the changes going on in the social relations of the building industry. Construction firms no longer bring a mass of directly-employed workers on to a site, but orchestrate a variety of subcontractors. The cost-control procedures necessary to bring order to such an organisation of the construction process, and enable contingency strategies should something go wrong, naturally lead to the arms-length management-consultancy form of management contracting. The weakened position of the architect also enables a management contractor to have clearly-defined responsibilities and obligations. Most importantly, from the building firm's point of view, their new role in the production process enables them to maintain their capital in a highly flexible form. All types of contracting, including those associated with the traditional contracting system, enable building firms to have only limited working capital tied up in projects, but the new forms of contracting mean that the minimum has been reduced considerably and that other incidental costs are avoided.

To summarise the shift in the role of the building contractor, it is perhaps best to see the change as one of contractors no longer being concerned with *production management*, which in its direct form is now often the prerogative of the subcontractor; instead, they are increasingly *project managers*. What this means is that now they only orchestrate the flow of activities on a site, and they organise their investments, market strategies and management teams with that in mind.

In Chapter 2 it was suggested that construction firms, more than most other capitalist enterprises, were merchant/producers, and later in Chapter 5 that the merchanting activities were detrimental to efficient and progressive methods of production. Today's major building firms in Britain have managed to emphasise the merchanting aspects of their activities even more strongly than in the past. What does this mean in practice though? One consequence is that there is limited investment in equipment and workers. It is replaced by large-scale speculative purchasing-and-selling activities (primarily in private housing) and, in contracting, the selling of management services which aim to tame the chaos of the building industry, a chaos arising from the social relations which building firms have been instrumental in creating. Could it now be true, at least for the building industry, that the tail is actually wagging the dog?

CHAPTER 12

Dilemmas in construction

In this final chapter it would seem ideal to follow a format which tries to draw up a balance-sheet of losses and gains arising from the transformation of the construction industry over the past twenty years. Unfortunately, such an approach is not practicable because whether a change implies a loss or a gain depends on whose perspective it is being considered from. What can be put in its place has to be more modest: an assessment of the potential flashpoints in the industry created by the changes, and commentary on the likely success of some of the current reforms suggested for the industry, especially large-scale reflation.

No detailed evaluation of policy options will be undertaken. Policy analysis requires too much contemporary detail, which dates rapidly and goes against the grain of a book that has tried to draw out longer-term trends from a mass of contemporary detail. I am also pessimistic and think that detailed policy-prescription in relation to the construction industry is futile at the moment. None of the key forces presently associated with construction seems genuinely interested in politically-induced change, and popular images of the industry are firmly grounded in beliefs in the hopelessness of the situation. The different images people have of the construction industry and its diverse parts have taken over from the reality of the industry. Within the diverse formulae of more money, state control, extra education and training, the power of market forces, and improved design, construction ends up as a political football conforming to everyone's varied beliefs about what needs to be done to the British economy and its workforce.

Has there been a revolution in construction productivity?

Table 1.4 (page 16) pointed out the substantial increase in construction productivity during the 1980s. The years of declining productivity in the 1970s seem to have been dramatically reversed. Although the apparent increases could be an artifact of the poor quality of statistics on the industry, earlier chapters have pointed out why such a productivity transformation might have occurred. Construction firms have been able to exert greater control over the construction process and in doing so have been able to increase productivity considerably. Such an argument has much to commend it. If contractor-induced productivity increases have actually taken place, they should start to trickle through to construction prices and completion times, and again there is evidence to suggest such trends. If the productivity improvement is sustained, the gains to the consumers of construction products could be considerable and the economy as a whole should benefit. Unfortunately, there are many aspects of the way in which construction firms have reorganised the building process which suggest that not all of the productivity gains are likely to be permanent.

A prime social change in construction over the past twenty years has been in project management. Although such statements are inevitably qualitative and so cannot accurately be specified, from the discussion in previous chapters it would appear that management has changed in a variety of interlinked ways.

First, building firms have extended their prerogatives against encroachments by organised labour and design professionals. However, neither shift has been achieved through a fundamental redrawing of the ways building workers or designers are brought into the construction process. Instead, contractors have gained by taking advantage of the weakened market position of the two groups to push outwards the boundary of their control.

Second, line management on a construction site is now further down the management hierarchy. This has not occurred through deliberate design but as a consequence of the switch away from directly-employed building labour to subcontracting. Contractors have been forced to adopt management techniques that put greater emphasis on coordinating and maintaining the flow of site activities, rather than relying on the rigours of direct supervision to get tasks done. Such a division of managerial labour has had beneficial effects on site productivity, as well as negative ones associated with the potential disruptiveness of an army of subcontractors.

Third, firms have taken longer-term strategic attitudes towards particular market-sectors. Associated with this, presumably, has been a more reasoned assessment of the scale of resources required for success in a sector, rather than a 'seat-of-the-pants', 'try-it-and-see' misallocation. Greater planning, both of site procedures and of company strategies, has been a necessary consequence of the accumulation techniques adopted by British construction firms.

Each aspect of the changes in construction management contains problems. The new space for management control has perhaps led to permanent changes, especially with regard to design professionals. But the situation is still in flux. The management ambiguities inherent in situations where the execution of design is distinct from production have not been negated. All that has happened is that architects have been forced back from a uniquely privileged position to a weaker situation long experienced by their US colleagues, amongst others (Saint, 1983). Conflicts of interest, confused or contradictory instructions, and plain bad design and building have not disappeared, as the catalogue of problems in the US and elsewhere testify.

On the labour side, a number of problems with the current situation were raised in Chapter 4. It is not true that unions, or even a strong shop-stewards movement, are necessarily bad things for employers. In trying to improve the position of their members, unions channel protest into circumscribed forms of action. A terrain is mapped out within which the two sides negotiate. Widespread subcontracting ruptures that terrain and replaces it with variable and uncharted territory. Here, workers still have grievances and adopt disruptive tactics; often their actions are against their own subcontract employer, but they have spillover effects on the whole building process. Obviously, the actions of the self-employed take different forms from those directly employed, but they still have an impact on production. As a result of the contractual relationship, management might not even perceive the disruptions as part of a capital/labour conflict. In such a terrain, productivity gains achieved are tenuous and easily reversed, particularly when labour markets tighten. Similarly, advances made by employers against organised labour might easily be lost if demand rises.

The forms taken by any new phases of worker militancy will not be reflex repeats of history. However, many of the productivity gains that have arisen from various types of work-speed-up could easily be threatened in the future. Whether their reversal is perceived as good or bad obviously depends on whose position is taken. An industry relying only on intensification of work to improve productivity can hardly be called socially beneficial, however, and it is unlikely to attract workers who can find more congenial employment elsewhere. In the long run, therefore, speed-ups could exacerbate the shortage of competent workers in the industry.

The state of demand has been a vital force in the transformations that have taken place, but construction demand is a fickle entity. Large contractors gained from the collapse of demand in the 1970s because they could squeeze their input costs. Their costs as a result fell faster than the prices at which they could sell their products, as Chapter 8 showed. In a sustained upturn, however, large builders could well feel the negative side of the relation. Dealing with large numbers of subcontractors, when pressed for time to complete work contractors could end up bidding against each other for an insufficient pool of resources. Then their input costs could rise much faster than their output prices, squeezing their profits. One consequence of the new organisation of production, therefore, could be a greater instability of construction input prices for any given variation in demand.

Pushing line management on to subcontractors has also helped to generate the much-publicised skills crisis in the industry. The catastrophic fall in apprenticeships has arisen because of the switch to subcontracting as well as because of the fall in workloads. It has reached such proportions that there are not enough skilled workers available to meet current levels of demand, let alone substantial increases in it. As the skills-shortage bites and there are insufficient new workers available to replace those who leave the industry, the bargaining position of building firms will progressively weaken. In addition, if skills-shortages worsen there will be a slow, but inevitable, decline in the speed and quality of work. One result will be a decline in productivity. The problem, of course, is not simply one for building firms. It is a disaster for workers who wish to enter the industry, and for consumers of building products who suffer higher input prices and quality deterioration.

Attempts are being made to confront the skills crisis. The government in early 1987, for instance, directed the Construction Industry Training Board (CITB) to find ways of training 4,000 extra people to meet the current skills-shortage in the industry. The extent of the skills-shortage, even at those contemporary levels of output, can be adduced from the fact that 4,000 represented over a fifth of the apprentices then undergoing training (*Financial Times*, 15 January 1987). Despite such optimistic governmental instructions, it is unclear at the time of writing how training is going to evolve in the industry, and what the level of competence achieved in the new schemes will be. British governments have been highly reluctant to adopt the state-sponsored full-time training schemes common in other Western European countries.

Construction firms have been exceedingly lucky in obtaining space to restructure their activities. Many, though not all, have taken some quite disastrous investment mistakes in their stride, because of involvement in buoyant markets elsewhere. It was argued in the previous chapter that a number of those markets were fortuitously in areas of work that were relatively simple, especially speculative housebuilding and much of the private commercial sector. Those markets strengthened building companies' position against professionals and workers by, in many cases, requiring lower design and building skill-inputs than other sectors. In addition, they were highly profitable, as data in Chapter 10 indicated.

Construction firms' flexibility of capital has enabled many of them to jump on the speculative-building bandwagon. Many now rely on such activities for large proportions of their profits, a reliance that could have limited their attempts to search for longer-term strategies of survival and expansion. Speculative markets do not rise for ever, and at the time of writing they have already been rising for over four years. Once the steam runs out of their booms, particularly the private housing one, a forced restructuring of firms in the industry might easily be on the cards again.

Repair and maintenance

One sector where all the problems of the building industry seem to coalesce into unmitigated disaster is private-sector repair and maintenance (R&M), especially the smaller-scale housing-related side. Repair and maintenance is now the most important sector of the building industry, so difficulties there are of considerable significance.

It was argued in Chapter 7 that the domination of R&M by small-scale builders, often themselves just informal link-ups between the self-employed, is a direct consequence of the employment structure created in the rest of the industry. Whilst that employment structure still exists, it is difficult to see how the situation in R&M can be significantly improved. Building workers will always have the chance to go freelance into R&M for no capital outlay and little danger of come-back if anything goes wrong. Given the flexibility with which the rest of the construction industry treats a worker's time, there are strong incentives for small jobbers to offer cut-price repair work. For them, labour is always readily available, and in the small doses usually required; that is, as long as the workers who are hired can be vague as to exactly when the job will be done and with what quality.

Large builders, not surprisingly, are furious at the activities going on in R&M. It squeezes them out of the sector, poaches scarce labour, and gives the industry a bad name. All the employers organisations in the industry have been campaigning for tough action against small-time R&M cowboys. Reports have been published (e.g. Building Employers Confederation, 1986b), and the government in 1986 set up an all-industry committee to review the situation. Self-regulation, tightening up of tax laws, and possibly some scheme of registration seem on the cards. Such schemes are unlikely to lead to serious improvements in R&M activity. Building employers' 'bona fide' firms, after all, are likely to employ exactly the same type of self-employed workforce as their so-called 'cowboy' rivals. And any product-insurance scheme will probably be ineffective, as the onus of proof is always on the consumer – an unskilled participant in a field where designating responsibility baffles even the experts.

Only through transforming employment conditions in construction as a whole is an improvement in R&M likely to be achieved. Then building workers will have less incentive to work in R&M in the way they currently do, and 'bona fide' firms will have a better chance of differentiating their product. The problems of R&M, in other words, could be one consequence of the low-wage labour-intensive regime that operates across the spectrum of construction work.

Quality blues

The R&M sector shows in its starkest form the general difficulties of construction firms in producing high-quality building products. A fairly extensive list of such problems was given in the first chapter, and the subsequent analysis of the ways in which the industry functions helped to explain why they occur. 'Technology' must partly be to blame, but far more important is the organisation of the construction process. Fragmentation of responsibility for production is a recipe for building failures, especially in a context where everyone has an incentive to work at speed and save time by cutting corners. The incentives are made all the stronger by the fact that so much poor work can be hidden with little chance of recrimination.

The changes that have taken place in construction over the past decade have heightened the tendencies encouraging poor quality described above. Some of the increase in productivity during the 1980s, in fact, could have been achieved through a deterioration in building quality. Within the current structure of the industry, it is difficult to see how the quality problem can be surmounted.

Reflation through the building industry

It is unnecessary to go through all the general problems of construction reflation here. The existence of severe capacity-constraints has been pointed out earlier in this book, and many times elsewhere (e.g. Building Materials Producers, 1984).

Any strategy of construction reflation must rely on bringing extra construction resources on-stream, rather than expecting to be able at the touch of a button to stimulate an industry with masses of spare capacity. As far as construction is concerned the excess capacity is simply not there; it has been 'restructured' away over the past decade.

217

In fact, if the argument about more volatile input costs is correct, cost inflation may rapidly hit even quite moderate expansions in demand. The construction boom in the South East led to construction costs rising five times as fast as those in the rest of the country in the eighteen months prior to October 1987, according to the Royal Institute of Chartered Surveyors. By January 1988, the rate of increase had slowed down, but in the South East it was still twice as high as the general rate of inflation (*Financial Times*, 5 January 1988). Cost, moreover, would not be the only indicator of strained resources; quality is also likely to suffer as one job is rushed through in order to start another.

The chances of dramatically reducing unemployment through expanding construction are unlikely to be achieved, at least in the short term, because of the industry's capacity constraints. One partial solution would be to direct more work to high-unemployment regions, and to concentrate on types of work where capacity shortages seem less acute. But such a strategy implies more state direction and public expenditure than most reflationists would like to envisage. Similarly, if particular types of building product are required, some element of diversion of resources from other construction sectors is required. Once again, if that is to be achieved without substantial inflation, state direction of one sort or another would be required.

One dark cloud looming over any construction-reflation strategy must be the threat of downturns in the private speculative sectors of housing and commercial development. Expansion of, say, public-sector demand then might merely compensate for demand losses elsewhere, though there could be wider implications in the implied shift in the structure of demand. It would be ironical, however, if a government intent on expanding construction in a planned and gradual way by initiating training schemes and much-needed public works found most of its construction expenditure allocations going to buy the products of builders in sectors facing sharp downturns in demand.

Towards regulation?

One factor that has characterised construction over the past two decades is a gradual slipping away of the notion that the industry should be closely circumscribed. Market forces and 'free' employment relations have been strongly at the forefront of developments. There are now indicators that many regard the pendulum as having swung too far. Of possible scenarios for the industry over the next few years, more regulation seems one that attempts to confront some of the industry's endemic problems and that might head off some of the conflicts within it.

Construction employers are keen to regulate the bits of the industry they do not like. 'Cowboys' are one category, the unknown quantity and quality of building-workers' skills another; building unions would like the industry decasualised; and everyone wishes things could be built better.

Joint negotiating bodies are common in the industry, so the scene may be set for some heavy negotiations over contentious issues that eventually bring greater regulation into the industry's affairs. It is unlikely, unfortunately, that any regulatory practice will halt the abuses it is aimed at, or transform key aspects of the industry. Even so, the changes that are taking place in construction might make such a path the most politically feasible and successful. But those very changes frequently mean that such controls are unworkable, because everything in the industry is so fluid that much can slip through any regulatory net.

Low wages, low productivity?

One final question must be left open in conclusion. A prominent feature of the British construction industry is that it has, like a number of other British industries, generally been a low-wage industry. Whenever construction firms are in difficulties, a prime response is to cut labour costs. The attempt is not made indirectly through new investments, but through a direct attack on workers' remuneration. Wage cuts, speed-ups which lower labour-costs per unit of output, and transformations of the ways in which workers are employed are all tactics that can be, and have been, used. Sometimes the government of the day will offer some help with the 'labour problem', but usually such assistance is not required.

Such a response to crisis fits in well with construction firms' desire to keep their capital employed in ways that are as flexible as possible. Low wages and low investment, therefore, have gone hand-in-hand. Workers then become not only the industry's main asset but also its main problem. Will they hang around, or get themselves adequately trained, in periods when nobody wants to employ them? Will they be reasonable and not ask for extra wages and better working conditions at times of high demand, when the laws of the market place say they should grab what they can? The low-wage, low-productivity cycle becomes a vicious circle in which both workers and consumers are trapped.

Higher wages might force construction firms and governments to consider workers as a precious asset, rather than a necessary nuisance. Higher wages would encourage firms to invest in more equipment to reduce labour costs. They might induce firms to gain greater control over this most-expensive asset by employing it directly and ensuring that it was healthy and adequately trained. Governments might find it expedient to deal with capital and labour in the construction industry on a more equal footing, initiating deals between them over a variety of issues.

In the first chapter it was pointed out that construction in Britain is one of the least efficient in Europe. Its productivity record trails way behind that of other Northern Europe countries. In many of those countries, construction wages are far higher. Spurious correlation or cause?

Notes

1 Construction: the image and the reality

1 Employment data for construction are notoriously unreliable as a result of widespread self-employment. See Chapter 7 for a greater discussion of the role of self-employment.

2 *United Kingdom National Accounts*, 1984, HMSO, London.

3 *Housing and Construction Statistics, 1972–82*, HMSO, London.

4 *Input–output Tables for the United Kingdom*, 1974, HMSO, London.

5 Association of Metropolitan Authorities evidence to The Inquiry into British Housing, September 1984, quoted in *Construction News*, 6 September 1984.

6 *Construction News*, 15 November 1984.

7 A 'World in Action' programme on ITV in July 1983 brought the faults of the system to public notice. The week previously 'World in Action' had shown the problems of Bison Wall-Frame.

8 *Construction News*, 23 April 1983 and *Financial Times*, 14 March 1984.

9 Report by Bickerdike Allen Partners, quoted in *The Times*, 17 August 1984.

10 Health and safety is an unresearched area. March *et al.* (1980), Leopold (1982), and the annual reports of the Health and Safety Executive, however, provided some useful information for construction.

11 Calculations were made using the purchasing-power-parity exchange-rate method. Sources are Eurostat (1983) and Kravis, Heston and Summers (1982), both quoted in Prais and Steedman (1985).

12 Hillebrandt (1974) attempted to apply such models with limited success to the construction industry, an approach she abandoned in her later and far more successful analysis of construction (Hillebrandt, 1984).

13 A similar case can be put against use of another development within neoclassical economics of seeing organisational differences in terms of transaction costs (Williamson, 1981). Winch (1986) produced some interesting arguments using the approach to explain the professionalisation of architects and their separation from building producers. His arguments unfortunately can only specify certain likely economic outcomes, given prespecified organisational divisions, not how those divisions emerged in the first place (and they were far from inevitable, as Chapter 4 will argue).

14 The Annual *Proceedings of the Bartlett International Summer School*, published by University College, London, are a good indicator of the type of Marxist-inspired work relating to the construction industry that has

taken place in recent years. Articles in those *Proceedings* also illustrate some of the fundamentalist tendencies referred to below.

15 See Fine and Harris (1979) for a general survey and critique of fundamentalist Marxist economics.

16 Price's illuminating book (Price, 1980) on the development of industrial relations in the nineteenth century has been criticised on these grounds. See Chapter 4 for details.

3 The different types of building enterprise

1 Since the mid-1970s, health and safety legislation has required that scaffolding be erected by trained scaffolders, encouraging firms of all sizes to subcontract the work and to hire the equipment. One of the most famous of the large independent scaffolding companies for many years was SGB plc, a company formed in the 1920s, whose initials stand for Scaffolding Great Britain (Savory-Milln, 1976). During the takeover boom of 1986 the company was acquired by Mowlem, ostensibly because of the benefits of increased company size – Mowlem's equity was doubled by the acquisition. The merger highlights the frequent 'family' ownership and management of many construction firms – the chairmen of Mowlem and SGB at the time of the merger were brothers, Philip and Clive Beck. For a background feature on the merger, see *Financial Times*, 18 April 1986.

2 To an extent, the combination of speculative and contracting activities is a new feature of the 1980s in Britain, arising from a situation where a number of previous contracting specialists have tried to cash in on the owner-occupied housing boom of the mid-1980s (see Chapter 10).

3 The tax situation of its founder, who only died in 1982, is likely to have been an important influence on the company's investment strategy until the early 1980s.

4 The development of class relations in the building industry

1 Some historians have tended to ignore the blurred, varying, but important distinction between the speculative and contracting sides of the building industry – conflating the economic forces in one with the other (cf. Price, 1980; McKenna and Rodger, 1985). In doing so, their analysis has been weakened, though not unduly because prime emphasis is placed by them on the inherent instability of activity in both sectors. However, it will be argued later that instability of demand in the construction industry can be exaggerated (see Chapter 6).

2 Dolan (1979) gives a brief history of the emergence of Joint Contracts Tribunal (JCT) Form of Contract. He also provides a useful introduction to the history of the building professions.

3 The principal references used in the section on building trade union

history are: Postgate, 1923; Price, 1980; Kingsford, 1973; Austrin, 1980; Wood, 1979; Drucker, 1980.

4 For criticisms of Price's interpretation of the development of nineteenth-century building trades unions see Melling (1981) and Read (1982).

5 See the National Federation of Building Trades Employers's evidence submitted to the Donovan Commission (1967) for the employers' attitude to the industrial relations situation at the time. Their basic attitude was that the unions were losing control.

6 The campaign of the employers organisations against direct labour is a good example of the lobbying activities that take place and their variety (see Direct Labour Collective, 1978 and 1980).

7 See also Richardson and Aldcroft, 1968, Table 5 and Feinstein, 1975, Table 4.21.

5 How construction firms organise production

1 *Building with Direct Labour* (Direct Labour Collective, 1978) gives many examples of cost and time overruns and subsequent claims and disputes in Britain, and of the practices that sustain them.

2 Beynon and Wainwright (1978) describe the impact of increased subcontracting in one particular engineering firm, Vickers. See also *Leyland Vehicles: the Workers' Alternative*, Leyland Vehicles Joint Works Committee, 1981.

3 See Phelps Brown Report (1968) and the results of a Construction Industry Manpower Survey study, the Construction Industry Mobility Survey, summarised in *Construction News*, 21 February 1980.

4 Cf. Gordon Bayley (1973). The Wood Report (1975) describes the effects of the loss of construction teams caused by the discrete nature of building contracts.

> It is arguable that contractors are more severely denied continuity by reason of current tender procedures than through uncertainties in total demand in their industry sector. The practice of seeking new tenders for each project results in a damaging lack of continuity for the individual firm. At site level, teams of men and managers built up during the progress of a job are often dispersed at the end of the contract. The advantages gained through learning particular constructional operations and sequences, understanding client attitudes and policies, and welding together effective management and site teams are lost ... Furthermore, the incentive for firms to innovate is weakened. (Wood Report, 1975, p. 47)

However, the Report's conclusion that forms of tendering can be altered to alleviate the worst problems of building-to-contract is highly dubious (see Direct Labour Collective, 1978).

6 Construction output: a thirty-year view

1 Calculated from *Housing and Construction Statistics.*

7 A hierarchical industry

1 Hillebrandt (1971) is a useful, but dated, survey.

8 Keeping up the profits

1 The complex industrial structure of the British construction industry makes any choice of firms a matter of personal judgment, and the sample here is no exception. Other well-known firms were excluded for the following reasons. Private companies (like Wates) obviously had to be excluded, as they publish little information about themselves. One firm, Barratt, was excluded because it is principally a speculative housebuilder. Three other firms were excluded because they were owned by firms operating primarily outside the industry; Trafalgar House, the Balfour Beatty subsidiary of BICC, and the Bovis subsidiary of P & O. Others are principally process engineers, e.g. Davy Corporation and Simon Engineering, whilst others are specialists with large interests outside construction, like Matthew Hall and Haden. The ten chosen are the most clear-cut building and civil engineering contractors – although frequently still hybrid enterprises. Tarmac, for instance, is equally active in private housebuilding, contracting and aggregates.
2 The price deflators (1975 = 100) used were the new construction output price index for turnover and the GDP deflator for profits. It was felt misleading to use the construction deflator for profits, as during the 1970s contractors have not necessarily reinvested their profits in construction (see later). The turnovers given include each firm's non-construction activities, as it is impossible to get a detailed breakdown of turnover from company accounts.
3 New management was not brought in to lead the company until 1983. The founder of Wimpey, Godfrey Mitchell, only died in 1982 and a long-term colleague of Mitchell's chaired the company until 1984. For the company's new strategy see the interview with Clifford Chetwood in *Construction News*, 29 March 1984.
4 *Source: Trade and Industry*, 23 March 1979.
5 Paradoxically the weakness of the financial packages offered to clients by British contractors has been cited in a series of industry reports as being a cause of UK firms' poor overseas performance.
6 If UK construction earnings are taken as a base of 100 in 1981, those of Italy were 114, the Netherlands 121, West Germany 142 and France 187. Korea at the same date weighed in at a remarkable 361, whereas in 1977 it had roughly the same earnings as the UK. *Source*: calculated using data from the Committee for European Construction Equipment reported in *Construction News*, 5 May 1983.

7   *Source: Financial Times* International Construction Survey, 9 November 1982. Of the top thirty international contractors listed there, twelve were from the USA, four from S. Korea, three from France and West Germany respectively, two from Italy, and one each from Britain, Brazil, the Netherlands, Israel, Belgium and Japan.

8   The ability of contractors to generate cash has proved attractive to firms outside construction. BICC took over civil engineers Balfour Beatty in 1969. In an interview with the *Financial Times,* BICC management explained the advantages of the link up:

> Balfour Beatty's ability to generate cash has been valuable to BICC in the last few years, but a contractor also benefits from being part of a large group. The asset backing is important, especially in large projects where performance bonds have to be lodged. There is scope for complementing Balfour Beatty's down-to-earth engineering skills with imaginative financial packages . . . the availability of finance on suitable terms is as important as the ability to handle the contract efficiently. (*Financial Times,* 8 April 1980)

9   *Source: Business Monitor MA3 Company Finance.* The ratio calculated is the proportion of net income distributed to shareholders or paid as interest on long-term loans. The lower payout ratio holds for the whole period of the *Business Monitor* data, so it is not a product of the downswing in construction since the late 1960s. Between 1961 and 1964, for instance, manufacturing firms paid out 44 per cent of net income and construction firms 36 per cent; for 1964–9 the average ratios were 46 per cent and 37 per cent respectively. The higher level of dividend payments prior to 1973 reflects the switch to the imputation system of dividend taxation in that year (see Kay and King, 1980).

10 Ball (1983), Chapter 3, discusses taxation and construction capital in more detail.

11 The variability of accumulation strategies between firms should be borne in mind here. Thus some firms have moved into property ownership in a substantial way to make up for lost contracting income. The firm of Gleeson, mentioned earlier, is a case in point; by the late 1970s rental income was more than twice as large as trading profits, and in 1982 the company dropped the word 'contractors' from its name to reflect the growing importance of its property portfolio (*Construction News,* 9 May 1983).

12 'Construction: the profits paradox', Fred Wellings of stockbrokers Laing and Cruickshank in the Financial Review Supplement, *Construction News,* 28 January 1982. Another analyst, Patrick Rogers, of stockbrokers Buckmaster and Moore provides a similar analysis in an article in *Construction News Magazine,* March 1982.

9 Takeovers for growth

1 This chapter and the following one draw heavily on Ball and Cullen (1980).

10 Sectoral restructuring

1 Good surveys of the development of the British plant-hire industry can be found in articles by J. A. Smith and especially C. Stratton in *Construction News* Plant Hire Supplement, 27 September 1979, and by D. Cole and R. Neale in *Construction News Magazine*, April 1978. *Construction News* Financial Review provides a useful annual update.

2 Stratton (*op. cit.*) suggested that such processes were a major reason why earth-moving equipment was in short supply in some localities in 1978 and 1979.

Bibliography

Aaronovitch, S. and Sawyer, M. (1975), *Big Business: Theoretical and Empirical Aspects of Concentration and Mergers in the United Kingdom*, Macmillan, Basingstoke.

Alford, B. (1981), 'New industries for old? British industry between the wars', in Floud, R. and McCloskey, D. (eds), *The Economic History of Britain Vol. 2: 1860 to the 1970s*, Cambridge University Press, Cambridge.

Ascher, F. and Lacoste, J. (1974), *Les Producteurs du Cadre Bati: vol 1*, Université des Sciences Socialies, Grenoble.

Austrin, T. (1980), 'The "Lump" in the UK construction industry', in T. Nichols (ed.), *Capital and Labour*, Fontana, London.

Ball, M. (1978), 'British housing policy and the housebuilding industry', *Capital and Class*, 4, pp. 78–99.

Ball, M. (1981), 'The development of capitalism in housing provision', *International Journal of Urban and Regional Research*, 5, pp. 145–77.

Ball, M. (1983), *Housing Policy and Economic Power: the Political Economy of Owner Occupation*, Methuen, London.

Ball, M. (1985a), 'Land rent and the construction industry', in Ball, M., Bentivegna, V., Folin, F. and Edwards, M. (eds), *Land Rent, Housing and Urban Planning: A European Perspective*, Croom Helm, London.

Ball, M. (1985b), 'The urban rent question', *Environment and Planning A*, 17, pp. 503–25.

Ball, M. (1986), *Homeownership: a Suitable Case for Reform*, Shelter, London.

Ball, M. (1988), 'The international restructuring of housing production', in Ball, M., Martens, M. and Harloe, M. (eds), *Housing and Social Change in Europe and the USA*, Routledge, London.

Ball, M. and Cullen, A. (1980), *Mergers and Accumulation in the British Construction Industry*, Birkbeck College Discussion Paper No. 73, London.

Banham, R. (1976), *Theory and Design in the First Machine Age*, Architectural Press, London.

Banwell Report (1964), *The Placing and Management of Contracts for Building and Civil Engineering Work*, Ministry of Public Buildings and Works, HMSO, London.

Bartlett Summer School (1979), *The Production of the Built Environment*, Proceedings of the Bartlett International Summer School, annually from 1979, Bartlett School, University College, London.

Bemis, A. (1936), *The Evolving House*, MIT Press, Cambridge, Massachusetts.

Beynon, H. and Wainwright, H. (1979), *The Workers' Report on Vickers*, Pluto, London.

Bishop, D. (1975), 'Productivity in the construction industry', in Turin (1975).

Bowley, M. (1944), *Housing and the State*, Allen & Unwin, London.

Bowley, M. (1960), *Innovations in Building Materials*, Duckworth, London.

Bowley, M. (1966), *The British Building Industry*, Macmillan, London.

Braverman, H. (1974), *Labour and Monopoly Capital*, Monthly Review Press, New York.

Building Employers Confederation (1986a), *A Fresh Look at the UK and US Building Industries*, Building Employers Confederation, London.

Building Employers Confederation (1986b), *Cowboys in the Black Economy*, Building Employers Confederation, London.

Building Materials Producers (1984), *The Economic Impact of Increased Public Spending on Construction*, National Council of Building Materials Producers, London.

Burawoy, M. (1985), *The Politics of Production*, Verso, London.

Butler, A. (1978), 'New price indices for construction output statistics', *Economic Trends*, 297, pp. 97–110.

Cameron Report (1967), *Report of the Court of Inquiry into Trades Disputes at the Barbican and Horseferry Road Construction Sites in London, 1966–67*, vol xxxvii, Cmnd 3396, HMSO, London.

Campinos-Dubernet, M. (1986), 'The rationalisation of labour in the construction industry: the limits of orthodox Taylorism', *The Production of the Built Environment*, 7, pp. 117–129, Bartlett School, University College, London.

Chartered Institute of Public Finance and Accounting (1975), *Direct Works Undertakings Accounting*, The Chartered Institute of Public Finance and Accounting, London.

Chartered Institute of Building (1982), *Project Management in Building*, Chartered Institute of Building, London.

Clarke, L. (1985), 'The production of the built environment: backward or peculiar?', *The Production of the Built Environment*, 6, pp. 2–3–2–7, Bartlett School, University College, London.

Coakley, J. and Harris, L. (1983), *The City of Capital*, Basil Blackwell, Oxford.

Colclough, J. (1965), *The Construction Industry in Britain*, Butterworth, London.

Coleman, T. (1968), *The Railway Navvies*, Penguin, Harmondsworth.

Construction News Financial Review 1986, International Thomson Publishing, London.

Cooney, E. (1955), 'The origins of the Victorian master builders', *Economic History Review*, VIII, pp. 167–76.

Cooney, E. (1974), 'High flats in local authority housing in England and Wales since 1945', in Sutcliffe, A. (ed.), *Multi-storey Living. The British Working Class Experience*, Croom Helm, London.

Le Corbusier (1970), *Towards a New Architecture*, Architectural Press, London.

Cullen, A. (1982), 'Speculative housebuilding in Britain. Some notes on the switch to timber-frame production method', *The Production of the Built Environment*, 3, pp. 4–12–4–18, Bartlett School, University College, London.

Davis, M. (1984), 'The political economy of late imperial America', *New Left Review*, 143, pp. 6–38.

Dickens, P., Duncan, S., Goodwin, M. and Gray, F. (1985), *Housing, States and Localities*, Methuen, London.

Direct Labour Collective (1978), *Building with Direct Labour*, Conference of Socialist Economists, London.

Direct Labour Collective (1980), *Direct Labour Under Attack*, Conference of Socialist Economists, London.

Dolan, D. (1979), *The British Construction Industry*, Macmillan, Basingstoke.

Drucker, J. (1980), 'The history of the construction unions: the process of structural change', *Production of the Built Environment*, 1, pp. 69–74, Bartlett School, University College, London.

Dunleavy, P. (1981), *The Politics of Mass Housing*, Clarendon Press, Oxford.

Dyos, H. (1961), *The Victorian Suburb. A Study of the Growth of Camberwell*, Leicester University Press, Leicester.

Economist Intelligence Unit (1975), *Housing and Land Availability in the South-East*, Economist Intelligence Unit, HMSO, London.

Economist Intelligence Unit (1978), *Public Ownership in the Construction Industries*, Economist Intelligence Unit, London.

Eichler, N. (1982), *The Merchant Builders*, MIT Press, Cambridge, Mass.

Bibliography

Emmerson Report (1962), *Survey of the Problems Before the Construction Industries*, HMSO, London.

Eurostat (1983), *Comparisons in Real Values of the Aggregates of ESA 1980*, Statistical Office of the European Communities, Luxembourg.

Feinstein, C. (1972), *National Income, Expenditure and Output of the UK, 1855–1965*, Cambridge University Press, Cambridge.

Fine, B. and Harris, L. (1979), *Rereading Capital*, Macmillan, Basingstoke.

Fishman, R. (1977), *Urban Utopias in the Twentieth Century: Ebenezer Howard, Frank Lloyd Wright, and Le Corbusier*, Basic Books, New York.

Fleming, M. (1966), 'The long-term measurement of construction costs in the UK', *Journal of the Royal Statistical Society*, series A, 129, pp. 534–56.

Foot, M. (1975), *Aneurin Bevan*, vol. 2, Granada, London.

Gamble, A. (1981), *Britain in Decline*, Macmillan, Basingstoke.

Gann, D. (1984), *Women in the Construction Industry*, Science Policy Research Unit, University of Sussex, Brighton.

George K. and Silbertson, A. (1975) 'The causes and effects of mergers', *Scottish Journal of Political Economy*, 22, 179–93.

Gillard, M. and Tomkinson, M. (1980), *Nothing to Declare: the Political Corruptions of John Poulson*, Platform Books, Sheffield.

Gordon Bayley, L. (1973), *Building: Teamwork or Conflict*, George Godwin, London.

Gottlieb, M. (1976), *Long Swings in Urban Development*, National Bureau of Economic Research, New York.

Higgin, G. and Jessop, N. (1965), *Communications in the Building Industry: the Report of a Pilot Study*, Tavistock Institute, London.

Hillebrandt, P. (1971), *Small Firms in the Construction Industry*, Committee of Inquiry on Small Firms, Research Report no. 10, HMSO, London.

Hillebrandt, P. (1974), *Economic Theory and the Construction Industry*, Macmillan, Basingstoke.

Hillebrandt, P. (1984), *Analysis of the British Construction Industry*, Macmillan, Basingstoke.

Hilton, W. (1968), *Industrial Relations in Construction*, Pergamon, Oxford.

Hinton, J. (1973), *The First Shop Stewards' Movement*, Allen & Unwin, London.

Hird, C. (1975), *Your Employers' Profits*, Pluto, London.

Hobhouse, H. (1971), *Thomas Cubitt: Master Builder*, Macmillan, Basingstoke.

Ingham, G. (1984), *Capitalism Divided?*, Macmillan, Basingstoke.

Jeremy, D. (ed.) (1985), *Dictionary of Business Biography*, volume 4, Butterworth, London.

Kay, J. and King, M. (1980), *The British Tax System*, Oxford University Press, Oxford.

Kingsford, P. (1973), *Builders and Building Workers*, Edward Arnold, London.

Kravis, I., Heston, H. and Summers, R. (1982), *World Product and Income*, Johns Hopkins University Press, Maryland.

Kuehn, D. (1970), *Takeovers and the Theory of the Firm*, Macmillan, London.

Lea, E., Lansley, P. and Spencer, P. (1974), *Efficiency and Growth in the Building Industry*, Ashridge Management College Research Unit, Ashridge.

Leeson, R. (1979), *Travelling Brothers*, Allen & Unwin, London.

Leopold, E. (1982), 'Where have all the workers gone?', *Building*, 22 October 1982, pp. 29–30.

Leopold, E. and Bishop, D. (1981), *Design Philosophy and Practice in Speculative Housebuilding*, University College, Building Economics Research Unit, London.

Lipietz, A. (1974), *Le Tribut Foncier Urbain*, Maspero, Paris.

Lipietz, A. (1985), 'Building and the crisis of Fordism: the case of France', *Production of the Built Environment*, 6, pp. 1-13–1-33, Bartlett, School, University College, London.

Littler, C. and Salaman, G. (1984), *Class at Work*, Batsford, London.

McKenna, J. and Rodger, R. (1985), 'Control by coercion: employers' associations and the establishment of industrial order in the building of England and Wales, 1860–1914', *Business History Review*, pp. 203–31.

Marriott, O. (1967), *The Property Boom*, Weidenfeld & Nicolson, London.

Marsh, A., Heady, P. and Matherson, J. (1980), *Labour Mobility in the Construction Industry*, OPCS, London.

Martens, M. (1985) 'Owner occupied housing in Europe: Postwar developments and current dilemmas', *Environment and Planning*, 17, pp. 605–24.

Marx, K. (1968), *Theories of Surplus Value*, Volume II, Lawrence & Wishart, London.

Marx, K. (1974), *Capital*, Volume III, Lawrence & Wishart, London.

Massey, D. and Catalano, A. (1978), *Capital and Land*, Edward Arnold, London.

Massey, D. and Meegan, R. (1982), *The Anatomy of Job Loss*, Methuen, London.

Melling, J. (1981), 'The workplace and the rise of labour', *Bulletin of the Society for the Labour History*, 42, pp. 44–7.

Merrett, S. (1979), *State Housing in Britain*, Routledge & Kegan Paul, London.

Middlemas, K. (1963), *The Masterbuilders*, Butterworth, London.

Monopolies Commission (1970), *A Survey of Mergers, 1958–68*, HMSO, London.

Monopolies and Mergers Commission (1977), *Architects' Services*, HMSO, London.

Morris, D. (1979), 'The behaviour of firms', in Morris, D. (ed.), *The Economic System in the UK*, Oxford University Press, Oxford.

National Economic Development Office (1970), *Large Industrial Sites*, HMSO, London.

National Economic Development Office (1976a), *Engineering Construction Performance*, HMSO, London.

National Economic Development Office (1976b), *Cyclical Fluctuations in the United Kingdom Economy*, NEDO Books, London.

National Economic Development Office (1978), *How Flexible is Construction?*, NEDO Books, London.

National Economic Development Office (1985), *Strategy for Construction R&D*, NEDO Books, London.

National Economic Development Office (1986), *Construction Forecasts, 1986–88*, NEDO Books, London.

National Plan (1965), *The National Plan*, Cmnd 2764, HMSO, London.

Needleman, L. (1965), *The Economics of Housing*, Staples Press, London.

Parry Lewis, J. (1965), *Building Cycles and Britain's Economic Growth*, Macmillan, London.

Parry Lewis, J. and Singh, D. (1966), 'Government policy and the building industry', *District Bank Review*, June, pp. 3–28.

National Association of Home Builders (1985), *Housing America – the Challenges Ahead*, NAHB, Washington, DC.

Pelling, H. (1976), *A History of British Trades Unionism*, Penguin, Harmondsworth.

Phelps Brown, E. (1968), *Report of the Committee of Inquiry into Certain Matters concerning Labour in Building and Civil Engineering*, Cmnd 3714, HMSO, London.

Postgate, R. (1923), *The Builder's History*, Labour Publishing, London.

Prais, S. and Steedman, H. (1985), *Vocational Training in Britain and France: the Building Trades*, Discussion Paper No. 105, National Institute for Economic and Social Research, London.

Price, R. (1980), *Masters, Unions and Men*, Cambridge University Press, Cambridge.

Ravetz, A. (1980), *Remaking Cities*, Croom Helm, London.

Read, A. (1982), 'Labour and society in modern Britain', *Historical Journal*, 25, pp. 493–500.

Richardson, H. and Aldcroft, D. (1968), *Building the British Economy between the Wars*, Allen & Unwin, London.

Roy, A. (1982), 'Labour productivity in 1980: an international comparison', *National Institute Economic Review*, 101, August, pp. 26–37.

Royal Institute of British Architects, (1962), *The Architect and His Office*, RIBA, London.

Rubinstein, W. (1977), 'Wealth, elites and class structure in Britain', *Past and Present*, no. 76.

Saint, A. (1983), *The Image of the Architect*, Yale University Press, London.

Savory Milln (1976), *Savory Milln's Building Book, 1976*, Savory Milln & Co., London.

Sayer, A. (1986), 'New developments in manufacturing: the just-in-time system', *Capital and Class*, 30, pp. 43–72.

Scott, G. (1976), *Building Disasters and Failures – A Practical Report*, Construction Press, Lancaster.

Short, J., Fleming, S. and Witt, S. (1986), *Housebuilding, Planning and Community Action. The Production and Negotiation of the Built Environment*, Routledge & Kegan Paul, London.

Simon Report (1944), *Report on the Management and Placing of Building Contracts*, Ministry of Works, HMSO, London.

Smith, A. (1776), *The Wealth of Nations*, Penguin edition (1970), Harmondsworth.

Smith, A., Hitchens, D. and Davies, S. (1982), 'International industrial productivity: a comparison of Britain, America and Germany', *National Institute Economic Review*, 101, August, pp. 13–25.

Smyth, H. (1985), *Property Companies and the Construction Industry in Britain*, Cambridge University Press, Cambridge.

Spender, J. (1930), *Weetman Pearson. First Viscount Cowdray, 1856–1927*, Cassell, London.

Stedman Jones, G. (1983), *The Language of Class*, Cambridge University Press, Cambridge.

Stone, P. (1976), *Building Economy*, Pergamon, Oxford.

Sugden, J. (1975), 'The place of construction in the economy', in Turin (1975).

Sugden, J. (1980), 'The nature of construction capacity and entrepreneurial response to effective demand in the UK', *The Production of the Built Environment*, 1, pp. 1–6, Bartlett School, University College, London.

Thompson, F. (1968), *Chartered Surveyors*, Routledge & Kegan Paul, London.

The Times 1000, 1978–79 (1978), Times Books, London.

Turin, D. (ed.) (1975), *Aspects of the Economics of Construction*, George Godwin, London.

Wallis, L. (1945), *The Building Industry: Its Work and Organisation*, Building and Society Series, Cooperative Building Society, London.

White, R. (1965), *Prefabrication: a History of Its Development in Great Britain*, HMSO, London.

Williams, N. (1981), 'Influences on the profitability of 22 industrial sectors', *Bank of England Discussion Paper no. 22*.

Williamson, O. (1981), 'The economics of organisation: the transaction cost approach', *American Journal of Sociology*, 87, pp. 34–55.

Winch, G. (1986), 'The construction process and the contracting system; a transaction cost approach', *The Production of the Built Environment*, 7, pp. 262–70, Bartlett School, University College, London.

Wood, L. (1979), *Building a Union*, Lawrence & Wishart, London.

Wood Report (1975), *The Public Client and the Construction Industries*, HMSO, London.

Wood, S. (ed.) (1982), *The Degradation of Work? Skill, Deskilling and the Labour Process*, Hutchinson, London.

Index